S0-BJU-242

Praise for CREATE A CULTURE OF KINDNESS IN MIDDLE SCHOOL

"*Create a Culture of Kindness* begins as if you are having a conversation with the wisest and most supportive teachers you have ever spoken to. This is worth the price alone, but you will soon see that the lessons also reflect wisdom and deep respect for children's competence and potential. This book gives you the tools needed to create an organized, respectful classroom filled with students who are more mindful and therefore more ready to engage in learning and positive relationships. Its lessons on compassion, in particular, should be mandatory in every middle school."

—Maurice J. Elias, Ph.D., Rutgers University and author of *Assessing Social, Emotional, and Character Development* and *Emotionally Intelligent Parenting*

"The vast majority of students we talk to agree that bullying is bad and kindness is cool. But they often lack basic strategies to show compassion to their classmates. This book offers dozens of practical, hands-on lesson plans educators can use to teach students how to be kind (and why that matters so much). The lessons encourage students to stand up for what is right, and give them the tools to do it. If you want to 'Create a Culture of Kindness in [your] Middle School,' this book is for you."

—Dr. Justin W. Patchin and Dr. Sameer Hinduja, codirectors of the Cyberbullying Research Center and authors of *Words Wound*

"This book is exactly what educators need, now more than ever: A blueprint for providing kids with the skills not only to prevent bullying, but to fundamentally change their schools and their world. With *Create a Culture of Kindness in Middle School*, Naomi Drew and Christa Tinari have added a timely and valuable resource to the literature on empathy, respect, school climate, and bullying prevention."

—Michele Borba, Ed.D., author of *The 6Rs of Bullying Prevention*

"*Create a Culture of Kindness in Middle School* is the single most impactful book I've seen on transforming a culture of bullying into one that reliably promotes kindness. It is essential reading for every middle school educator and for every parent of a middle school student. It takes intention, courage, and powerful protocols to create a school culture that empowers students to flourish, both emotionally and academically. Naomi Drew and Christa Tinari deliver the goods in this practical, wise, and inspiring guide."

—Marilee Adams, Ph.D., best-selling author of *Teaching That Changes Lives: 12 Mindset Tools for Igniting the Love of Learning*

"*Create a Culture of Kindness in Middle School* brilliantly covers all the bases, with a hands-on approach to building important skills like compassion, empathy, listening, anger management, coping tools, personal responsibility, and respect for diversity. This timely and important manual includes practical activities, questions, and resources to engage students and help them recognize their interconnectedness, their capacity to change deeply held beliefs, and the potential they each have to make a difference—all while helping to preserve civility, respect, and common decency in our world."

—Jane Bluestein, Ph.D., author of *Creating Emotionally Safe Schools* and *The Win-Win Classroom*

Create a Culture of Kindness in Middle School

48 Character-Building Lessons to Foster Respect and Prevent Bullying

Naomi Drew, M.A.,
with Christa M. Tinari, M.A.

Text copyright © 2017 by Naomi Drew, M.A., and Christa M. Tinari, M.A.
Illustrations copyright © 2017 by Free Spirit Publishing Inc.

All rights reserved under International and Pan-American Copyright Conventions. Unless otherwise noted, no part of this book may be reproduced, stored in a retrieval system, or transmitted in any form or by any means, electronic, mechanical, photocopying, or otherwise, without express written permission of the publisher, except for brief quotations or critical reviews. For more information, go to freespirit.com/permissions.

Free Spirit, Free Spirit Publishing, and associated logos are trademarks and/or registered trademarks of Free Spirit Publishing Inc. A complete listing of our logos and trademarks is available at freespirit.com.

Library of Congress Cataloging-in-Publication Data
Names: Drew, Naomi. | Tinari, Christa.
Title: Create a culture of kindness in middle school : 48 character-building lessons to foster respect and prevent bullying / Naomi Drew, Christa Tinari.
Description: Minneapolis, MN : Free Spirit Publishing, 2017. | Includes bibliographical references and index.
Identifiers: LCCN 2016046253 (print) | LCCN 2017005904 (ebook) | ISBN 9781631980299 (paperback) | ISBN 1631980297 (paperback) | ISBN 9781631981609 (Web PDF) | ISBN 9781631981616 (ePub)
Subjects: LCSH: Bullying in schools—Prevention. | Middle school education—Activity programs—United States. | Character—Study and teaching (Middle School)—Activity programs—United States. | Classroom management—United States—Handbooks, manuals, etc. | BISAC: EDUCATION / Leadership. | EDUCATION / Classroom Management.
Classification: LCC LB3013.3 .D738 2017 (print) | LCC LB3013.3 (ebook) | DDC 371.5/8—dc23
LC record available at https://lccn.loc.gov/2016046253

Free Spirit Publishing does not have control over or assume responsibility for author or third-party websites and their content. At the time of this book's publication, all facts and figures cited within are the most current available. All telephone numbers, addresses, and website URLs are accurate and active; all publications, organizations, websites, and other resources exist as described in this book; and all have been verified as of April 2021. If you find an error or believe that a resource listed here is not as described, please contact Free Spirit Publishing.

Edited by Alison Behnke
Cover and interior design by Emily Dyer

10 9 8 7 6 5 4
Printed in the United States of America

Free Spirit Publishing Inc.
6325 Sandburg Road, Suite 100
Minneapolis, MN 55427-3674
(612) 338-2068
help4kids@freespirit.com
freespirit.com

SFI label applies to the text stock

Free Spirit offers competitive pricing.
Contact edsales@freespirit.com for pricing information on multiple quantity purchases.

Every student who walks through your door is an unpolished gemstone. Every facet you create will stay with that student for life. Your work is that important. So we want to dedicate this book to you and your students. And we want to thank you. Thank you for the hard work you do every day. Thank you for the heart you bring to the students you educate. And thank you for caring enough to use this book. We know it is in good hands and you will teach its lessons wisely and well.

Now, go and help your students shine. Our deepest hope is that their collective light will someday change the world.

—Naomi Drew and Christa M. Tinari

Acknowledgments

Heartfelt thanks to my family and friends for all their love, support, and belief in my work. A special thanks to Christa for all her insight and knowledge, plus for all the fun and laughter we shared as we brainstormed, wrote, researched, and edited. Many thanks to Cornerstone Health and Fitness for being one of my favorite places of grounding, and for all the hours spent writing in their light-filled lobby. Additional thanks from both Christa and me to the Eagle Diner, the Zen Den, and Jamie Hollander Café for providing us with great places to caffeinate and write.

—Naomi

I can't possibly name all the people who have influenced my passion for peace education over the course of my career, yet each one of them is part of this book. Thanks to my parents, Frank and Barbara Tinari, who were my first teachers and also career educators. Not only did you shape my thinking and character, but you instilled in me a joyful love of learning that provides me unlimited opportunities for discovery and growth. I'm grateful for your constant support. Thanks to my sisters (also professional educators!) for your constant friendship, honesty, empathy, humor, and encouragement. Thanks to Heather Herrington for sparking my journey on the path of nonviolence over twenty years ago. Special thanks to my friend and colleague Naomi Drew, who has been a pioneer in the field. Without your generous invitation to collaborate on this book, none of this would be possible. I'm grateful for our shared passion for this work, for your gentle guidance, and for the deep conversations we had while writing and editing that ventured beyond the subject matter of the book. Thanks also to the educators with whom I've worked, as they all have shaped the content and purpose of this book. At their core, teaching and learning are about transformation. The fact that each of us can change for the better throughout our lives keeps me hopeful for the future. Finally, thanks to the students I have known over the past twenty years. This is all for you!

—Christa

We also want to acknowledge the following people and organizations:

- Stan Davis and Charisse Nixon for their insightful feedback and for allowing us to use their Youth Voice Project research
- Researcher David Yeager for sharing his vast knowledge and data about mindsets
- Middle school teacher Kiren Chanda for sharing her inspiring story, and principal Steve Roos for sharing his knowledge and expertise
- Whitney Kropp for sharing the story of her experience of being bullied
- The Allen-Stevenson School for allowing us to use their book list
- Eileen Quinn, guidance counselor at Delaware Township School, for setting up many wonderful student interviews and for sharing her vast knowledge

- Geoff Hewitt, former principal of Lambertville Public School, for setting up student interviews and for his continuous support
- Heartfelt thanks to all the great people at Free Spirit who made this book possible, especially Marjorie Lisovskis and Judy Galbraith. You make Free Spirit a publishing house we are proud to be associated with. We also want to thank Free Spirit's crackerjack design team, copyeditor, and publicity team, as well as blog editor Eric Braun. Our warmest thanks to editor extraordinaire, Alison Behnke, for her wisdom, insight, and meticulous editing of our book. We felt so lucky to have you, Alison!
- Maurice Elias, Jane Bluestein, Marilee Adams, and Michele Borba for reviewing our book
- Justin Patchin and Sameer Hinduja for advising us on cyberbullying
- The many teachers and counselors whose voices inform the pages of this book
- The many schools that participated in our surveys, including Arts & Letters Middle School, Carl Sandburg Middle School, Frances E. Willard School, Lawrence Intermediate School, the Math and Science Exploratory School, Ponce de Leon Middle School, Poquessing Middle School, Sampson G. Smith School, and Somerset Intermediate School
- All the students who shared their stories during interviews

Contents

List of Reproducible Forms

Customizable digital versions of all reproducible forms can be downloaded at **freespirit.com/kindness-forms**. Use password **4respect**.

Introduction

"The mission of schools must include teaching kindness. Without it, communities, families, schools, and classrooms become places of incivility where lasting learning is unlikely to take place. . . . Kindness can be taught, and it is a defining aspect of civilized human life. It belongs in every home, school, neighborhood, and society."

—Maurice Elias, director of the Social-Emotional Learning Lab, Rutgers University

Creating a Culture of Kindness in Your School

One of the most important jobs educators have is to teach, model, and reinforce respect, compassion, kindness, and other prosocial skills. Doing so builds a school climate and culture where kids feel more connected to their teachers and to one another. It leads to greater emotional health for students and teachers alike. And it can create a fundamental shift in school climate—a tipping point at which bullying and cruelty become a rarity. Academic gains will likely follow. According to the American Institutes for Research, "Positive school climate is tied to high or improving attendance rates, test scores, promotion rates, and graduation rates." Better test scores and higher rates of student achievement are inextricably related to a school climate of kindness and support.

Changing a school's culture can start with a single teacher. We saw a great example of this when we interviewed eighth-grade teacher Kiren Chanda. When she started teaching her students about social responsibility, they came up with the idea of doing random acts of kindness for the entire school—from teachers and administrators to custodians, support staff, and students. Motivated by the intrinsic value of doing good for others, Kiren's class transformed into a team on a mission. And the impact went way beyond the walls of their classroom. Ripples of kindness started spreading through the entire school. Before long, kids were holding open doors for each other, writing thank-you notes to teachers, and giving each other compliments. Kiren says, "A feeling of niceness and camaraderie started popping up all over the building. Kids were feeling so good about what was being done for them, they wanted to do good for others." And the recipients of these pay-it-forward acts of kindness were inspired to do similar acts themselves. Ultimately, the climate of the entire school changed. As Kiren's principal, Steve Roos, said: "We don't have a bullying problem in our school. Our kids feel accepted here. People take care of one another." And it all started with one teacher and a bunch of eighth graders who were inspired to do good.

Better test scores and higher rates of student achievement are inextricably related to a school climate of kindness and support.

This story is a perfect demonstration of how, when seeds of peace, kindness, and compassion are planted, they can spread through an entire school.

Making Kindness Contagious

What happened in Kiren Chanda's school is a great example of something researchers have quantified and documented: Kindness is contagious. A study by James Fowler and Nicholas Christakis published in the *Proceedings of the National Academy of Sciences* revealed that "cooperative behavior is contagious and spreads from person to person to person. When people benefit from kindness they 'pay it forward' by

THE REVEALING POWER OF SURVEYS

In order to find out what students are experiencing when it comes to conflict, bullying, and other negative and unkind behaviors, we studied the research and also conducted two national surveys of our own. In total, we surveyed over 1,000 students in schools throughout the United States in sixth through eighth grade. We surveyed kids in different demographic areas, of varying races and socioeconomic groups, and from cities as well as suburbs and rural areas. Our participating schools were both public and private. Because our surveys were anonymous, students often revealed things they hesitated to speak of face-to-face in the dozens of one-on-one interviews we also conducted. On pages 244–247, we have included a similar student survey that you can use at your school.

helping others who were not originally involved, and this creates a cascade of cooperation that influences dozens more in a social network."[1]

Planting the seeds of compassion and respect in classrooms and schools is essential, not only to reduce bullying and other cruel behaviors, but because empathy and kindness are so essential to all human relationships. But just as these positive behaviors spread, so can cruelty and callousness. As a Harvard study of 10,000 middle school and high school students reported, 80 percent were more concerned about their own success and happiness than they were about others. The report states something all of us have seen: "When caring takes a back seat, youth are at risk for being cruel, disrespectful, and dishonest."[2] As one eighth-grade boy told us, "I was a bully because I never put myself in the other person's shoes. I never stopped to think what the other kid was feeling."

On the other hand, when kids start standing up for others, more are likely to follow. That's partly because "mirror neurons" in the brain prompt people to mimic other people's behaviors. According to neuroscience researchers Sourya Acharya and Samarth Shukla, mirror neurons are activated when people observe others' actions. This helps explain why kids learn through imitation. Mirror neurons also spark the spread of empathy and emotions. This is why it's so important to fill classrooms and hallways with enough empathy, kindness, and respect to motivate every student.[3]

The Need to Foster Acceptance of Diversity

Day by day the world is becoming visibly more diverse. People from different cultures interact in schools, communities, workplaces, and online more than ever before. Schools strive to meet the needs of diverse students, including dual language learners, students with learning differences and disorders, students with disabilities or behavioral challenges, students who identify as gender variant, and those whose families have recently immigrated.

Yet the challenges are many. Racism, sexism, classism, homophobia, ableism, and other forms of bias and bigotry impact students on a daily basis. People who are not part of a society's dominant group (or groups) may be subject to unfair treatment, restrictions on rights, physical attacks, bias-motivated crimes, and more. And particularly relevant to educators is this fact: The FBI reports that 33 percent of all hate crime offenders, and a similar percentage of victims, are under age eighteen.

A study published in the *American Journal of Public Health* about the negative impact of bullying on kids concludes that "bias-based harassment is more strongly associated with compromised health than general harassment."[4]

Helping kids develop respect and appreciation for diversity decreases their likelihood of harming others due to perceived differences. Teaching students to respect and value differences is therefore a critical part of bullying prevention. In tandem with these goals, educators can also help kids see their many similarities as human beings on a shared planet. This is why this book includes certain key understandings and skills, such as fostering empathy and appreciation of differences, cultivating awareness of our own biases, and developing the fine art of perspective-taking. Lessons 25 and 26, for example, raise awareness of the ways bias, stereotyping, and prejudice bring harm. The lessons provide strategies for students to use in preventing bias-based bullying behaviors and reinforcing a culture of care and respect.

Encouraging Upstander Behaviors

Along with building empathy, compassion, and acceptance, another critical piece in creating an atmosphere of kindness is teaching kids how to step out of the role of passive bystander and into the role of upstander. Taking this step is often challenging for kids of all ages for a variety of reasons. A study published in the *Journal of Early Adolescence*, for example, found that bystanders often don't step into the role of upstander "because they lack the skills that are needed to help victims and because they are afraid of retaliation."[5]

"It's not our job to toughen our children up to face a cruel and heartless world. It's our job to raise children who will make the world a little less cruel and heartless." —L.R. Knost

Many lessons in this book help build the necessary skills, providing practical strategies to help you teach kids how to effectively intervene when peers are mistreated. Some of these skills may be different from what you expect. For example, the first step is instilling the understanding that our actions matter. A National Institutes of Health (NIH) study shows a direct link between kids' mindsets and their willingness and ability to support peers who are mistreated. If students believe they can make a difference, and feel capable of doing so, they're more likely to take action when someone's being picked on.[6] (For more information on mindsets, see page 5.)

The NIH study also gave the following key actions that educators can use to foster upstander behavior:

- *Clearly communicate* to kids that they are expected to include and support anyone who's mistreated.
- *Show kids* how to include, support, and encourage others so they feel confident in doing so.
- *Encourage the understanding* that bullying is wrong and that helping others is the right thing to do.[7]

Kids also have a lot to say about what works based on their personal experiences. The Youth Voice Survey looked at data from more than 13,000 students in fifth through twelfth grades to find out what helped most in responding to bullying and victimization. This study's findings challenge some conventional wisdom and shed light on the strategies that really work best. Here's some of what the survey revealed.[8]

The single most helpful strategy for kids who are targets of bullying:
Seek support from an adult at school or from a friend.

Another highly effective strategy for kids who are targeted:
Don't think like a victim. Kids who told themselves that the bullying wasn't their fault, and that there was nothing wrong with them, proved to be more resilient in the face of bullying.

The least helpful strategies for kids being targeted:

- Telling or asking the person bullying them to stop.
- Telling the person how they felt.

The most helpful things bystanders can do when they witness others being bullied:
Include and support those being bullied in the following ways:

- Walk with them and spend time with them at school.
- Give them advice and hope.
- Help them get away.
- Distract the person who's bullying them.
- Help them tell adults.
- Encourage them.
- Talk to them at school to give support and show that you care.
- Call them at home to give support.
- Listen to them.
- Hear their concerns without judgment.
- Show that you care.

The most important *adult* strategies to help kids who are bullied:
Kids surveyed by the Youth Voice Project also addressed adult behaviors that made a difference. They reported that the three most helpful things any adult can do are:

- Listen to them.
- Encourage them.

- Check back later and over time to see if they're okay.

The *least* helpful things adults might do:

- Say, "You should have . . ."
- Tell a student that the bullying wouldn't have happened if he or she had acted differently.
- Tell a student to stop tattling. (This was the most harmful adult action.)

Communication, problem-solving, emotional management, and perspective-taking are just a few of the many prosocial skills you will find explored throughout the book.

Other recommendations for adults from the Youth Voice Project:

- Reduce or eliminate the following messages in bullying prevention: "Stand up for yourself" and "Just pretend it doesn't bother you."
- Teach kids ways to support and include those who are picked on or excluded, rather than confronting the person doing the bullying.
- Build student and school cultures that encourage inclusion and belonging for all.
- Give kids skills that foster connectedness and resiliency. Building prosocial skills that connect kids to each other and to the school as a whole will help prevent bullying and also enable kids to respond proactively when it does happen.

The lessons in this book will help you adopt these recommendations. Communication, problem-solving, emotional management, and perspective-taking are just a few of the many prosocial skills you will find explored throughout the book.

Two more factors that studies show prompt upstander behaviors:[9]

- *Having effective strategies for standing up for and supporting others.* For example, simply standing next to the person who's being bullied is a powerful way of giving nonverbal support. Through the lessons in this book, your students will learn how and when to employ this strategy and many more.
- *Perceiving that others are likely to intervene.* When bullying takes place, kids are most likely to give support in schools where upstander behavior is more prevalent. Additionally, students who partner up with others are more likely to offer help.

Understanding the Middle School Brain

During early adolescence, the brain goes through some of the most intense changes it will ever experience. At this critical time in young people's lives, the choices they make, attitudes they adopt, and actions they take will affect their capacity to learn, remember, handle stress, stay healthy mentally and physically, and control impulses *for the rest of their lives.*

Additionally, what kids do now has the potential to either raise or lower their IQ and prepare them to fulfill every ounce of their promise—or not.[10]

Research shows that the frontal lobe—the part of the brain that governs reason, judgment, insight, self-control, decision making, and other higher-level thinking skills—doesn't fully develop until age twenty-five. That's why adolescents can be impulsive, disorganized, flighty, and prone to making careless decisions. To a degree, they simply can't help it.

» » » **Online Resource** » » » » » » » » » » » »

To hear more about the teen brain, listen to the NPR interview with Frances Jensen by searching online for, "Why Teens Are Impulsive, Addiction-Prone and Should Protect Their Brains."

» »

The teen brain is busy eliminating excess neural connections left over from childhood. This process of "pruning" is more active now than at any other time of life. Which neural connections get eliminated from any person's brain depends largely on what he or she spends time doing. "Those cells and connections that are used will survive and flourish," says teen brain expert Jay Giedd. "Those cells and connections that are not used will wither and die. So if a teen is doing music or sports or academics, those are the cells and connections that will be hardwired. If they're lying on the couch or playing video games . . . those are the cells and connections that are going [to] survive."[11]

The "brain sculpting" that happens during teen years sets up patterns for life. It's important to let students know this and to make sure they appreciate the implications. For example, if they binge-eat, overdose on video games, drink, or use drugs, their neural pathways become more prone to long-term addiction. At the same time, however, a teen's neural pathways for *healthy* life patterns are also uniquely primed. Kids who nurture intellectual, artistic, and physical talents will be stronger in these areas for life. The same is true when it comes to social and emotional skills. Kids who learn them now may, in fact, have them forever. The pages of this book are filled with ways to expand your students' capacities for kindness and empathy, as well as for self-control, problem-solving, moral courage, and altruism. These skills are essential to a kinder climate and culture, within your school and as your students go out into the world.

Note: For important information and current research on the impact of electronic media, which you may choose to share with parents, see "The Impact of Media Violence" in the digital content for this book.

Stress is another major issue for many kids this age. One seventh-grade girl from our survey said, "In middle school, people have mood swings and get angry more easily than when we were younger. We're getting more homework and have after-school pressures, plus other stuff, too. It's easier to release stress toward other people than deal with it ourselves." The teen brain is especially susceptible to stress and its side effects. Family issues like illness, divorce, money problems, and substance abuse can take a huge toll, and some kids have the added strain of acting as substitute parents for younger siblings. Others may be dealing with physical and emotional abuse. All of this can lead to a sense of powerlessness. Since bullying is commonly driven by a need for power, some kids will be more apt to bully as a result. Others will be more susceptible to being bullied, especially those being victimized at home. For kids who already feel overwhelmed by stress, bullying can sometimes feel like too much to bear.

Thankfully, most adolescents are resilient. But when multiple risk factors exist at the same time, some teens will gravitate toward drugs, alcohol, promiscuity, self-harm (such as cutting), and isolation. Some will develop eating disorders. And some will develop suicidal thinking. Again, bullying can be the factor that pushes them beyond their limits—whether they are observing, being targeted by, or carrying out the bullying.

These are among the many reasons why it's important to create the compassionate, kind, and connected school culture the lessons in this book explore, build, and reinforce. Doing so will not only decrease bullying but can also provide kids who need help with a greater sense of support and connection.

The Importance of Mindsets

This book is fundamentally about change. When we believe change is possible, it is. When we believe it isn't, we close off to possibility and act accordingly. The brain actually changes when our mindset is open to growth. That's neuroplasticity in action.

Some of the first lessons in this book are designed to help your students create a growth mindset—and the understanding that every new strategy they learn will literally change their brains.

Neuroscientists are giving us new ways to use this plasticity and to harness the power of the brain as problem-solver. Helping kids develop a "growth mindset"—as opposed to a "fixed mindset"—is critical. Stanford University neuroscientist Carol Dweck found that growth mindsets enable us to see our abilities as ever-evolving. And this has enormous potential for counteracting bullying and fostering kindness. For example, a study by Dweck's colleague David Yaeger revealed that kids who'd learned about the power and plasticity of the brain showed a 40 percent decrease in depressive and aggressive responses to bullying.[12] Acquiring a growth mindset helped them understand that change is possible—for kids who've bullied, for kids who've been bullied, and for themselves.

Based on this science, some of the first lessons in this book are designed to help your students create a growth mindset—and the understanding that every new strategy they learn will literally change their brains. Take a look at the "Brain Graphic" on page 30. It's used in many lessons to help kids grasp new concepts. These lessons contain strategies and information to help kids understand how their brains work. In turn, this understanding can lead to greater resilience in the face of conflict, bullying, and more.

WHY IS IT SO HARD FOR KIDS TO TAKE RESPONSIBILITY?

This is a question that frustrates many educators as they witness kids' denials, excuses, and justifications for bullying and other cruel behaviors. New research sheds light on this phenomenon, revealing that the fear of getting in trouble isn't the only reason kids avoid accepting responsibility for negative actions. A new study in the *Proceedings of the National Academy of Science* reveals that denials and justifications of morally questionable acts are common because of something termed "unethical amnesia"—the tendency to forget or justify acts too uncomfortable to confront honestly. This allows people to perceive certain bad things they do as "morally permissible." Perpetrators of cruel acts, for example, might say the other person deserved it. They justify "dehumanizing the victim."[13] And this is a common practice among kids who bully.

While this study was conducted with adults, other research shows that its implications extend to people of all ages. For example, a 2011 study of kids ages nine to thirteen showed that those who bullied were "woefully deficient" in moral compassion, and easily justified their actions.[14] Additionally, a study by the Centers for Disease Control and Prevention (CDC) found that adolescents, whose prefrontal cortexes are still developing, are more susceptible than adults to making bad decisions, including harming others.[15] Being aware of these factors gives educators a starting point for guiding their students toward the right path. You'll find many exercises in the lessons of this book that will help kids take responsibility and make good choices. You'll also find two lessons and three handouts to foster conscience (Lessons 27 and 28), and one lesson on moral courage (Lesson 46).

What Student and Teacher Surveys Tell Us About Bullying, Conflict, and School Violence

Let's start with the good news: Educators, parents, and communities are making real, tangible progress in the mission to reduce bullying and violence in our schools. According to the National Institutes of Health, the rate of bullying among teens in U.S. schools has dropped more than 9 percent since 1998. The latest National Crime Victimization Survey tells us that the rate of bullying among students ages twelve to eighteen is now 21.5 percent—the lowest rate ever reported in this survey. (Past years' rates were 28 percent in 2005, 2009, and 2011, and 32 percent in 2007.)[16]

Additionally, fewer middle school students are afraid of being harmed at school than in the past. The rate of students who report feeling fearful of physical harm at school has fallen by 8 percent overall since 1995. The drop is even more dramatic for students of color, among whom the rate has fallen by 15 percent.[17]

The work that educators are doing across the country is paying off! Yet there's still room for progress. That's why we wrote this book. We want cultures of kindness to be the norm in middle schools, not the exception. All kids need to feel safe, supported, and accepted. The fact that 21.5 percent of twelve- to eighteen-year-olds still report being bullied is unacceptable.

Listen to the words of students from the two national surveys we conducted:

- "I was bullied because I was small and I really had no one to go to. I used to self-harm with a razor blade." —7th-grade girl
- "They call me weird, emo, and a weird gay person. They say, 'You suck at everything!' and 'You're horrible at sports!' Sometimes I can't take it." —6th-grade boy
- "There are kids in our class who go home and cry every night over things that people do to them. Some of them have family problems and the problems at school make it worse. The teachers don't even know." —8th-grade girl

- "They say, 'lesbian, stupid idiot, go back to where you came from. You should just end it.'" —8th-grade girl
- "Things go viral sometimes. Some kids make fun of people in a really mean way. They'll send screenshots of personal texts that are meant just for them. It's like bullying and harassing at the same time." —7th-grade boy
- "Kids say I'm bad and shouldn't be allowed to go to this school. I'm so sad that I can't sleep. Why do they treat me this way?" —7th-grade boy

As we read through our survey results and as we interviewed middle schoolers, we repeatedly saw how deep the pain of bullying goes for far too many. Often, kids hide this pain as they sit in classrooms and walk through the halls. Yet it interferes with their learning and affects their emotional and physical well-being. Here is some of the other information our surveys revealed:

Frequency of mean words, conflicts, and rumors:

- 81% of the kids surveyed said that they hear kids saying mean things to one another every day.
- 64% said that they see conflicts happening at their school sometimes, often, or every day.
- 42% said that they hear kids spreading rumors or mean gossip every day.
- 14% said that other kids say things to hurt their feelings every day, and 19% said that this happens one to three times a week.

Going beyond this overarching information, our surveys asked students to select their top three choices for each of the items that follow. Here is what their answers revealed.

The top reasons kids said they are teased or bullied:

- looks or body size: 59%
- how they dress: 41%
- physical ability or disability: 28%
- race: 14%

The top places where kids said bullying and teasing occur:

- at lunch: 84%
- in the hallways: 55%
- on the bus or walking to school: 43%
- in the bathrooms: 33%

The top conflict starters:

- rumors and gossip: almost 60%
- being teased or made fun of: about 46%
- name-calling: 40%

Note: Although conflict can lead to bullying, the above refers to more common conflicts that tend not to escalate into bullying.

People kids said they would go to if they were being bullied:

- a parent: 33%
- a friend: 20%
- a counselor: 16%

One piece of information that especially concerned us was this: Only 14 percent of the kids we surveyed said they would go to their teachers if they were being bullied. When we delved deeper, we found out why. Some kids are ashamed to admit what's happening, or they're afraid of getting in trouble. Others don't want to risk being seen as a tattletale or snitch. And, sadly, some kids simply don't believe their teachers can or will help. Unfortunately, the data support this view in many cases. In their 2012 report, "Bullying in U.S. Schools," two of the world's top bullying experts, Susan P. Limber and Dan Olweus, found that 41 percent of middle schoolers say their teachers have done "little or nothing" or "fairly little" to cut down on classroom bullying. Limber and Olweus also found that 39 percent of kids who reported being bullied said it lasted for over a year.

Equally troubling are the following statistics from the *2013 National School Climate Survey* of students by GLSEN (Gay, Lesbian, Straight Education Network): "56.7 percent of LGBT students who were harassed or assaulted in school did not report the incident to school staff, most commonly because they doubted that effective intervention would occur or the situation could become worse if reported." Furthermore, "61.6 percent of the students who did report an incident said that school staff did nothing in response." The same survey revealed that "51.4 percent of students reported hearing homophobic remarks from their teachers or other school staff." Additionally,

"74.1 percent of LGBT students were verbally harassed (e.g., called names or threatened) in the past year [at school] because of their sexual orientation and 55.2 percent because of their gender expression." The same study reported that "36.2 percent were physically harassed (e.g., pushed or shoved) in the past year because of their sexual orientation and 22.7 percent because of their gender expression."[18]

Another disturbing piece of data comes from the National Center for Educational Statistics: 20 to 30 percent of kids who were bullied didn't tell *any adult*. Yet telling an adult is one of the most effective tools kids have against bullying. As one teenage boy said in retrospect, "I wish I'd spoken up sooner, because it really would have made life a lot easier. If I had just spoken up after the first day, or first couple of days, I could have ended the whole thing."

One of the most important insights we gained in the process of talking to students and conducting our national surveys was this: Although many schools have anti-bullying assemblies and give kids the clear message that bullying and other mean behaviors are not acceptable, kids are too rarely given enough specific, practical information on how to handle real-life bullying situations. They know the why-nots, but not the how-tos. The main message often tends to be simply, "You shouldn't do it." And even if they *do* have more detailed how-tos, they often aren't given enough time—or any time at all—to practice implementing what they've learned.

Kids are too rarely given enough specific, practical information on how to handle real-life bullying situations. They not only need the right words, they need time to role-play and rehearse using them. Without this practice, kids often end up vulnerable and unprepared.

What became clear is that kids not only need the right words to use to confront and prevent bullying, they also need time to role-play and rehearse using them. Without this practice, kids often end up vulnerable and unprepared. Assemblies aren't enough. Imagine doing an assembly on baseball, talking about it in class a few times, then sending kids out on the field to play the game. This tends to be how schools and districts often approach teaching anti-bullying strategies.

In addition, many kids we talked to described ways bullying and conflict interfere with all aspects of their lives at school and beyond. A theme that came up over and over in our student interviews was that many middle schoolers feel stressed out and distracted by conflicts they can't resolve. This often leads to lost friendships, larger conflicts, and—especially in the case of many girls—time wasted replaying the details in their heads. For girls and boys, conflict and anger can lead to incidents of bullying. For example, one kid might get mad at another and want to get even. He might engage friends in harassing the person he's mad at. Before long, texts are flying, the classroom is buzzing with rumors, and the put-downs continue online. The kid who's been targeted can feel as though there is no escape.

Here are a few more things the kids we talked to expressed:

- Many believed that talking to a teacher about a bullying situation actually made things worse.
- Most didn't feel comfortable intervening when they saw someone being picked on.
- Many didn't feel like they had the right skills for dealing with an angry person.
- Quite a few wished that their classes allowed time for weekly lessons that would help them get better at skills for dealing with bullying.

One of the biggest changes we hope this book will make is to help kids feel more hopeful and less powerless in the face of bullying—especially those who are bullied, but also bystanders and the kids who do the bullying.

A Word About Crisis Situations

According to the Centers for Disease Control and Prevention (CDC), most kids who are bullied *do not* engage in suicide-related behaviors. However, as mentioned earlier, bullying *can* increase the risk of self-harm when combined with other risk factors, such as exposure to violence, family conflict, emotional distress, problems in relationships, feeling a lack of connectedness to school or not feeling supported at school, alcohol or drug use, physical disabilities, and learning or behavioral differences.[19] It's also important to remember that kids with physical disabilities or learning differences are among the most vulnerable. And, as stated earlier, gay, lesbian, bisexual, and transgender kids are bullied far more often than their peers. In addition, suicide rates among LGBT kids are much higher than the average.[20] According to another CDC study, gay, lesbian, and bisexual students in seventh through twelfth grade were "more than twice as likely to have attempted suicide as their heterosexual peers." Studies have also shown a significantly elevated suicide risk among transgender youth.[21]

Whether bullying takes place in person or online, it can take a steep toll on kids, contributing to problems ranging from depression to disengagement in school, and, in some rare cases, suicide. This is true not just for those who are targeted, but for those who target others. Kids who bully are at an elevated risk for depression, suicide, substance use, trouble with the law, and violence as they grow into adulthood.[22]

Bystanders—those who witness bullying—are adversely affected as well. According to a report by the Centers for Disease Control, "Even youth who have *observed but not participated in bullying* behavior report significantly more feelings of helplessness and less sense of connectedness and support from responsible adults (parents/schools) than youth who have not witnessed bullying behavior." And kids who both bully and are bullied are at greatest risk of experiencing negative repercussions. The CDC notes, "Youth who report both being bullied and bullying others (sometimes referred to as bully-victims) have the highest rates of negative mental health outcomes, including depression, anxiety, and thinking about suicide."[23]

One of the most important protective factors against suicide and despair for any young person, including those affected by bullying, is a sense of connection and support. School is absolutely critical in this regard. This is true for all kids. But it's especially important for kids with difficult home lives and other risk factors. Feeling connected to and accepted by teachers, counselors, and peers can spell the difference between hope and despair. The lessons in this book will help you foster this connection and acceptance. In addition, we've included the lesson "When Bullying Leads to Self-Harm" (page 230) to help you address the difficult topics of suicide and self-harm.

HANDLING CONFLICT VS. BULLYING

Schools with a lot of conflict—such as peer disagreements, fights, name-calling, or an overall atmosphere of mistrust—tend to have more bullying. And while conflict can lead to bullying, the two issues can't be solved in the same way. In fact, it is *never* appropriate or helpful to try to mediate a bullying situation or to get kids to "talk it out" using conflict resolution skills. In bullying situations, which often involve a serious power imbalance, putting the involved parties face-to-face can be damaging to the student who's being targeted. For more information on handling bullying situations, see "Addressing and Preventing Bullying" on page 14.

You'll find tools and resources for your students, as well as a handout for parents. And at the end of this book (page 248) is information for hotlines and other sources of support.

About This Book

All forty-eight lessons in this book are designed for teachers, counselors, group leaders, social workers, religious educators, and facilitators of out-of-school activities. Each one is based on current research and information gleaned from our national surveys as well as from our face-to-face interviews with middle school kids, teachers, principals, and counselors. Additionally, the lessons and strategies in this book can mesh with any existing anti-bullying program you may be using in your school, such as Olweus Bullying Prevention Program, Second Step, or Responsive Classroom.

Each lesson takes thirty minutes or so, and contains discussion topics, activities, and concrete strategies that foster critical thinking and language development. Optional follow-ups at the end of each lesson can be completed on another day or as homework. You'll also find creative, thought-provoking enrichment activities that support, reinforce, and expand the content of each lesson. These, too, are optional, and how you use them is up to you. Some lessons also list helpful online resources that expand on key points.

Every lesson also has handouts for kids to complete during your meeting time or as homework. The handouts are designed to help students apply what they've learned. If at all possible, make time to talk about the handouts after they're completed. (These handouts are available as downloadable digital content. See page ix for details on how to access this material online.)

Also, to help you meet your district's character education goals, the "Character Connections" section at the top of each lesson indicates the key character traits related to the lesson.

Some lessons also include accompanying "10-Minute Time Crunchers." These quick activities reinforce and extend the concepts presented in their corresponding lessons. You can do these time crunchers immediately after completing the corresponding lesson or at a later date.

Here's the layout of the rest of this book:

Section 1: The Core Lessons
These twelve activities have been carefully designed to reshape the way your students think, react, and interact, and many activities are rooted in current neuroscience. They set the stage for all the lessons and skills that follow.

Section 2: Fostering Courage, Kindness, and Empathy
The ten lessons in this section give kids specific strategies and understandings that foster greater kindness, empathy, and courage.

Section 3: Celebrating Uniqueness and Accepting Differences
These eight lessons challenge mindsets that lead to cruelty. They also help kids honor their own uniqueness and the uniqueness of others, fostering respect and the understanding that individual differences enrich us all.

Section 4: Dealing with Conflict
This section's nine lessons are full of practical strategies and understandings to help students handle conflict and anger respectfully, peacefully, and productively.

Section 5: Coping with and Counteracting Bullying
These nine lessons are filled with real-life stories and realistic strategies to prevent bullying and address it when it happens. Some of the lessons will help kids stop bullying.

Writing Prompts
In this section you'll find bonus writing prompts to help students reflect on concepts in each section of the book and gain deeper understanding of certain topics.

Student Survey
The survey on pages 244–247 is similar to the one we used in our research. It will help you learn how your students are affected by conflict, bullying, and other mean behaviors—as well as how kind, caring, and willing to do the right thing students might be.

Recommended Resources
At the end of the book is an annotated list of high-quality books, websites, organizations, and other resources. There's also hotline information in the event that you need to handle crisis situations.

Using This Book

We highly recommend doing at least one lesson a week. If that's not possible, try to aim for three a month. Many teachers find advisory period to be the best time. Others find it helpful to alternate with colleagues on their team, each teaching a lesson a month wherever they can fit it in. That way, students get several lessons a month, and each teacher or counselor has to lead only one. The material in each lesson ties in with many content areas, including language arts, social studies, and health. So if you're a classroom teacher, you may choose to align these lessons with the curriculum. Or, if you're a school counselor, you might join classrooms and teach these lessons there or pull out kids for group lessons. Decide what works best for you, your students, and your school. However you do it, we are confident you'll find that the results are worth the effort.

Getting Started

The climate of your building can change if everyone gets on board. Chat with your principal about the prospect of using this book schoolwide so everyone can reap the benefits. If you're using this book on your own, know that you may be planting seeds of change that reach beyond your classroom. People who notice positive changes in your students will likely ask what you're doing. That's when the possibilities start expanding.

The following recommendations will help you use this book in ways that maximize its rewards and suit you, your students, and your school.

You'll need the following for most lessons:

- **Student journals and pens or pencils.** Ask each student to designate a notebook as his or her journal for these lessons. These journals will be confidential unless students choose to share certain entries with you or the group.
- **Agreement for Classroom Discussions.** You'll create this agreement with your students in Lesson 2 (page 20).
- **"Brain Graphic" poster.** This graphic is introduced in Lesson 4 (page 27) and is also included in this book's digital content.

If everyone in your school is using this book, consider doing a whole-school launch. Kids receive a powerful message when their entire school commits to common values and strategies. Starting the school year with a unified activity gets kids excited and creates enormous motivation. For example, one of the best start-of-the-year kickoffs we've heard of linked the entire community, bringing home the message that kindness, respect, acceptance, and decency were highly valued and expected within the school and beyond. Each year at this school, students, staff, administrators, and support personnel were joined on the school's lawn by the mayor, chief of police, board of education chair, parents, and selected town dignitaries. The local press reported on the event and published photos of the festivities, including a processional in which kids from each grade marched out with huge handmade banners representing different character education traits. All students were given the unmistakable message that their school and community valued respect and kindness.

Another school's launch engaged students in team-building activities at the start of the year, emphasizing the expectation that respect was paramount. Every kid knew they could go to designated adults for support throughout the year, and every adult was ready to deliver. Kids who otherwise might have feared being labeled snitches felt safe to speak up if they were being bullied, buoyed by the collaborative environment initiated on day one. As weeks went on, student-led morning announcements about respect and kindness echoed messages on student-made posters that were posted around the school. Lessons on compassion, kindness, and anti-bullying strategies were just part of this school's

AN INNOVATIVE SOLUTION TO THE TIME CRUNCH

If you're using this book schoolwide, and if your administrator's open to creative solutions, read on for one of the most ingenious time crunch solutions we've heard about. Middle school principal James Walsh shared with us his creative approach to a scheduling challenge. When he realized that regular class meetings might be the way to reduce bullying and other bad behaviors, he wracked his brain to figure out how teachers could fit two meetings a month into an already packed schedule. That's when an inventive idea came to him: shortening the day's eight class periods by four minutes every other Tuesday, thus freeing up the necessary thirty minutes for the "Tuesday Talks" that teachers conducted. He adjusted the bell schedule accordingly, and set his plan in motion.

Says Walsh, "Everyone got on board, and teachers started seeing changes right away. Now, four years later, kids look forward to these meetings, and it never feels like a chore for any of us." Walsh reports that the results at his school far outweigh the effort it takes to juggle the schedule. He says, "We all agree we're getting better classrooms, better behaved kids, and more time to teach due to fewer discipline distractions. It's really working."

Your school may want to consider Walsh's method. If it's not possible to implement it schoolwide, work with your team or department to come up with an innovation that works for your particular setting. A little creativity can go a long way!

commitment to peace and harmony. The theme was carried out in countless other ways throughout the year, spearheaded by a student-teacher committee that met monthly.

Start with the first twelve core lessons. These lessons set up and support the other lessons in the book. They provide foundational concepts, foster growth mindsets, and help students see their connection to the larger world. Laying the groundwork with these core lessons will better ensure the long-term results you're looking for. Once these lessons are completed, you can choose others based on the needs and priorities of the class or group.

Create agreements for group discussions. Lesson 2 (page 20) walks you through creating agreements that will enable any discussion to go smoothly. We recommend laminating and posting these agreements in a prominent place if you can. If you can't, make copies and distribute the agreements to students to keep in their journals. Refer to the agreements at the start of each meeting period and whenever necessary.

You can also display a digital image of the guidelines at the start of each period, or consider giving your students copies on business cards to keep handy. Revisit the guidelines often and help kids assess where they've shown growth and where they have room to improve.

Begin each lesson with deep breathing. Start each lesson with deep breathing and use it at times of transition, especially when the energy in your room is chaotic or distracted. Your students are likely to end up liking this process and asking for more, even if they resist at first. Let them know that athletes and performers use deep breathing to get calm and focused, and that the practice will do the same for them. Don't be deterred by middle schoolers' natural cynicism and silliness when you introduce this. If you stick with it, they will, too. Lesson 7, on page 41, tells you how to teach the process.

» » » Online Resource » » » » » » » » » » »
To learn more about the efficacy of deep breathing, search health.harvard.edu for "relaxation techniques: breath control."
» »

Harness the power of visualization. A number of lessons in the book incorporate visualization. Introduced in Lesson 1 (page 18), this process helps kids mentally rehearse applying many concepts and strategies in this book, thus positioning them to better use them in life. Author and psychology professor Barbara Fredrickson explains, "Visualization has been shown to activate the same brain areas as actually carrying out those same visualized actions." That's why visualization has been such a powerful tool for winning athletes and other successful people. Seeing oneself accomplishing a specific goal or action strengthens the neural pathway for achieving the goal or action in real life. For example, in Lesson 17, "The Courage to Be Kind" (page 86), students practice building their "courage muscles." They're asked to envision standing tall and conveying strength in the face of meanness. Visualizing themselves doing this makes it easier to do so in real life.

Bring your unique style to each lesson. Teach the content in this book in a way that feels natural to you. If you like gathering students in a circle, go for it. Or you may prefer to have them remain seated at their desks or tables and to look at whomever is speaking. That's fine, too. Also, since some of the lessons deal with deeply sensitive issues, you might want to let students occupy their hands while they listen (by doing things such as drawing, doodling, or modeling clay). This may sound counterintuitive, especially when you want kids to tune in. However, letting students occupy their hands can actually help some of them focus better. Recent research conducted by the University of California-Davis and funded by the National Institutes of Mental Health encourages teachers to allow nondisruptive movements, because this helps many kids with ADHD think more clearly.[24] This may be true for some kids without ADHD as well. Hands-busy activities can take the edge off difficult topics while helping kids stay more engaged. Again, see what feels right to you.

Introduce and use automatic writing. This technique is introduced in Lesson 9, "Your Actions Create Ripples," and is included in many other lessons. It helps kids rapidly get their thoughts and feelings on paper and release what's inside, rather than pondering every word they write. To conduct an automatic writing activity, have your students open their journals and pick up their pens. Tell them that when you say *go,* they're going to write for one to three minutes without pause. Spelling and neatness don't count, and no one else will see what they write unless they choose to share. This is a great way for kids to unblock and channel thoughts they didn't even know were there.

Enforce confidentiality. Make sure students understand that they should not bring other people's personal information into group discussions or role-plays. Remind students not to use real names when describing bullying or conflict experiences or other sensitive situations. Coach them to say things like, "Someone I know," "This kid," or "A relative of mine." In addition, ensure that student journals are confidential unless kids choose to share certain entries with you or the group.

Have students share in pairs. Many lessons in this book include sharing with a partner. This practice increases communication between students who otherwise might not interact socially and fosters openness in kids who are reluctant to share in front of the group. To optimize your paired sharing time, here are some tips:

- Put students into pairs. (Pick partners for them rather than having them choose their own.)
- Remind them to listen respectfully and to take turns speaking.
- Share the question, prompt, or topic for discussion before partners begin their discussion.
- Announce the allotted time frame. Cue pairs to switch halfway through, so they each get a chance to share.
- Circulate and give coaching where needed.
- When the time has elapsed, have partners thank each other.

Try the circle configuration. Most lessons in this book can be done in a circle if you so choose. The advantage of a circle is that it allows kids to see each other's faces, and helps them tune in and listen attentively. However, if a circle doesn't work for you, use whatever configuration does. Some middle school teachers pass a "talking object" to each speaker, which alleviates interrupting and fosters greater focus. You can use any object that can easily be passed from hand to hand. One middle school teacher we know uses a koosh ball. Another uses a soft globe. Or you might use a "talking stick," decorated with bright colors by a student. (To see examples, search online for "talking stick.")

KNOWING WHEN AND WHAT TO REPORT

There are, of course, limits on confidentiality. Certain things need to be reported, depending on the rules in your area and depending on whether you are a mandatory reporter. Follow your school or district protocol for notifying proper personnel if a student reveals red-flag issues such as cutting, suicidal thoughts, or abuse.

Honor diversity. Model and reinforce an attitude of acceptance and respect toward all differences—in ethnicity, race, gender, sexual identity, culture, ability, or any other area of diversity. Emphasize that people's unique differences bring richness and texture to our world, to your school, and to students' individual lives. Many lessons in the book incorporate these ideas. When welcomed, diversity in any form is one of our greatest strengths, leading to deeper understanding, greater compassion, and more expansive ways of thinking. When students embrace diverse people and perspectives, they become better prepared to thrive and succeed in a changing world.

Have kids use the strategies you teach in real life. It is critically important to check in regularly with students about how they're applying what they've learned. Each time you conduct a lesson, be sure to remind students you'll be asking how they're applying the strategies in their relationships at home, in school, on the playing field, and elsewhere. Many of the lessons and handouts in this book include "Real-Life Challenges." Let your students know that you expect them to try these challenges, and that during parent conferences, you may discuss with family adults how students are applying what they've learned.

Addressing and Preventing Bullying

In truth, this entire book is about preventing bullying. The more adults model and foster kindness, compassion, respect, and acceptance, the less bullying will occur. That said, it's still important to address bullying directly. Here are key steps in this process.

Survey students to learn what's really going on. You can use the survey on pages 244–247 several times a year to find out what your students are experiencing behind the scenes. This will help you chart progress, note changes, and record data. The survey will also help you see what topics, challenges, and strategies you most need to zero in on. Talk with an administrator about doing this schoolwide. You may be surprised at what it reveals!

Talk to your administrator about arranging comprehensive staff training. As we've shared, when the entire staff of a school shares common goals, it sends a powerful message to students and encourages them to take what you're teaching more seriously. When values, attitudes, and expectations are shared and modeled by *everyone* in the building, a climate of respect is a lot easier to create. This includes teachers, counselors, bus drivers and monitors, security personnel, cafeteria workers, custodians, secretaries, substitutes, and parent volunteers. Although this book can be used without special training, arranging for a comprehensive staff training can provide additional benefits.

Make parents your partners. Keep parents in the loop. They are among your most powerful resources. On your school website, share information for parents on fostering compassion and preventing cruel behaviors. Talk to your principal about arranging parent workshops that reinforce the ideas in this book. Not all parents are able to attend evening workshops, so provide them with related information they can access easily. Many of the resources provided in this book are perfect for parents. If you create the kind of student-staff committee suggested in Lesson 48, "Ending Bullying in Your School Starts with You," have this committee also find or develop helpful information to send home to parents.

Give students a voice in the process. Kids *have* to be an integral part of creating change—and they want to be. Middle schoolers want their opinions heard and honored. The best way to encourage students to buy into change is to make them a key part of it. Educators can plant the seeds, but it's students who will make those seeds grow. When kids are empowered to contribute ideas and follow through with concrete actions, real change can take root. For example, Lesson 48, "Ending Bullying in Your School Starts with You" (page 238), gives students a chance to come up with specific actions to initiate a schoolwide anti-bullying campaign. In this lesson, students form groups to consider the following questions as a way of prompting creative ideas:

- What messages of kindness do you want to share with others? How can you spread these messages at school?
- How can you use the power of social media and the Internet to spread your message even further?
- Do you want to take your campaign out into the community? If so, how do you want to get people outside the school involved?
- What kind of ongoing committee do you need to carry out these ideas? Who should be part of this committee, and how often should the committee meet?
- What questions do you have about how to carry out your plans and ideas? Who can you talk to about these questions?

Your support in helping students implement their ideas is critical.

Model what you want to see in your students. Words affect the way the brain functions, and every member of the school community can be mindful of this. Choose kind words over critical ones, and avoid sarcasm. Be empathetic, too. Young people watch adults for cues on how to behave, and empathy should top the list of modeled traits.

»»» **Online Resource** »»»»»»»»»»»»
To see an example of the power of empathy, search online for "I Wish My Teacher Had Known" in *Yes!* magazine.
»»»»»»»»»»»»»»»»»»»»»»»»»

Talk to your administrator about positioning staff in "hotspots" in your school. Your surveys will reveal where most bullying takes place. Adult presence in those spots is a powerful preventative measure. Whoever is there should be trained in how to respond if bullying occurs.

Know what to do if you see bullying taking place. By conducting the lessons in this book, you will hopefully have fewer and fewer instances in which you'll need to directly intervene. However, it's important to know what to do, should those cases arise. Here are the steps we recommend:

- Intervene immediately.
- Separate the students.
- Offer support to the target of the bullying.
- Refer to your school's anti-bullying policy for designated disciplinary consequences. This may vary from school to school. Consequences are generally based on the severity and frequency of the bullying and the degree of harm it causes. Examples include temporary removal from the classroom, losing certain privileges, behavioral assessment, counseling, peer support groups, conferences with parents, detention, or restitution.
- Follow up with the student who was bullied. Check in the following day at a minimum, and more often if the bullying has been ongoing.
- Contact the parents or caregivers of each student.
- Offer continued follow-up to the student who was bullied. Checking back in is critical.
- When necessary, provide remedial counseling to the student who did the bullying.

Provide easy, confidential ways to report bullying. Let kids text in reports of bullying. Many schools set up a special number for kids. You can also provide blank index cards kids can use to report bullying. Position boxes around the school where kids can place their cards, and check the boxes at least once a day. And make sure all staff members give a clear message that they'll support any student who comes to them.

Acknowledge and reward kindness and positive behaviors. Certificates, bulletin boards, special assemblies, coupons, fun events, and verbal compliments—kids love to be acknowledged, and it works! Punitive measures, on the other hand, often don't. You'll create and strengthen an atmosphere of kindness by using positive feedback to reinforce the behaviors you most want to see.

One Last Thing

We wish you all the best as you undertake this mission, and we would enjoy learning about your journey. Please feel free to contact us in care of our publisher at help4kids@freespirit.com. We would love to hear your experiences, thoughts, and ideas.

In peace,

Naomi Drew and Christa M. Tinari

Section 1

The Core LESSONS

Creating a Vision of a Peaceful School

CHARACTER CONNECTIONS
personal responsibility / kindness

Lesson 1 guides students to envision the kind of school atmosphere they'd like to create and the kind of world they hope to have.

Students will

- engage in the process of visualizing a peaceful school
- specify actions that would lead to a more peaceful atmosphere in their school
- understand their connection to the larger world and their role in creating a more peaceful future

Materials

- student journals

Introduction

Say: **Imagine going to school each day in an atmosphere of kindness, respect, and acceptance. What would that be like?** Accept responses, and then say: **Well, it's possible for us to create what you've described. There have been breakthrough studies proving that kindness is actually contagious. It goes from one person to the next. We have the power to start the chain of kindness.**

Read aloud the following quote: **"Researchers from the University of California, San Diego and Harvard provided the first laboratory evidence that cooperative behavior is contagious and that it spreads from person to person to person. When people benefit from kindness they 'pay it forward' by helping others who were not originally involved, and this creates a cascade of cooperation that influences dozens more."**[25]

Say: **You are the leaders, innovators, teachers, and parents of the future. What you do matters. Creating the kind of school—and the kind of world—that you want starts right here, right now.** Invite student responses to these ideas.

Discussion and Activity

Say: **Here's what one middle schooler said about kindness and conflict at school: *"Without kindness and respect, society would break down and there would be fights everywhere. That's one of the reasons I like my school. There are rarely conflicts and kids get along with each other."***

Ask: **What are some ways you'd like to see our school change in terms of how kids treat each other?**

Say: **Envisioning what we want is an important part of making it happen. And having a clear vision of what we want—who we want to be, how we want to treat others, what kind of school we want to have—helps us take concrete steps to turn these visions into reality. Every great idea starts with a picture in the mind's eye!**

Share this quote from social and behavioral scientist Frank Niles: *"Visualization works because neurons in our brains . . . interpret imagery as equivalent to a real-life action. When we visualize an act, the brain generates an impulse that tells our neurons to 'perform' the movement. This creates a new neural pathway—clusters of cells in our brain that work together to create memories or learned behaviors—that primes our body to act in a way consistent to what we imagined. All of this occurs without actually performing the physical activity, yet it achieves a similar result."*[26]

Say: **Let's try visualization now.** Ask students to close their eyes. If some prefer not to close their eyes, have them look down and concentrate on a focal point as they visualize. Let them know that the key to visualization is to mentally picture what they wish to create, and then imagine the steps it would take to get there.

Say: **Take a slow, deep breath: in through the nose, then out through the mouth. Allow your body and mind to totally relax. Do this again, a little slower, lingering on the breath out.** Have students continue to breathe slowly and deeply as you speak.

Say: **Now, imagine coming to school every day and feeling safe, respected, and welcome. Take another deep breath as you picture this.** (Allow about twenty seconds of silence.) Say: **Picture people being nice to each other regardless of differences. Imagine being able to walk through any part of this school, inside or out, feeling secure, accepted, and happy. Envision it being this way every day.** Give students another minute to visualize this in silence.

When the visualization process is complete, say: **In your journals, please write down the details of what you pictured. You're going to be sharing this with a partner. Don't worry about spelling or neatness. Just let your thoughts run free.** After several minutes, have students get into pairs. Say: **Please share with your partner what you visualized.** Caution kids to listen with an open mind and not to judge or criticize what they hear. Say: **This is an important first step in creating the kind of atmosphere we all want at school.**

Give pairs about three minutes to share. Then have students reconvene in the large group and have a few students discuss what they envisioned. On the board, list the key elements of these ideas and visions. Next, ask students what specific actions people could take to make your school the way they visualized it. List these ideas on the board, as well.

Wrap-Up

Tell students that each lesson you do as a group will move you closer to the kind of school atmosphere everyone envisioned. Say: **The future depends on you! You have the power to create the kind of classroom, school, community, and world you want. That's what we're going to be working on together.**

Follow-Up

If you have time to follow up on this lesson, put your students in "vision groups" of three to five people. Ask them to agree on two specific actions that can start bringing the entire school closer to what they envisioned. How can they get the word out about their goals? Have them put together an action plan. After they've had a few minutes to discuss ideas, reconvene the large group and invite groups to share what they came up with.

Choose a few representative students to share these ideas with your principal. If you like, go with them and ask permission for your students to take steps toward implementing some ideas that emerged from vision groups. If other educators at your school are using this book, chat with them and see how your groups could pool ideas. If you're using this book on your own, help your students select a few activities that might appeal to the rest of the student body. This is critical. Students need to know they really have the power to change their school, and that adults are taking their ideas seriously. Also, consider ideas that apply just to your group or classroom. What can your students start doing right now to create a kinder culture?

Enrichment Activity

If you can fit this into the schedule in a way that works for you, have vision groups continue to meet regularly during class or advisory time and start putting their plans into action. Feel free to customize this for your students, your group, and your school. For example, some schools have formed kindness groups, peace groups, and respect groups that are open to anyone who wants to join. They have monthly activities initiated by students and supported by staff. If you have a School Climate Committee or something similar, see if you can work together to create a plan for your school. Be sure to include some students when you meet. This is very empowering for them, and further reinforces that they are being heard and their ideas are valued.

LESSON 2

Creating Group Agreements for Classroom Discussions

CHARACTER CONNECTIONS

assertiveness / collaboration / respect / responsibility

Lesson 2 has students create a group agreement that ensures emotionally safe, productive discussions and interactions.

Students will

- reflect on what makes discussions positive or negative
- identify the behaviors and conditions that facilitate positive, productive discussions
- pledge to follow the "Agreement for Classroom Discussions"

Materials

- handout: "Overcoming Obstacles to Productive Classroom Discussions" (page 22)

Introduction

Say: **When we met to talk about creating a vision of a peaceful school, we discussed creating an atmosphere in our school where people are kind, respectful, and accepting of others. How would you feel if we could really make this happen?** Take responses. Say: **Throughout the coming weeks, we'll be having many more discussions that will help us make this a reality. In order for our discussions to go well, what are some things we can always do?** Entertain a few answers. You'll be getting back to this question in greater detail later in this lesson.

Discussion and Activity

Ask: **What things can prevent classroom discussions from going well?** Take some responses. Then distribute the "Overcoming Obstacles to Productive Classroom Discussions" handout to each student. Have kids think about the two prompts on the handout: "Classroom discussions don't go well when . . ." and "It's difficult for me to participate in a classroom discussion when . . ." Give students three to four minutes to circle the responses that are true for them and answer the questions at the end.

Afterward, ask students what they circled and discuss these responses. Then ask how they answered the questions at the end.

Say: **Now let's talk some more about what makes discussions go well.**

Write the following prompts on the board:

- *Classroom discussions go well when . . .*
- *It's enjoyable for me to participate in classroom discussions when . . .*

Ask students to share their responses to each prompt. As students share, have several student volunteers record responses on the board.

In a new spot on the board, write, *Agreement for Classroom Discussions.*

Next, have students look at the list on the board and think about which ideas are the most important agreements they can make as a group. Point to each item listed on the board and ask students to give a thumbs-up if they find it really important, a thumbs-down if it's not important, or a thumb to the side if they think it is somewhat important. Have a volunteer count the thumbs-ups for each item. Have another volunteer list the number next to the item. Circle the top seven or eight. Tell students that these will become your agreement for group discussions. Either have a student copy the top choices onto the board or do so yourself. Tell students that during the next lesson you'll be asking them to sign this as a way of showing their willingness to honor these agreements.

Wrap-Up

Ask: **Why do you think this agreement is important? How might it help us all have a really great year together? How might it help us both academically and socially?** Discuss.

Follow-Up

- Type up the agreement and give copies to all students to keep in their notebooks or folders for the rest of the year or semester. Have each student sign his or her copy.
- If possible, make the agreement a permanent fixture in your space. You might make a copy on poster paper that you laminate and label with the name of your class or group.
- Send copies of the signed agreement home for family adults to sign as well. Write a brief cover letter explaining to family adults how the purpose of this agreement ties in with the purpose of these lessons. Encourage family adults to contact you with any questions they might have. Have students bring signed copies back to school.
- For the next several group discussions on any topic, ask a student to read the agreement aloud before beginning. After a few meetings, you should be able to simply refer to the agreement before beginning a discussion, without needing to read the whole thing.
- Regularly check in with students on how well they're abiding by each of the agreement's terms. Are there areas they need to work on? Are there areas anyone is really struggling with? From time to time, have students rate themselves as a group on a scale of 1 to 5, with 1 being the lowest and 5 the highest, on how well they're following the agreement as a whole. Ask students to consider areas where they personally may need to improve. Give coaching where needed.

Overcoming Obstacles to Productive Classroom Discussions

Check the choices that stand out to you in the lists below. Then answer the questions that follow.

Classroom discussions don't go well when:

- ☐ we go off topic
- ☐ people feel afraid to give their opinions
- ☐ only some people talk
- ☐ kids goof off or fool around
- ☐ people can't hear each other
- ☐ people aren't respectful
- ☐ people aren't listening
- ☐ the topic is difficult to discuss
- ☐ anyone is criticized or made fun of
- ☐ kids exchange looks or make gestures in response to what someone else is saying

It's difficult for me to participate in classroom discussions when:

- ☐ I'm afraid I'll say something wrong
- ☐ I'm not interested in the topic
- ☐ I can't form my thoughts or opinions clearly enough
- ☐ I'm worried about confidentiality
- ☐ I have to talk in front of the whole group
- ☐ I've been criticized, made fun of, or given a look
- ☐ I feel like I'll be judged for things I say
- ☐ I feel uncomfortable speaking my mind in my own words

What else?

Now, what are the *best* classroom discussions like? How do people conduct themselves? How do they act toward others? How can we continue having positive group discussions where everyone is heard? What is the value of doing so?

Classroom discussions go well when:

It's easier for me to participate in classroom discussions when:

From *Create a Culture of Kindness in Middle School* by Naomi Drew, M.A., with Christa M. Tinari, M.A., copyright © 2017. This page may be reproduced for individual, classroom, or small group work only. For all other uses, contact Free Spirit Publishing Inc. at www.freespirit.com/permissions.

Respectful Listening

CHARACTER CONNECTIONS

respect / personal responsibility / compassion

Lesson 3 teaches respectful listening skills that can be used all year long.

Students will

- understand the attitudes and behaviors of respectful listening
- reflect on how it feels to be listened to respectfully
- practice respectful listening skills

Materials

- handouts: "Respectful and Disrespectful Listening Chart" (page 25) and "Respectful Listening Checklist" (page 26)

Preparation

Before you begin, choose a student volunteer and have him or her think of a story to tell you for the "bad listening" role-play in this lesson. The story can be about a fun activity he or she did with a friend recently. Alert him or her to the fact that you will be interrupting and demonstrating other disrespectful listening habits. (If the volunteer you choose needs a more specific topic, feel free to brainstorm briefly with him or her.)

Introduction

Ask: **How do you feel when people care about what you have to say and show it by the way they listen?** Take responses. Say: **That's why listening to one another is a really important skill. There are lots of ways people listen. (Student's name) has volunteered to help me demonstrate one style of listening. Please watch us carefully. Afterward, I'll be asking you about specific things you noticed.**

Have the student you recruited tell his or her story as you display elements of disrespectful listening, such as interrupting, exhibiting closed body language, fidgeting, checking your phone, adopting negative facial expressions, using a sarcastic or bored tone of voice, and changing the subject.

Discussion and Activity

Pass out the "Respectful and Disrespectful Listening Chart" handout. Ask students to quickly jot down things they noticed you doing in the "Disrespectful Listening Habits" column.

Then ask: **What did you notice about my body language? Facial expressions? Tone of voice? Words? General attitude?** After receiving a variety of responses, ask your student volunteer how he or she felt about being on the receiving end of bad listening. (Possible answers: ignored, hurt, or angry.) Stress that bad listening can send signals of disrespect and lack of care, and that this can result in conflicts and damaged relationships.

Say: **On the other hand, respectful listening is a gift we can give to anyone.** Ask: **How do you feel when someone really listens to you?** Accept and discuss responses.

Say: **Consider this quote by Simon Sinek: *"There is a difference between listening and waiting for your turn to speak."*** Ask: **How is good listening more than just "not speaking"?** After taking some responses, have students list specific things good listeners do on the "Respectful Listening" side of the chart. After a few minutes, ask several students to share their responses with the group. See if any other respectful listening behaviors need to be added.

Now demonstrate a respectful listening role-play with another student volunteer, with this student also telling a story about a fun activity with a friend. This time, use the respectful listening behaviors students mentioned. Afterward, review the tenets of respectful listening that students noted, making sure they understand that attitude, body language, facial expression, tone of voice, and word choice all play an important part in being an attentive and respectful listener.

Next, break students into small groups of four or five. Hand out copies of the "Respectful Listening Checklist," giving one to each student, plus one extra per group. Have group members compare their individual lists on the "Respectful and Disrespectful Listening Chart" and then combine their ideas into one "Respectful Listening Checklist" that they fill out for their small group. Remind students to practice respectful listening skills as they do this activity.

Throughout this activity, observe how well students are listening to each other, and coach them as needed by offering tips such as, "Remember to face one another."

Here's an example of what a completed "Respectful Listening Checklist" might look like:

Attitude of a Respectful Listener

- Open-minded
- Curious
- Caring

Body Language and Facial Expressions of a Respectful Listener

- Good eye contact (not looking at a phone, for example)
- Facing the speaker; engaged
- Nodding

Words and Voice Tone of a Respectful Listener

- Interested, alert tone of voice
- Not interrupting or changing the subject
- Asking relevant questions

Wrap-Up

Reconvene as the large group and have each small group share their "Respectful Listening Checklist." Discuss why students chose to focus on the items they did. Also give small groups a chance to amend their charts as they see fit.

Follow-Up

- Have students do the Real-Life Challenge at the bottom of their "Respectful Listening Checklist" handouts.
- Refer to the "Respectful Listening Checklist" during group discussions. Have students rate themselves on how well they are listening.
- When students need a respectful listening reminder, ask someone to read aloud specific items on the "Respectful Listening Checklist."

Enrichment Activities

- In small groups, have students work together to design and create Respectful Listening posters that include words and graphics to represent respectful listening skills (for example, a cell phone with a slash through it). Have students sign their posters. Posters can be displayed in classrooms, hallways, or other areas of the school.
- Have students write "Respectful Listening Tips" that students can read during all-school morning announcements if that works in your setting.

Respectful and Disrespectful Listening Chart

"There is a difference between listening and waiting for your turn to speak."
—Simon Sinek

Respectful Listening Habits	Disrespectful Listening Habits

From *Create a Culture of Kindness in Middle School* by Naomi Drew, M.A., with Christa M. Tinari, M.A., copyright © 2017. This page may be reproduced for individual, classroom, or small group work only. For all other uses, contact Free Spirit Publishing Inc. at www.freespirit.com/permissions.

Respectful Listening Checklist

"You never really understand a person until you consider things from his point of view."
—Atticus Finch in *To Kill a Mockingbird* by Harper Lee

Respectful listening means listening with an open mind, giving your full attention, and caring about what the other person says. Brainstorm the qualities of a respectful listener.

Attitude of a Respectful Listener

Body Language and Facial Expressions of a Respectful Listener

Words and Voice Tone of a Respectful Listener

REAL-LIFE CHALLENGE

» Try to catch yourself when you are being a distracted or disrespectful listener. Then, refocus your attention, care, and concern on the speaker. Take note of how it feels to make that shift in attention.

» Use respectful listening skills with your family and friends. Notice how they respond when you listen respectfully.

» Pay attention to how your family and friends listen to others. Thank or compliment someone who is a respectful listener.

 From *Create a Culture of Kindness in Middle School* by Naomi Drew, M.A., with Christa M. Tinari, M.A., copyright © 2017. This page may be reproduced for individual, classroom, or small group work only. For all other uses, contact Free Spirit Publishing Inc. at www.freespirit.com/permissions.

Train Your Brain to Be More Compassionate

CHARACTER CONNECTIONS
compassion / kindness / personal responsibility

Lesson 4 introduces an exercise documented by neuroscience to increase compassion.

Students will

- understand that neuroplasticity gives us the power to change our brains
- reflect on the meaning of compassion
- engage in a practice that has been studied by researchers and found to expand the brain's capacity for compassion

Materials

- one ball of clay about the size of your fist and a ballpoint pen or pencil with a sharp point, OR a ball of clay and a pen or pencil for each student
- student journals
- handouts: "Brain Graphic" (page 30), "Compassion Exercise" (page 31), and "Changing Our Brains: How the Process Works" (page 32)

Preparation

Distribute the "Brain Graphic" and "Compassion Exercise" handouts at the beginning of the lesson. If you like, you can also display the "Brain Graphic" at the front of the room.

» » » **Online Resource** » » » » » » » » » » » » »

For an article about the impact of mindfulness meditation that includes a mini-meditation, search "What Does Mindfulness Meditation Do to Your Brain?" by Tom Ireland on the *Scientific American* blog. You may also want to show students a video segment on the teen brain by Dr. Daniel Siegel. Search YouTube for "The Great Opportunity of the Teen Brain and Empathy." To maximize your time, start the video at 3:36 and end at 8:11.

» »

Introduction

Ask: **Have you noticed how different you are now compared to just a few years ago?** Take responses.

Say: **These changes are happening because your brain is going through some of the most rapid changes it will ever experience.**

Write the word *neuroplasticity* on the board. Say: **This word refers to the fact that our brains are constantly changing. *Neuro* means "nerves." In this case it refers to the nerves in our brain. And *plasticity* means "the quality of being easily shaped or molded." We can actually change our brains—for better or for worse—through the thoughts we think and the actions we take.**

Say: **Later today we're going to do a powerful exercise that will change how our brains feel and experience compassion.** Write the word *compassion* on the board.

Ask students what compassion means to them. (Possible answers: Being caring in a way that allows us to understand and feel the feelings of others; experiencing sadness when we see someone who's sad, or happiness when we see someone who's happy.) Talk with students about the idea that compassion is not feeling sorry *for* other people, but feeling sorry *with* them. Ask: **Why is it important to be compassionate?**

Take a few responses. Ask: **How would our world be different if there were more compassion?**

Discussion and Activities

Say: **Compassion helps us relate to other people with greater kindness and acceptance. It helps us get along better with other people.** Tell students that the meaning of the word *compassion* is similar to that of *empathy*, and that people sometimes use the words interchangeably.

Ask students if they know anyone who's especially compassionate. Ask for an example.

Say: **The activity we're going to do in a few minutes has been studied by researchers and proven to expand the brain's capacity for compassion. First let's take a look at how the brain changes.** Have students form their hands into fists and then put their fists together side-by-side with thumbs touching, tips of thumbs up. Say: **This is the approximate size of your brain. See the lines where your fingers are creased? You can picture these creases as similar to the neural pathways that form in your brain every time you learn or practice something new—whether it's a subject, a sport, a song, an attitude, or a thought.**

Say: **Here's how it works.** Hold up your ball of clay and form it into an approximation of a brain. (If you have clay for every student, pass it out. Have students form their clay into small models of the brain and do each of the following steps along with you.) With your pen or pencil, draw a line in the clay brain to represent a neural pathway that's formed each time we learn something new.

Say: **Each time we practice something new, the line—or neural pathway—gets deeper. When that happens, whatever we're learning starts to feel more natural, and we get better at it.** (Deepen the line in the clay as you speak.) Say: **Attitudes are the same way. The more we practice holding positive attitudes, the better we get at it. This is true for negative attitudes, too.**

Say: **Now we're going to do the exercise I mentioned, which will strengthen your brain's capacity for compassion.** Direct students' attention to the "Compassion Exercise" handout. Ask several students to read aloud two lines apiece.

Say: **In a moment we're going to go through each of these steps. Which one do you think might be challenging for you?** Take responses. Ask: **How might directing compassion toward someone you don't like be helpful?**

Say: **When we hold onto anger, hatred, or resentment, it can end up hurting *us*. As Nobel Peace Prize–winner Nelson Mandela said, *"Resentment is like drinking poison and hoping it will kill your enemies."*** Ask students what this quote means to them. Ask: **How can resentment and anger hurt us?** (Possible answers: When we hold onto anger we can become bitter; we might feel sad or distracted; we might even become depressed.) Say: **We can also hurt ourselves physically by holding onto anger. It can increase our risk for heart trouble over time. Letting go of anger can improve our health and our happiness. Having compassion for someone you don't like actually helps *you!*** Remind students that being compassionate helps us have healthier friendships and makes people feel more comfortable being around us. It also helps us feel more peaceful.

Note: If some students express excessive anger, talk with a school counselor or other appropriate personnel about how to help them manage this issue.

Now have students close their eyes, cover them, or look down. Say: **Take some slow deep breaths, and focus your attention on your heart. Feel it beating inside your chest.** Now read the "Compassion Exercise" aloud slowly, section by section. Ask them to focus on the words and their meanings. Allow for about thirty seconds of silence between each section.

Wrap-Up

Ask students how it felt to engage in this exercise. Ask, in particular, how it felt when they pictured someone they didn't like. Address their concerns and let them know that each time they do this exercise it gets easier, since they'll be creating and strengthening new neural pathways.

Say: **This exercise has been proven to help us build our "compassion muscles." Brain researchers show that the more we do this, the easier it will get—and the stronger our compassion will be.** Pass out copies of the "Compassion Exercise" and encourage students to practice it at home.

Pass out the "Changing Our Brains: How the Process Works" handout. Have students complete it as homework. Tell them you'll be collecting the second page of the handout, and that no one will see their answers but you.

Follow-Up

- In about a week, have students journal about how the repetition of this exercise is affecting them. Are their feelings toward certain people shifting in any way? Are they feeling more compassionate toward anyone in particular? Are they feeling more compassionate toward themselves?
- Talk with students about how the compassion exercise has changed the way they look at people in their lives.

Enrichment Activity

Take on this six-week challenge: For several minutes each day (or each time you meet), have students continue doing this compassion exercise. Help them observe and consider any changes they notice in themselves. At the end of six weeks, take time together to reflect on the overall impact of this exercise. Consider continuing this practice with them all year or all semester.

Brain Graphic

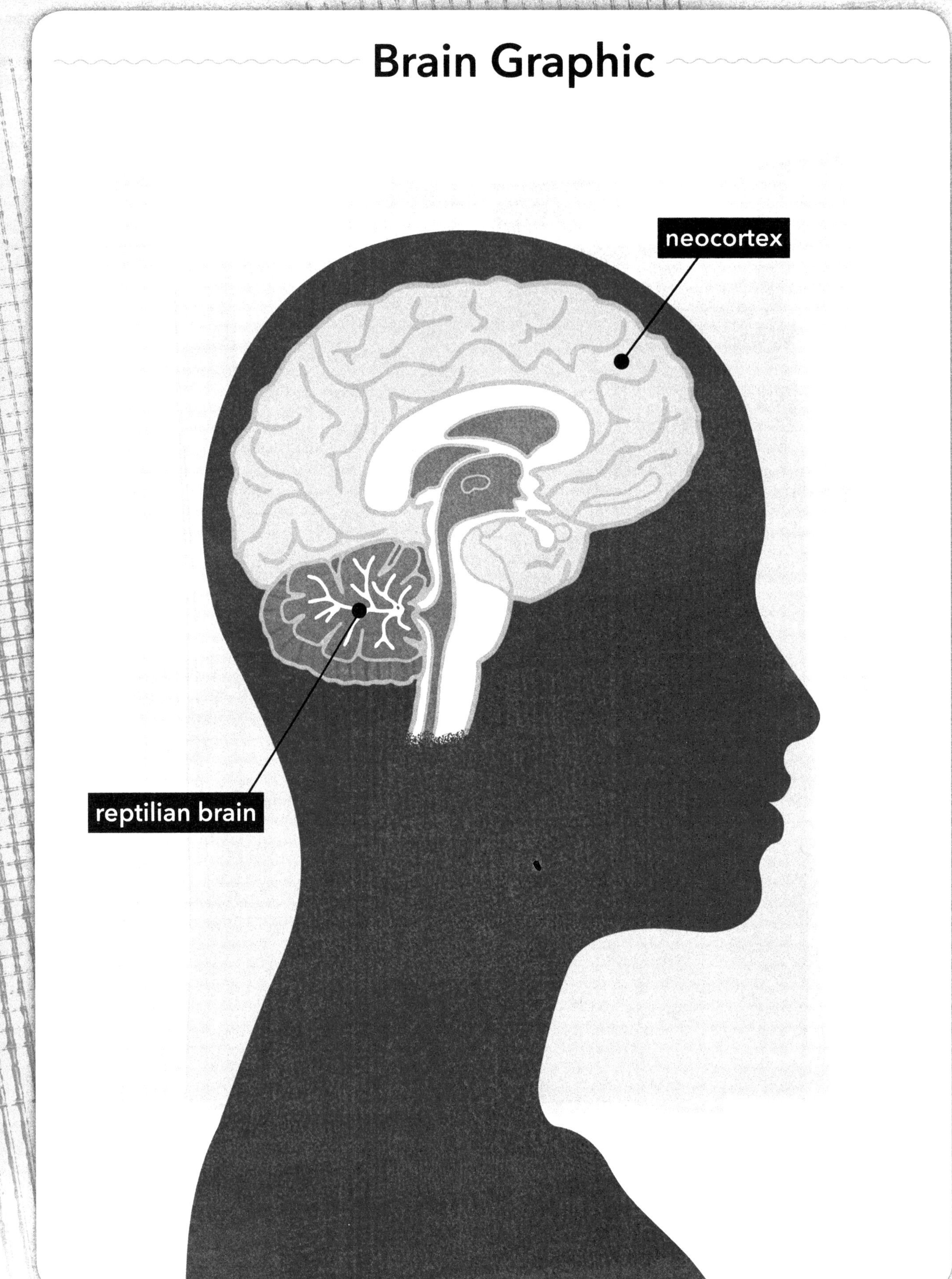

 From *Create a Culture of Kindness in Middle School* by Naomi Drew, M.A., with Christa M. Tinari, M.A., copyright © 2017. This page may be reproduced for individual, classroom, or small group work only. For all other uses, contact Free Spirit Publishing Inc. at www.freespirit.com/permissions.

Compassion Exercise

This exercise is adapted from an ancient mindfulness practice. Take some deep breaths, close your eyes, and focus on the beating of your heart as you do each step.

(Picture yourself as you hear or think these words.)

May I be safe, well, and happy.

May I be fully accepted and respected.

(Picture someone you love and care about and silently say his or her name in place of the blank below.)

May ______ be safe, well, and happy.

May he/she be fully accepted and respected.

(Identify and picture someone you really don't know but see fairly regularly, such as the person who serves you lunch in the cafeteria or a student you often pass in the halls.)

May ______ be safe, well, and happy.

May he/she be fully accepted and respected.

(Picture someone you don't like or are in conflict with and silently say his or her name.)

May ______ be safe, well, and happy.

May he/she be fully accepted and respected.

(Picture people all over the world.)

May all people be safe, well, and happy.

May they be fully accepted and respected.

From *Create a Culture of Kindness in Middle School* by Naomi Drew, M.A., with Christa M. Tinari, M.A., copyright © 2017. This page may be reproduced for individual, classroom, or small group work only. For all other uses, contact Free Spirit Publishing Inc. at www.freespirit.com/permissions.

Changing Our Brains: How the Process Works

Imagine that you never used to help when you'd see someone being picked on. You feel bad about this, so you promise yourself that you're going to start helping now, even if it's just standing by someone's side or saying something simple like, "Are you okay?"

Here's what would start to happen in your brain. Each time you helped someone, neurons would start sending out electrical messages through nerve cells called dendrites. The dendrites would form new neural pathways for "helping." At first the new pathways would be kind of wispy, like lines thinly sketched with a light pencil. But each time you spoke up, the new pathway would get more defined, like when you press down firmly with a heavy pencil. The new pathway would start connecting with other parts of your brain. Soon your old pathway—the one that formed back when you *didn't* help people who were mistreated or bullied—would start to fade away, and the new pathway—the one created when you *do* help—would become stronger. Over time, helping people would feel easier and easier. It would become a part of your life.

Many successful athletes and musicians know about these pathways. That's why they practice so much. Practicing deepens their neural pathways and helps them get better and better at what they do. That's why they look so natural when they perform. Through practice, they've made their pathways very strong.

Here's another way to think about creating new neural pathways. Imagine that you've always taken the same path through the woods to get to your friend's place. Because you've used it so often, that path is very distinct. But one day a tree falls and blocks the path. Now you have to cut through the woods a different way. You have to create a new path. At first, you can barely see your footprints, but each time you walk the new path, it becomes more and more defined, and you start feeling more and more sure of yourself. Over time, the old path starts disappearing, and the new path becomes well-defined. You feel more and more confident each time you walk it.

This is how it works with the brain. Each time we practice a new habit, behavior, or attitude, we create a stronger neural pathway in the brain. By practicing the "Compassion Exercise" again and again, you'll strengthen your brain's neural pathways for compassion. Imagine what our world would be like if everyone did this!

"As a single footstep will not make a path on the earth, so a single thought will not make a pathway in the mind. To make a deep physical path, we walk again and again. To make a deep mental path, we must think over and over the kind of thoughts we wish to dominate our lives."

—Henry David Thoreau

Take a few minutes to think about this quote. In the space below or on a separate sheet, write about what it means to you. What kinds of thoughts do *you* wish to have in your life? Choose positive ones, and you'll be glad to have them keep you company for a long time!

From *Create a Culture of Kindness in Middle School* by Naomi Drew, M.A., with Christa M. Tinari, M.A., copyright © 2017. This page may be reproduced for individual, classroom, or small group work only. For all other uses, contact Free Spirit Publishing Inc. at www.freespirit.com/permissions.

Train Your Brain to Handle Anger

CHARACTER CONNECTIONS

self-control / self-awareness / anger management / personal responsibility

Lesson 5 helps students gain more self-control in the face of anger.

Note: Complete Lesson 4, "Train Your Brain to Be More Compassionate" (page 27), prior to this one.

Students will

- identify body sensations they experience when angry
- learn about the neocortex (the brain's seat of rational thought) and the reptilian brain (the brain's seat of reaction)
- understand that choosing a rational response rather than reacting creates far better outcomes

Materials

- two pieces of chart paper and markers (one black, one red)
- student journals
- handouts: "Brain Graphic" (page 30), "Anger Checklist" (page 36), and "Take Charge of Your Anger" (page 37)

Preparation

On the board, write the word *ANGER* in large letters. In a different area of the board, write the following quote:

> *"Holding onto anger is like drinking poison and hoping it kills your enemy." —Nelson Mandela*

In addition, display the "Brain Graphic" handout, have students bring back their copies of the "Brain Graphic" handout from Lesson 4, or distribute new copies.

Introduction

Ask: **What words come to mind when you think of anger?** Have students come to the board and write their words under the "ANGER" heading.

Ask: **What are some hurtful things people do when they're mad?** (Possible answers: Yell, curse, hit, threaten, withdraw, send mean texts, spread rumors, bully.) **If we hold onto anger—especially if we do it for a long time—who does it end up hurting the most?** (Answer: Ourselves.) Refer to the Mandela quote, and ask a volunteer to read it aloud. Ask students if they agree with the quote. Why or why not?

Say: **Changing behaviors like the ones you just described starts by becoming aware of how anger affects us and how we normally react. It's only by being aware that we can start to change. We can actually change our brains when it comes to how we handle anger.**

Discussion and Activity

Have students look at the "Brain Graphic" handout. Ask if anyone knows which part of the brain anger reactions come from. (Answer: The reptilian brain.) Have students touch the base of their skull, at the top of the neck. Tell them that this is the home of the reptilian brain. Say: **The reptilian brain is not a rational, thinking part of the brain. It's the source of *automatic reactions*, like fighting, fleeing, or freezing up.** Tell students that most animal brains have this region, too. Point to the "Brain Graphic" chart as you discuss this area of the brain.

Ask: **Does anyone know which part of the brain enables us to think clearly and make good choices rather than simply react?** (Answer: The neocortex.) Have students locate the neocortex on their "Brain

Graphic" handouts. Tell students that scientists believe the neocortex only exists in the brains of mammals.

Have a student come to the front of the room. Have the student point to the area of the neocortex on his or her head. Say: **You have the ability to use this part of your brain when you get mad.** Ask: **Which part of the brain do most animals act from?** (Answer: the reptilian brain.) Say: **Since we're human beings, we can use the higher part of our brain to handle anger and conflict. We have the capacity to make choices and not simply react.**

Say: **But sometimes it's hard not to react. Sometimes the sensations we feel in our bodies and the thoughts we think tempt us to react really fast. That's our reptilian brain working, the same way it does in animals. Think about the last time you got really, really mad. What sensations did you feel in your body?** (Possible answers: pounding heart, pressure in the head, heat in the face or body, shakiness, faster breathing.) Take some student responses and share examples from your own experience. Then share these quotes from other middle schoolers:

> *"I get pressure in my head. It's kind of like the headache I get when I'm dehydrated."*
>
> *"I get sweaty palms when I'm really mad."*
>
> *"When I get mad it's like adrenaline, like a rush, like I was just running and my heart's racing. I can't think straight."*

Say: **Now think back to that angry situation you pictured a moment ago. What were some of the angry thoughts that went through your mind when you were most upset?** Have a few students share. Then say: **Angry thoughts fuel angry feelings and actions. Do you have any strategies you use to calm yourself when you're really mad?** (Possible answers: Take deep breaths, get a drink of water, or remind yourself that the issue isn't worth getting into a big argument over.) Accept and discuss student responses.

Say: **I can remember a time when I let my reptilian brain take over. Here's what happened.** (Briefly explain.) Tell students how you felt afterward. Then say: **If you've ever let your reptilian brain take over—which happens to all of us sometimes—how did you feel afterward? How did the other person react? Did things get better or worse?** Entertain responses and guide students to understand that even though unleashing anger might give us momentary relief, we're often left with regret, guilt, and bad reactions from the other person.

Say: **Sometimes we freeze up in the face of anger, like a deer in a car's headlights. Then, afterward, we start thinking about what we *could* have said or done. Has that ever happened to you?** Entertain responses.

Say: **The wonderful thing is that we can change our brains' old patterns. Remember what we learned about forming new neural pathways?** Invite descriptions. Then say: **We're actually forming new neural pathways for handling anger right now, just by talking about it.**

Pass out the "Anger Checklist" handout. Say: **Being aware of how we've reacted to anger in the past is another really big step.** Have students fill out the checklist as honestly as possible. Then have them partner up and briefly talk about which of their anger reactions they most want to change.

Give pairs a few minutes to share. Then ask: **Which items on this list are healthy responses to anger? Go over the list with your partner and underline as many as you can find.** Take responses. Then have students write in their journals one or two responses they want to start working on now. Tell them what your own goals are, as well.

Wrap-Up

Say: **During our next lesson you're going to learn the secret of getting *out* of your reptilian brain and *into* the neocortex. That's going to help you *respond* rather than *react* when you get mad.** Ask: **If we want to create more peaceful relationships, a more peaceful school, and a more peaceful world, why is this so important?** Entertain responses.

Distribute the "Take Charge of Your Anger" handout and instruct students to complete it at home. Let them know that you believe in them and in their capacity to change and grow.

Follow-Up

Go over student responses to the "Take Charge of Your Anger" handout. Ask students what they learned about themselves from doing this exercise. What are some areas they want to improve? Ask if anyone thinks that might be difficult. Discuss. Ask if they've made any changes—even small ones—as a result of what they learned from this activity. Discuss.

Enrichment Activity

Make three copies of the "Take Charge of Your Anger" handout for each student. Have them fill out one per week for the next three weeks. At the end of the three weeks, discuss the experience together and explore how kids' reactions to anger are changing. Invite them to envision the new neural pathways forming in their brains as a result of the work they're doing. How do they feel about the process and the effect it's having on them?

Anger Checklist

Take a look at the reactions in this list and put a check mark next to all the ones that apply to you.

When I'm angry at someone, I usually . . .

- ☐ react first and think later
- ☐ push, hit, punch, or kick
- ☐ use a put-down
- ☐ yell
- ☐ roll my eyes or give a nasty look
- ☐ lose my ability to think straight
- ☐ say or do something I regret later
- ☐ refuse to talk
- ☐ gossip about the other person
- ☐ send an angry text or email
- ☐ get even
- ☐ take responsibility for my part and try to work things out
- ☐ sulk
- ☐ stuff my feelings down and try to ignore them
- ☐ talk to someone I trust and think of solutions together
- ☐ cry
- ☐ take it out on someone else
- ☐ take it out on myself
- ☐ do something healthy to release my anger, like exercise
- ☐ decide not to be friends with the person who made me mad
- ☐ walk away and cool off
- ☐ talk it out with the person
- ☐ listen to what the other person has to say and work toward a fair solution
- ☐ other:
- ☐ other:
- ☐ other:

Now look at the list again and put stars next to the items that are the healthiest ways to deal with anger.

- Which behaviors do you want to change?

- Which behaviors might be the hardest for you to change? Why?

- What can you do to help yourself change these behaviors despite the challenges?

- Who can help you do this?

From *Create a Culture of Kindness in Middle School* by Naomi Drew, M.A., with Christa M. Tinari, M.A., copyright © 2017. This page may be reproduced for individual, classroom, or small group work only. For all other uses, contact Free Spirit Publishing Inc. at www.freespirit.com/permissions.

Take Charge of Your Anger

Noticing our reactions is the first step to changing our brains when we get angry. Observe yourself the next time you get mad. Afterward, answer the following questions.

- Who did I get mad at?
- Why was I angry?
- On a scale of 1 to 10, how angry did I get?
- What sensations did I feel in my body?
- What thoughts went through my mind?
- Did I let myself react, or did I consciously choose a response? Describe what happened.
- What was the outcome of my actions? Did things get better or worse? Why?
- What other feelings were underneath my anger? Did I feel hurt, embarrassed, betrayed, disrespected, ignored? Something else?
- If I'm still mad, do I know a trusted person I can talk to? Who?
- What do I wish I'd done differently in terms of how I handled this situation?
- If I managed to choose a response instead of just reacting, how did I do that? (For example, did I take deep breaths or do something else to calm down?) What did I say to myself?

From *Create a Culture of Kindness in Middle School* by Naomi Drew, M.A., with Christa M. Tinari, M.A., copyright © 2017. This page may be reproduced for individual, classroom, or small group work only. For all other uses, contact Free Spirit Publishing Inc. at www.freespirit.com/permissions.

Words Can Change Your Brain

CHARACTER CONNECTIONS

personal responsibility / kindness / integrity

Lesson 6 helps students recognize that words affect how the brain functions. This lesson also helps students take responsibility for negative words they use, whether they use these words consciously or without thinking.

Students will

- understand the specific ways negative words affect the brain
- make a list of mean words they know, then destroy that list
- list and share the most positive words they can think of

Materials

- at least ten large sticky notes for each student
- a piece of blank paper for each student
- several markers for each student
- shoebox
- construction paper to cover shoebox with
- tape or glue to affix paper to shoebox
- student journals
- handouts: "Brain Graphic" (page 30) and "Words Can Change Your Brain" (page 40)

Preparation

Cut an opening in the top of the shoebox large enough for notes to be slid through. Cover the box with paper, or ask a student to do so and to decorate it. Write the words "Compliment Box" on the side.

Display the "Brain Graphic." Also have students bring back their copies of the handout, or distribute new copies. On the board, write the following quote:

> *"I've learned that people will forget what you said, people will forget what you did, but people will never forget how you made them feel."*
> *—Maya Angelou*

Introduction

Say: **Have you ever noticed the impact angry, critical, and mean words can have? How do you feel when you hear negative words—even if they're directed at someone else?** Tell your students how *you* feel when you hear someone trying to hurt another person with words. Say: **Angry and unkind words actually affect the way our brains function. We're going to talk about that now.**

Discussion and Activity

Pass out the "Words Can Change Your Brain" handout. Ask: **Can you remember a time when you weren't able to think straight because someone attacked you with angry words? The following quote from a book called *Words Can Change Your Brain* explains how this can happen.** Ask a student to read the following quote from the handout: "Angry words send alarm messages through the brain, and they partially shut down the logic-and-reasoning centers located in the frontal lobes."[27]

Explain that the frontal lobe of the brain is where the neocortex is located. Have another student point to the neocortex on the Brain Graphic poster. Have students point to it on their foreheads. Say: **When this part of the brain shuts down, it's impossible to think straight.** See if anyone is willing to share an experience of this with the group. Share one yourself.

Say: **"Alarm messages"—that's how the authors of *Words Can Change Your Brain* describe the effect of angry words. What do you think they mean by that?** (Possible answer: Angry words put us on high alert, like when a siren goes off. That's why the heart pounds faster when we hear them.)

Now look at your group and say something sincerely complimentary and kind to them. Speak from the heart. Ask: **How did hearing those words make you feel?** Explain that kind words and compliments spark the release of healthy hormones called endorphins. Endorphins create a warm feeling around the heart, a relaxed feeling in the body, and a sense of lightness. Endorphins are the antidotes to cortisol—the stress hormone that is produced when we hear mean words.

Pair up students and have them share something kind, complimentary, or affirming that someone's said to them in the past. Tell them to think specifically of things that "lifted them up." It could be as simple as hearing "Good job" from a coach or teacher, or "I love you" from a family member or friend. Share a personal example to get the ball rolling.

After several minutes, see if anyone wants to share with the whole group. Discuss, stressing that kind and sincere words boost our brains, help us feel good, and build stronger, healthier relationships. They also contribute to our overall health and well-being. Share this information from psychology professor and researcher Barbara Fredrickson: "The biggest news is that we're able to change something physical about people's health by increasing their daily diet of positive emotion."[28]

Say: **Since mean, critical, or angry words do the opposite, it's important to eliminate them as much as humanly possible. We're going to do this symbolically right now.** Pass out a blank sheet of paper to every student. Give students one minute to brainstorm and write every negative, critical, or hurtful word or phrase they can think of. (Tell them no one will see what they write.) Then have them tear the papers into tiny pieces and toss them in the recycling bin.

Now pass out the sticky notes. Have students use markers to write one positive affirming word on each note (or on as many of the ten notes as they wish) in large, clear letters. They can decorate around the edges if they wish. Have them hang the notes in visible places around the room or in a special spot you've designated.

Wrap-Up

Select a few students to read aloud one of their favorite words from the sticky notes on display. Then have them turn to the person they were paired up with earlier and offer a sincere compliment. End by complimenting the group as a whole one more time for something you sincerely feel. Ask a student to read aloud the Maya Angelou quote on the board.

Follow-Up

Privately, give every student in the group the name of another student. Have students write anonymous notes of affirmation, sincerely complimenting that person for something they've observed. It can relate to a talent, a personal quality, or the way this person treats others—*not* about his or her appearance or clothing. Here are some qualities that often fly under the radar in middle school: helpful, considerate, good listener, caring, good at overcoming challenges, brave, kind, has high integrity, knows about interesting things, hard worker. Have each student fold up the note, write the name of the person to whom it was written on the outside, and put it in the Compliment Box. Distribute the notes to students before they leave for the day.

Enrichment Activities

- Have students journal about how they felt after receiving the notes from the Compliment Box.
- Tell students to be on the lookout for positive traits in each other as they go through the coming days because they'll be repeating the Compliment Box activity with someone new. Tuning in to people's positive qualities will help them notice things they might ordinarily miss. On another day, repeat the activity, pairing up students differently. You can do this as many times as you like.

Words Can Change Your Brain

"Angry words send alarm messages through the brain, and they partially shut down the logic-and-reasoning centers located in the frontal lobes."
—Andrew Newberg, M.D., and Mark Robert Waldman, authors of *Words Can Change Your Brain*

"I've learned that people will forget what you said, people will forget what you did, but people will never forget how you made them feel."
—Maya Angelou

Write your responses to the questions and prompts below.

- How do you feel when you hear mean or critical words? They can be words that were directed at you or at someone else.

- Think of someone you directed hurtful words at. (This may include adults in your family.) How do you think the person felt after hearing your words?

- Why is it important to think about what we say before we say it, text it, or type it?

- Create a "Promise Statement" spelling out what you plan to do to eliminate mean, hurtful, or critical words and increase kind words every day. For example, "I promise not to criticize anyone for their appearance or anything else. Instead, I will offer compliments to people when they say or do something I admire."

REAL-LIFE CHALLENGE

» Copy your Promise Statement on a notecard or paper and put it in a spot where you will see it every morning and every night.

» Thank and compliment the people you live with, even if it's for small things. Notice what happens when you do this. Now keep doing it!

From *Create a Culture of Kindness in Middle School* by Naomi Drew, M.A., with Christa M. Tinari, M.A., copyright © 2017. This page may be reproduced for individual, classroom, or small group work only. For all other uses, contact Free Spirit Publishing Inc. at www.freespirit.com/permissions.

Using Your Breathing to Calm Your Brain

CHARACTER CONNECTIONS
personal responsibility / compassion

Lesson 7 introduces deep abdominal breathing as a key strategy for achieving calmness and focus, especially when dealing with negative feelings.

Note: Complete Lesson 5, "Train Your Brain to Handle Anger" (page 33), prior to conducting this one.

Students will

- review the functions of the reptilian brain and the neocortex
- understand that they have the power to calm themselves when they feel angry, stressed, fearful, or upset
- learn and practice deep abdominal breathing as a strategy for becoming calmer and less reactive

Materials

- handouts: "Brain Graphic" (page 30) and "Deep Breathing Instructions" (page 43)

Preparation

Remind students to bring back their "Brain Graphic" handouts or distribute new copies.

Introduction

Say: **Today you'll learn a valuable strategy for calming down in the face of anger, stress, fear, or any other negative or difficult feeling that you confront.** Remind students that the rapid changes in their brains and bodies might be causing them to feel moodier and be quicker to lash out—or to react in other negative ways—than they did when they were younger. Emphasize that it's perfectly normal to feel this way and that learning ways to calm themselves when tense or angry can make their lives a lot less stressful.

Share this student quote: "Kids get self-conscious. They start questioning everything about themselves—what they wear, what they should say—everything!" Invite responses to the quote. Tell students that these kinds of feelings, although perfectly normal, can cause us to feel irritable, insecure, and defensive. Emphasize that these feelings are normal and almost everyone who's gone through adolescence has had them.

Say: **The strategy you're about to learn will help you manage some of these uncomfortable emotions. It's a healthy tool for handling anger, too.**

Discussion and Activity

Have students refer to the "Brain Graphic" handout. Review what they've learned by asking: **Which part of the brain reacts most to anger, stress, and fear?** (Answer: The reptilian brain.) Have students locate the reptilian brain on their handouts. Ask: **How many of you have ever felt trapped in the reactions of your reptilian brain?** Talk a little about how being tired, hungry, or overscheduled can also cause us to feel more confined by our reptilian brain.

Say: **The strategy you're about to learn is going to help you access the part of your brain that helps you think clearly and get calmer. Which part is that?** (Answer: The neocortex.) Have students locate it on their handouts. Have them touch the fronts of their foreheads to locate it on themselves. Say: **This practice will also help you become less reactive when you're faced with conflicts or anything else that upsets you.**

Entertain questions briefly. Then say: **The strategy you're about to learn is similar to the ones many**

professional athletes and performers use before games or performances to become calm, focused, and less susceptible to reacting, no matter what happens. It's called abdominal breathing. Ask if anyone practices this already. Kids who take martial arts, yoga, or singing lessons will probably be familiar with it.

Share this quote from a middle schooler in our survey: "I think we all know that we're not always the nicest we can be. If somebody says something mean about me, I'm going to get defensive. But other times I just take a deep breath and then I can let it go." Tell students that this experience is a common one. Abdominal breathing soothes the body and the brain.

Say: **We've talked before about two things that fuel anger. What are they?** (Answer: The sensations we feel in our bodies and the thoughts we think.) Say: **This breathing strategy will help you manage and control your reactions to anger.**

1. Have students sit up tall and, without tensing, place their hands on their lower abdominal muscles, just below their belly buttons.
2. Have them imagine a balloon in the lower abdomen that fills with air as they inhale. (Make sure no one has anything in their mouths before beginning, such as food, gum, or any another object that could cause choking.) Together, take a slow, deep breath all the way down into the imaginary balloon. Together, hold the breath for a few seconds. (This should be a gentle, quiet breath, not the kind kids take when they're about to swim underwater.)
3. Now have students slowly, quietly, and gently breathe out, "deflating" the imaginary balloon as they exhale. Repeat three times, extending the length of each exhalation. Say: **The greatest calming power is in the exhalation of the breath.**
4. After they've taken three deep breaths, have students remove their hands from their abdomens and take two more slow, deep breaths with hands resting in their laps.
5. Now have them take a few regular cleansing breaths, rolling shoulders and neck to release any areas of tension.

Ask students how they feel. Next, show them how to do abdominal breathing "invisibly." (Hands free, just focusing on the breath.) Have them try it. Let them know they can do this practically anywhere. Tell them that focusing on a "centering" word can help. Examples are *calm*, *peace*, or *chill*. Some kids like to use names of places, pets, or people that have a calming effect on them. Ask for suggestions of other words they can use as focal points.

Note: If anyone gets dizzy, tell them not to inhale quite as deeply next time, particularly if they have asthma.

Wrap-Up

Ask students to think of situations where deep breathing might come in handy. (Possible answers: Before tests, before bed, before a big game, or other times when they need to focus or relax.) Pass out the "Deep Breathing Instructions" handout and tell students to practice deep breathing when they go to bed tonight, when they wake up in the morning, as well as any time they feel stressed throughout the day. Let them know you'll be following up with them and will want to hear about results they're getting from the practice of abdominal breathing.

Follow-Up

When you conduct your next lesson with students, begin with deep breathing. Consider doing so whenever possible. Have students write in their journals about how the deep breathing affects their thoughts, moods, and actions. Discuss this together.

Enrichment Activities

- Have each student teach abdominal breathing to a friend or family member.
- Ask students to do a fourteen-day challenge in which they do several minutes of deep breathing every morning and every night. Encourage them to journal about how this affects their day.
- Encourage students to add a statement when they do their breathing. Thich Nhat Hanh (Nobel Peace Prize nominee and author of *Peace Is Every Step*) suggests using the following statement: "I breathe in and I calm my body. I breathe out and I smile." Invite students to try it. This statement is comforting, and the smile that comes afterward triggers a sense of warmth and happiness.

Deep Breathing Instructions

1. Sit up tall with your hands resting on your lower abdominal muscles, just below your belly button.

2. Imagine a balloon in your lower abdomen that slowly fills with the air you breathe in. Take in a slow, deep breath, breathing all the way down into the imaginary balloon. Hold the breath gently for a few seconds.

3. Slowly, quietly, and gently breathe out, "deflating" the imaginary balloon as you exhale. Repeat this process of deep breathing three times. Each time, exhale a little more slowly.

4. After three deep breaths, remove your hands from your lower abdomen and place them in your lap. Take two more deep breaths.

5. Finish with a few regular, cleansing breaths. Roll your neck and shoulders to help release tension.

REAL-LIFE CHALLENGE

» Practice abdominal breathing every night before bed and every morning, plus during the day whenever you feel stressed.

» Practice doing abdominal breathing "invisibly." Take some deep breaths the way you've just learned, but leave your hands at your sides. Now try it in a busy room. Breathe slowly, fully, and deeply. No one but you needs to know what you're doing. This way you can use abdominal breathing at any time. It's kind of like having a secret power.

» In your journal, write about what happened when you did abdominal breathing in a busy room. Did it help you feel calmer? Were you able to better cope with challenging situations?

From *Create a Culture of Kindness in Middle School* by Naomi Drew, M.A., with Christa M. Tinari, M.A., copyright © 2017. This page may be reproduced for individual, classroom, or small group work only. For all other uses, contact Free Spirit Publishing Inc. at www.freespirit.com/permissions.

LESSON 8

Using Stop, Breathe, Chill to Respond, Not React

CHARACTER CONNECTIONS

self-control / personal responsibility / anger management

Lesson 8 teaches students how to do Stop, Breathe, Chill, a powerful brain-based anger-management strategy that expands the impact of abdominal breathing.

Note: Complete Lesson 7, "Using Your Breathing to Calm Your Brain" (page 41), prior to this one.

Students will

- understand the brain mechanics of the Stop, Breathe, Chill strategy
- practice using Stop, Breathe, Chill
- understand that Stop, Breathe, Chill will give them more control over their reactions when they get angry, upset, or stressed

Materials

- handouts: "Brain Graphic" (page 30), "Get a Handle on Anger with Stop, Breathe, Chill" (pages 46–47), and "Calming Statements" (page 48)

Preparation

On the board, write these three words, one above the other: *Stop, Breathe, Chill.* Draw a stop sign next to the word *Stop.* Display the "Brain Graphic," ask students to take out their copies, or distribute new copies.

Introduction

Say: **We've been practicing deep abdominal breathing as a way to calm ourselves in the face of anger or stress. What kind of results are you getting from doing this?** Entertain several answers. Say: **Today we're going to take abdominal breathing a step further by adding some steps that will calm the mind and body even more. This is called Stop, Breathe, Chill.**

Discussion and Activity

Refer to the "Brain Graphic." Ask: **What two main things fuel anger?** (Answer: The sensations in our bodies and our thoughts.) Ask: **What part of the brain is activated when we're angry?** (Answer: Our reptilian brain.) Ask: **What does the neocortex help us do?** (Answers: Think clearly, make good decisions, have good judgment as opposed to being reactive.)

Direct students' attention to what you've written on the board. Say: **When anger strikes, this is a powerful strategy for getting *out* of the reptilian brain and *into* the neocortex.** On the "Brain Graphic" poster, use your finger to trace a path from one to the other.

Pass out "Get a Handle on Anger with Stop, Breathe, Chill." Say: **Here's how some middle schoolers say Stop, Breathe, Chill has helped them.** Have volunteers read the quotes from the handout beginning with, "Knowing how to stop" and, "In touch football."

Say: **Let's try Stop, Breathe, Chill now.** Have students close or cover their eyes and think of a time they got really mad. It could have been at a friend, a parent, a sibling, or someone at school. Say: **Recall where you felt the anger in your body.** (Pause to allow students time to think and remember.) **Think about what the person said or did that made you so angry. Recall some of the angry thoughts that popped into your head.** (Pause.) Say: **Imagine you're still mad and the person is standing in front of you now. Imagine you're about to say or do something you'll regret, but instead, you stop. Now bring into your mind a big red stop sign, and as you do, take several slow abdominal breaths.** (Pause.) **Breathe the oxygen deep into your lungs. Feel it calming your body and mind. Imagine**

the breath going all the way down to your feet, then up to the top of your head. Now imagine replacing your angry thoughts with a word or phrase that calms you down. Say the word or phrase in your head. (Pause.) **Now picture yourself walking away, getting a drink of water, then coming back and talking to the person when you're calmer.**

After a few more seconds have students open their eyes. Ask what they pictured. Ask how they felt during the process. Ask for questions and reactions. Discuss.

Now have students get into pairs. Say: **Knowing how to cool off is critical. As one middle schooler said, "Sometimes when I'm angry I need to get away from everyone because if I do something negative I feel really bad about it. If I have time to cool off, I can think the situation through and find a way to make it better."**

Say: **Getting some space is one way to cool off. Having a drink of water is another. With your partner, brainstorm other things that would help *you* calm down and chill out. Then list at least five of these "chill out" ideas in your journals. You don't have to write the same thing down as your partner does. Just see what new ideas come up from the process of brainstorming.**

After about two minutes of discussion and writing, reconvene the large group. On the board, write "Cooling Off" and list students' "chill out" suggestions under this heading. Have them add additional ones they like into their journals.

Next, have students turn to new pages in their journals and each write down a specific word or phrase they can use to calm their brains whenever they're faced with anger. Tell them to frame their word or phrase in the positive. For example, they might say, "I can keep my cool," rather than, "I won't lose my temper." After a minute or two, ask for volunteers to share some of these words or phrases they can use to calm themselves when angry. List them on the board, too, under the heading, "Words That Help Us Chill."

Wrap-Up

Pass out copies of both handouts for students to complete at home. Tell students that you'll be checking in with them on a regular basis to see how they're using Stop, Breathe, Chill. Stress the importance of applying what they learn in real life. Remind them that using this strategy will get easier over time. As new neural pathways form, it will begin to feel more natural.

Follow-Up

Go over completed handouts and give coaching where needed.

Enrichment Activity

Have students do the Stop, Breathe, Chill challenge: Pledge to use Stop, Breathe, Chill every single time they get angry for the next seven days. Ask them to take note of what happens when they do this, and to write about it in their journals. Discuss their observations and invite reflection on the experience. If you like, pose the following questions:

- When do you find it most difficult to use Stop, Breathe, Chill in real life?
- What do you think could make it easier for you to use Stop, Breathe, Chill regularly?

Get a Handle on Anger with Stop, Breathe, Chill

Stop, Breathe, Chill can make a big difference in every area of your life. Below are some things middle schoolers have said about how Stop, Breathe, Chill helps them. Read each quote, then think about the questions that follow. On the next page are some other questions to answer in writing.

"Knowing how to stop, breathe, and chill really helps me handle my anger. I can control myself better now. Before, I would do things when I got mad that I'd feel guilty about. Sometimes I would get punished. Now I can calm myself down and make a better choice. I feel better about myself now."

Think about this: Do you ever get punished for things you say or do when you get mad? How might your life be different if you could choose a better way to handle yourself when you feel angry?

"In touch football, this kid pushed me and yanked the ball out of my hand. I was ready to fight him for it, but I knew I'd get in trouble for that. So I stopped and breathed and decided to play even harder and better. I ended up scoring three touchdowns."

Think about this: This is a great example of how the energy of anger can be rechanneled into something positive. This boy transformed the energy of anger into the energy of determination. How might you do something similar in your life?

"Stop, Breathe, Chill helped me with my annoying sister. She started getting on my nerves the other day, and I almost called her a name. But then I stopped, took some breaths, and reminded myself that she's only four."

Think about this: What did this girl remind herself of that enabled her to resist name-calling? What can you remind yourself of the next time you're mad at a sibling or friend?

"I used Stop, Breathe, Chill with my mother. She was yelling at me to clean my room, and instead of talking back, I stopped and breathed. Then I told myself to just do it. I was going to have to do it anyway. I avoided a fight with my mom and I didn't end up getting punished."

Think about this: How did this person benefit from using Stop, Breathe, Chill with his mother? What are ways you could benefit by doing something similar with the adults in your life?

"I was in the cafeteria when someone rolled their eyes at me. Usually I would roll my eyes back at them. This time, I reminded myself to stop and breathe. Then I chilled out by saying the name of my dog. That always calms me down. I was able to just walk away and forget about it then, instead of getting into a big thing."

Think about this: What statement or word could help you calm down when someone does or says something that really bothers you?

From *Create a Culture of Kindness in Middle School* by Naomi Drew, M.A., with Christa M. Tinari, M.A., copyright © 2017. This page may be reproduced for individual, classroom, or small group work only. For all other uses, contact Free Spirit Publishing Inc. at www.freespirit.com/permissions.

- What happens when you get angry? Describe the physical sensations you experience.

- What thoughts pop into your head when you get mad?

- List three things you can do to calm yourself next time you're angry or upset:

- Write down a few words or short phrases that you can use to calm yourself every time you get mad or stressed:

REAL-LIFE CHALLENGE

» Next time you get mad, do one of the "chill out" things you listed in your journal and use your calming word or phrase. Write in your journal about what happened after you did this.

» Ask an adult to share his or her favorite "chill" idea with you. Is that something you would use? Why or why not?

From *Create a Culture of Kindness in Middle School* by Naomi Drew, M.A., with Christa M. Tinari, M.A., copyright © 2017. This page may be reproduced for individual, classroom, or small group work only. For all other uses, contact Free Spirit Publishing Inc. at www.freespirit.com/permissions.

Calming Statements

Did you know that calming statements can help you free your brain of the angry and reactive thoughts that pop into it when you're mad? Calming statements help you chill out when you need it most. Even a single word, like "chill," can send a message to your brain. Calming statements can be longer than just one word, though. And they should always be framed in the positive: "I can handle this," or, "I know how to stay calm," rather than, "I'm not going to lose it!"

Create a calming statement that works for you. Use it every time you're mad. Doing so creates a new pathway in the brain and will make it easier for you to calm down and take control of your anger. Now answer the following questions:

- How do you tend to react when you get mad?

- How would you *prefer* to respond to anger?

- What is your calming statement?

REAL-LIFE CHALLENGE

» Next time you feel yourself getting mad, instead of reacting, remind yourself to stop, repeat your calming statement silently several times, and do some deep breathing.

» Notice what happens when you use your calming statement and deep breathing. Write about it in your journal. Did doing this help you not react as much as you usually do? If it didn't help, why do you think that was the case? If it *did* help, please explain what happened after you stopped yourself from reacting, used your calming statement, and took a breath.

From *Create a Culture of Kindness in Middle School* by Naomi Drew, M.A., with Christa M. Tinari, M.A., copyright © 2017. This page may be reproduced for individual, classroom, or small group work only. For all other uses, contact Free Spirit Publishing Inc. at www.freespirit.com/permissions.

Your Actions Create Ripples

CHARACTER CONNECTIONS

personal responsibility / compassion / kindness

Lesson 9 helps build greater awareness that every word we speak and every action we take affects others.

Students will

- understand that our words, actions, attitudes, and choices send either positive or negative ripples into the "pond of life"
- consider the concept that every ripple we create affects others
- reflect on the understanding that if we want the atmosphere around us to be healthy and respectful, creating this atmosphere starts with each one of us

Materials

- a piece of unlined paper (8½" x 11" or larger) and a red and blue marker for each student
- handout: "What Kind of Ripples Did I Create in the Pond of Life Today?" (page 51)

Preparation

Write the following quote on the board:

> *"Never forget, no matter how overwhelming life's challenges and problems seem to be, that one person can make a difference in the world. In fact, it is always because of one person that all the changes that matter in the world come about. So be that one person." —R. Buckminster Fuller*

Also on the board, draw a large oval representing a pond. Above it write,

The Pond of Life

»»» Online Resource »»»»»»»»»»»»
If desired, search YouTube for "The Ripple Effect" by Just Do 1 Thing and show this video to students.
»»»»»»»»»»»»»»»»»»»»»»»»»»»»

Introduction

Pass out the paper and markers to each student. Ask them each to draw a large oval outline of a pond, leaving about two and a half inches of space on each side of the oval.

Say: **Hold out your hand with your palm open and facing up.** Do this yourself as you speak. Say: **Imagine that in your hand is a small pebble. This pebble represents every word you speak, every action you take, and every attitude you have. What happens when you throw a pebble into the center of a pond?** (Answer: It creates ripples.)

Say: **Imagine throwing your pebble into the center of a pond.** Have students pretend to do this. As they do, make a mark in the center of the "pond" on the board, indicating where an imaginary pebble might land. Have students mark their "ponds" with a blue dot in the center. Say: **Whatever energy or feelings your pebble contains are now rippling all the way out to the edges of the pond.**

Discussion and Activity

Say: **If your pebble contains mean words, attitudes, or actions, that's exactly what will ripple out.** Ask: **What are some other negatives someone's pebble might contain?** (Possible answers: Anger, hatred, prejudice, jealousy, exclusion, gossip, bullying.) As each negative word is spoken, draw a ripple in red. Have students do the same. Choose a student volunteer to list these words on the board. At the same time, have students write down every negative word they can think of, writing in red ink on the left side of their papers.

Ask: **How might those negative ripples affect the lives of other people?** Entertain responses. Say: **Here's a real example from one middle schooler: *"Kids get into arguments over texts. Some kids make fun of people for liking the person they like. They send screenshots of texts that are meant just for them. Some kids end up getting really mad. Then more people get mad, and more mean texts get sent."***

Ask: **In this case, how did the negative ripples get started? What was the effect on the people involved? How about other people who weren't directly involved but knew what was going on? How do you think those negative ripples affected them?**

Ask: **What happens to a pond when toxic chemicals get dumped into it? How are negative words, actions, and attitudes like toxic chemicals?** Entertain responses. Ask: **Can you think of times when toxic words or actions polluted the atmosphere around you?** If students share anecdotes, remind them not to use real names or other identifying details.

Say: **Here's how one middle school boy put it: *"If one person isn't respectful to someone else, then that person won't be respectful to other people. It's just like, 'An eye for an eye and the whole world goes blind.'"*** Ask students if they've ever observed something like this happening. How did it feel to witness the spread of negative ripples?

Say: **There is some good news, though. Even the most polluted ponds and lakes can be cleaned and the pollution replaced with healthy substances.** Have students think about positive words, attitudes, and actions that can create healthy ripples. (Possible answers: Kindness, acceptance, inclusion.) As students give specifics, trace over the "polluted" red ripples with a blue marker and have students do the same at their seats. Cross out the negative words listed on the board and write positives on the other side of the pond. Have students list positive words and actions on the right side of their papers and cross out the negative ones on the left.

Direct students' attention to the sign with the R. Buckminster Fuller quote and invite a volunteer to read it aloud: "Never forget, no matter how overwhelming life's challenges and problems seem to be, that one person can make a difference in the world. In fact, it is always because of one person that all the changes that matter in the world come about. So be that one person."

Ask students what this quote means to them. Ask: **If there's a lot of negativity and mean behavior going on around us, how can we each "be that one person" who creates positive ripples? What can we do specifically?** Have students open their journals and do two minutes of automatic writing on this idea. Tell them to let the ideas flow without judgment and without pause. Let them know that the process of automatic writing can help them uncover and unlock thoughts and feelings they didn't even realize they had. After the two minutes are up, ask for a few students to share what they wrote. Acknowledge that when a lot of negativity is present in a school or other environment, shifting the tide can be challenging, but that if we all work together, it becomes easier.

Wrap-Up

Have students pair up and think of one positive ripple they're going to add to the pond of life today. Have them write it down in their journals. Ask a few students to share what they chose. Tell students about a positive ripple you yourself have added to the pond of life.

Pass out the self-observation handout, "What Kind of Ripples Did I Create in the Pond of Life Today?" Instruct students to complete it at home.

Follow-Up

Try to make some time in the days following this lesson to go over the handout, and give coaching where needed. Doing so will deeply expand the value of self-observation for your students.

Enrichment Activity

Have students create a visual presentation with some form of written description depicting a healthy pond of life. Students can use technology, artwork, or any other creative medium. Have them bring in what they create and share it with the group. Students can also complete this activity in pairs.

What Kind of Ripples Did I Create in the Pond of Life Today?

"Never forget, no matter how overwhelming life's challenges and problems seem to be, that one person can make a difference in the world. In fact, it is always because of one person that all the changes that matter in the world come about. So be that one person."

—R. Buckminster Fuller

Observe yourself during the day. Then answer these questions as honestly as possible:

- Describe a negative ripple—even a small one—that you might have sent into the pond of life today at school, at home, or elsewhere.
- Describe how someone else's negative ripple or ripples affected you today.
- Describe at least one way someone else's positive ripples positively impacted you today.
- Describe at least one way you positively affected others with the positive ripples you sent out today.
- Looking ahead to tomorrow, what can you do to send out more positive ripples and fewer negative ones?
- What can you do to "be that one person" who does something supportive if you hear negativity or see someone being mistreated?

REAL-LIFE CHALLENGE

» Think of one positive thing you can do tomorrow to send out a positive ripple. If you're having trouble coming up with something, talk to a friend and come up with ideas together. Promise yourself to do that one thing, even if it's small. Every ripple makes a difference!

» Write a thank-you note or email to someone who made a positive ripple in your life. Explain what he or she did and how it affected you.

From *Create a Culture of Kindness in Middle School* by Naomi Drew, M.A., with Christa M. Tinari, M.A., copyright © 2017. This page may be reproduced for individual, classroom, or small group work only. For all other uses, contact Free Spirit Publishing Inc. at www.freespirit.com/permissions.

LESSON 10 The Power of Each Individual

CHARACTER CONNECTIONS

self-worth / respect / personal responsibility / compassion / kindness

Lesson 10 helps students understand that every one of us has worth and dignity and that we all hold the keys to peace.

Note: Complete Lesson 9, "Your Actions Create Ripples" (page 49), prior to doing this one.

Students will

- revisit the concept that, depending on our words, attitudes, and actions, we send either positive or negative ripples into the world
- reflect on ways each of us can be a key to peace
- consider ways they hold the keys to peace at school, especially if someone is being mistreated

Materials

- handouts: "I Am an Individual" (page 54) and "Write Your Own Poem" (page 55)

Preparation

On the board, write the R. Buckminster Fuller quote from Lesson 9:

> *"Never forget, no matter how overwhelming life's challenges and problems seem to be, that one person can make a difference in the world. In fact, it is always because of one person that all the changes that matter in the world come about. So be that one person." —R. Buckminster Fuller*

Also write the following definition:

> ***dignity:*** *the state of being worthy of respect*

Introduction

Say: **Today we're going to talk about the importance of each individual person.** Ask: **Do you know how much your life makes a difference to the people around you? What thoughts and feelings do you have when you hear me say that?** Take some responses.

Review the concept that we each send either positive or negative ripples out into the world depending on our words, actions, and attitudes. Ask for examples. Remind students that we have the power to choose which kind of ripples we send out. Ask for a volunteer to read aloud the R. Buckminster Fuller quote. Ask students to describe what Fuller's words mean to them.

Discussion and Activity

Say: **Along these same lines, I want to share a short poem with you.** Pass out copies of "I Am an Individual." Say: **This poem is actually about every single one of us.** Before reading the poem, direct students' attention to the definition of *dignity* on the board and make sure they understand the meaning. Then, with conviction in your voice, read the poem aloud. Ask students what part of the poem most resonated with them and why. Discuss.

Now ask a student to read the poem aloud to the group. As the poem is read, ask students to circle the lines with the most meaning to them. At the end of the reading, have students take out their journals. At the top of a blank page, direct students to copy down the single statement of the poem that has the greatest meaning for them. Then have them do several minutes of automatic writing in response to the text they chose.

Afterward, ask for volunteers to share some of their responses. Say: **Imagine if all people lived by the words of this poem. How do you think the world would be different? How might our school be different?** Elicit responses to each question.

Read aloud the following line again: "I deserve respect, and I respect others." Say: **Now let's listen to the words of a middle schooler: *"Some kids don't care how much their words hurt you—partly because they don't know how it feels, but mostly because they don't care."*** Ask for student responses. Ask: **Why is it important to be respectful toward all people?** Ask students to think of times when this might be challenging. Entertain responses.

Ask: **If we don't get along with someone, what are some ways we can still be respectful toward that person?** (Possible answers: Refrain from making negative expressions or comments, being as neutral as possible.)

Say: **When considering the idea of being the key to peace, here's what one middle schooler said: *"You shouldn't just watch someone getting hurt. You should stand up for them."*** Talk with students about the idea of being an "upstander" rather than a "bystander" in situations like this, and ask if they've been upstanders in the past. Ask: **What might stand in the way of people standing up for others? When we're working toward creating the kind of school and the kind of world we want to have, why is it important to support people who are being mistreated?**

Wrap-Up

Ask: **What are other specific ways you can be the key to peace at home and in school? Why is this important? How you think your positive actions can make a difference in the lives of people you know?**

Follow-Up

Distribute the "Write Your Own Poem" handout and have students compose their own "I Am an Individual" poems. Depending on your schedule, it can be completed on a day following this lesson or as homework. Invite volunteers to share their poems with the group.

Enrichment Activities

- Have students set "I Am an Individual" to music. Again, give students the option of sharing their compositions with the group.
- Invite students to share their poems and songs with other groups or classes in the school.
- The United Nations Declaration of the Rights of the Child states that every child should be able to live in an atmosphere of peace, dignity, understanding, tolerance, freedom, and equality. Have students look up the definitions of these words and write in their journals about what each word means to them. Ask how we can honor this declaration at school and in life.
- Do the 10-Minute Time Cruncher "Seeds of Change" on page 56.

I Am an Individual

by Naomi Drew

I am an individual.

I have dignity and worth.

I am unique.

I deserve respect,
and I respect others.

I am part of the human family.

I have something special
to offer the world.

I am committed to
a peaceful world for all of us.

I make a difference,
and so do you.

I can accomplish
whatever I set out to do,
and so can you.

I am the key to peace.

Permission to copy for classroom use. Copyright © Naomi Drew, 2014. From *Learning the Skills of Peacemaking*. Jalmar Press, 1987.

 From *Create a Culture of Kindness in Middle School* by Naomi Drew, M.A., with Christa M. Tinari, M.A., copyright © 2017. This page may be reproduced for individual, classroom, or small group work only. For all other uses, contact Free Spirit Publishing Inc. at www.freespirit.com/permissions.

Write Your Own Poem

Based on the poem, "I Am an Individual," write your own poem. You can use the format below, or create your own structure. If you use the one below, fill in the blanks with whatever words you choose. You can also add more lines if you wish. Or, if you prefer a different verb than some listed below, cross out the verb you see and substitute the one you like better.

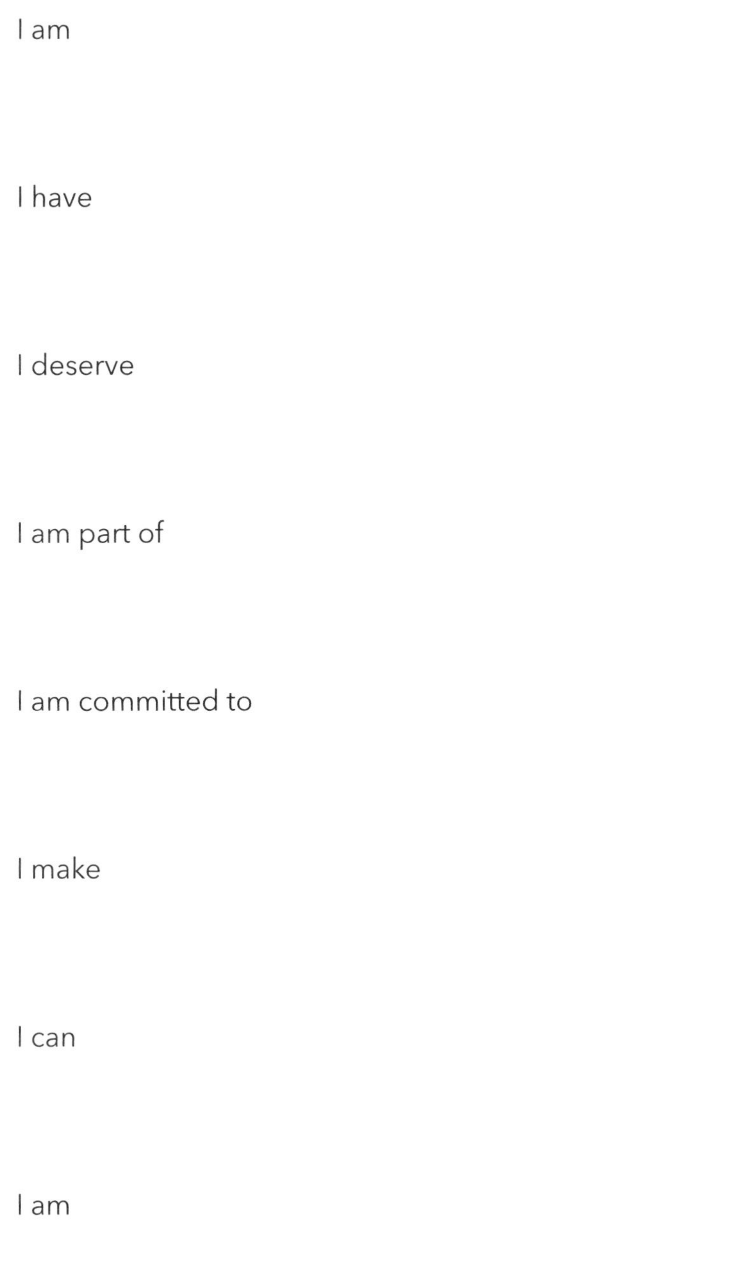

I am

I have

I deserve

I am part of

I am committed to

I make

I can

I am

Now copy your poem onto unlined paper and decorate around the edges, or type it on a computer and decorate it digitally. Share it with someone important to you. Then bring it to school to share with the group.

From *Create a Culture of Kindness in Middle School* by Naomi Drew, M.A., with Christa M. Tinari, M.A., copyright © 2017. This page may be reproduced for individual, classroom, or small group work only. For all other uses, contact Free Spirit Publishing Inc. at www.freespirit.com/permissions.

Seeds of Change

CHARACTER CONNECTIONS

self-worth / respect / personal responsibility / compassion / kindness

This time cruncher coordinates with Lesson 10, "The Power of Each Individual" (page 52). It helps students see and understand the power each of them has to change the world around them.

Materials

- handouts: "The Seed Inside Each of You" (page 57)

Directions

Distribute handouts. Ask a volunteer to read aloud the quote at the top, and briefly discuss the questions that follow.

The Seed Inside Each of You

"Kids don't realize that they're sitting there with this seed inside them that's going to change the world."

—Bryan Collier

Consider this quote and what it means to you. Then answer the following questions here or in your journal.

- What three things in this world most need to be changed?
- If you had the power to change one of these things, which one would it be? Why?
- If you had unlimited power and resources, what would you do to make this change happen?
- Close your eyes and imagine that this change happened. The world is different now. Describe what it would be like.
- The seed for creating this changed world is inside of you now. What are you going to do with it?

From *Create a Culture of Kindness in Middle School* by Naomi Drew, M.A., with Christa M. Tinari, M.A., copyright © 2017. This page may be reproduced for individual, classroom, or small group work only. For all other uses, contact Free Spirit Publishing Inc. at www.freespirit.com/permissions.

LESSON 11

The Interconnected Web

CHARACTER CONNECTIONS
acceptance / respect

Lesson 11 helps students understand that we are all interconnected. It creates a tangible experience of being connected to every member of the group.

Students will
- understand that all people are connected
- reflect on the idea of being connected to every other being on earth
- create a representation of an interconnected web

Materials
- large ball of yarn, plus another of the same color in case the first one isn't long enough
- camera (a cell phone camera is fine)
- a large clear jar

Preparation

Copy, or have a student copy, the following quotes onto the board:

> *"We cannot live for ourselves alone. Our lives are connected by a thousand invisible threads."*
> *—Herman Melville*

> *"In nature nothing exists alone." —Rachel Carson*

> *"The reality today is that we are all interdependent and have to co-exist on this small planet."*
> *—the Dalai Lama*

Introduction

Write the word *interconnected* on the board. Ask students what it means to them.

Discussion and Activity

Refer to the quotes on the board and ask two students each to read one aloud.

Ask students what resonates for them when they hear these words. Then ask two more students to read the same quotes aloud a second time. Ask the group to tune in to other insights they have as they listen again. After the second listening, ask students what additional thoughts, understandings, or questions revealed themselves.

Now ask: **What are some things we all have in common? These are the invisible threads that connect us.** Here are some examples to discuss. We all:

- share the same planet
- experience feelings
- have blood coursing through our veins
- want to be accepted
- have a heart that beats every minute of our lives
- want to be cared for and treated with respect
- need to eat, drink, and sleep to stay alive
- experience sadness when someone dies
- love others

Tell students they're going to engage in an activity where they'll be creating a visual representation of the web that connects all of us.

Have students move desks to the sides of the room. In the open space created, have students stand in a large circle. Hold the ball of yarn in your hands and join the circle. You will be using the yarn to form a web that connects every student.

Say: **When it's your turn to throw the ball of yarn, say one word or phrase that describes something we all have in common—a way we are all connected.**

Holding one end of the yarn, throw the ball to a student across from you. This is the beginning of the web. Say a word or phrase as you throw.

Now instruct that student to hold onto the other end of the piece of yarn you have in your hand, and throw the ball to another student.

Note: Ask students to try to make eye contact with the person to whom they are going to throw the ball before throwing it.

Keep this going until every student is holding onto a section of the yarn. Encourage students to throw the ball to someone across the circle, rather than next to them. Caution everyone to hold tightly to their sections of yarn as the ball is being tossed. When the web is complete, have your students observe what they've created. Ask them to look at the faces of every person who is a part of this web. Ask them how it feels to "see" the interconnected web that binds them. Let them know that we are always connected to others by the invisible threads of our common human existence.

After a few minutes of discussion, have a student you're standing next to hold your section of the yarn. Leave the circle and read the following quote aloud:

> ***"All things are connected like the blood that unites us. Man did not weave the web of life, he is merely a strand in it. Whatever he does to the web, he does to himself." —Chief Seattle***

Next, take some pictures of the interconnected web. Make sure to include every student, even if it takes several pictures. If you have any students who are not comfortable being photographed, here's something else you can do: Holding onto their pieces of the web, have students kneel and extend the hands that hold the web. Position yourself above so you can get a picture of their hands. You might not get every hand, but you'll capture an image of the web being held by most students.

Wrap-Up

Have students journal about the experience of being part of an interconnected web. Ask them what they learned from this activity. For example, do they have a new sense about themselves in relation to others? Did they think differently about the impact of each person on the world at large.

Follow-Up

After printing the pictures you took of the interconnected web, give photos to each student so they can incorporate them into posters or artwork if they wish. They can also incorporate the quotes from this lesson or find quotes of their own that speak to the idea of connection.

Enrichment Activities

- Have students create a Group Charter that enumerates how they want to treat each other as members of the interconnected web. They might want to include things such as, "We will do our best to treat each other with respect," or, "We will agree not to laugh at each other's mistakes."
- After creating your web, say: **In order to preserve a representation of our web, we're going to gently lay it down and very carefully push the whole thing together toward the center of the floor.** Next, have several students work together to carefully put the condensed web into a large clear jar. (By now it might look more like a cocoon.) Break students up into groups of four or five. Have students brainstorm creative ways to transform the condensed web into a piece of artwork or another type of display representing interconnectedness. If time allows, have students share their ideas with the large group. Ask students to vote on which idea to execute. Choose a team of students to follow through on completing the project. In the meantime, keep the "web" in the jar and label it with a sign, "Our Interconnected Web," and your group's name or period. If you like, invite your art teacher to help students fine-tune ideas for creating something special. Once the project is complete, display it somewhere in your room or building.

Honoring Uniqueness

CHARACTER CONNECTIONS

self-acceptance / respecting differences / kindness

Lesson 12 guides students to understand that we're all unique in our own way and that everyone's differences are worthy of respect.

Students will

- reflect on the idea that all people, no matter how seemingly different, deserve to be respected
- understand that our uniqueness is what makes us special
- explore things they can do if someone, including themselves, experiences mistreatment because of differences

Materials

- student journals
- handout: "Uniqueness, Differences, and Respect" (pages 62–63)

Preparation

Make one copy of the first page of the handout, and cut it into five strips, each containing one of the five quotes.

On the board, write the following words:

Uniqueness

Being different

Respect

Introduction

Say: **Today we're going to talk about uniqueness and differences. We're all different in one way or another. How can differences be positive? How can they create challenges?**

Ask a student to read aloud the words on the board:

Uniqueness

Being different

Respect

Make sure everyone understands the meaning of uniqueness: the quality of being one of a kind. Ask students what comes to mind when they hear these three terms together. Ask: **In middle school, what happens when kids are seen as different? Can you think of some examples of negative reactions to being different? Please don't use real names if the examples relate to people you know.**

Discussion and Activity

Say: **Let's consider another perspective on being different. Let's think about it in the context of being unique.** Give the Martha Graham sentence strip to a student. Tell students that Martha Graham was an iconic dancer who rose to the top of her profession in part because she was so different, so unique that she stood out from everyone else. Have the student read her words aloud: *"There is a vitality, a life force, an energy, a quickening that is translated through you into action, and because there is only one of you in all of time, this expression is unique. And if you block it, it will never exist through any other medium and it will be lost. The world will not have it."* Have the student read the quote again so your group can fully digest it. Then ask: **What do you think when you hear these words?** Take responses.

Say: **Now let's hear what a few middle schoolers have to say about differences.** Pass out the remaining four sentence strips. Have students read them aloud to the group.

Ask students to do three to five minutes of automatic writing on whatever thoughts come up relating to these quotes. Then ask for volunteers to share some insights and feelings that arose.

Next, pass out the "Uniqueness, Differences, and Respect" handout and place students in pairs. Have them read the quotes together. Then ask them each to choose one quote on the handout that is most meaningful to them and explain to their partners why they chose as they did.

Reconvene the large group. Ask students to share thoughts and insights they had during this process. Say: **Think about the student who said, *"Everybody deserves respect. No matter who you are or how you do things, you deserve respect."* Do you agree with this statement? Why or why not?** Have students share their thoughts. Guide students to understand that all people, regardless of differences, deserve respect. Ask: **Why is it so important to show respect toward others, no matter how different they might be from you?**

Ask: **What conscious choices can we make when we see someone being mistreated for being different? What can we do if this happens to us?** Discuss, emphasizing that we all deserve respect. Also let students know that if any of them are facing mistreatment or exclusion, that you care and want to help. Ask who else students can talk to if they need help dealing with a difficult or upsetting situation.

Wrap-Up

Ask: **If we notice ourselves about to say something derogatory about someone we perceive as different, what can we do? If we witness someone making a mean comment about a person perceived as different, what can we say or do?** Explore ideas and options as a group.

End by having the group read the R. Buckminster Fuller quote on the handout in unison: *"Never forget that you are one of a kind. Never forget that if there weren't any need for you in all your uniqueness to be on this earth, you wouldn't be here in the first place."*

Follow-Up

Have students complete the written part of the handout. Make time on another day to discuss their responses.

Enrichment Activities

- Have students create signs, collages, or posters based on one of the quotes on the handout. Tell them they can keep these creations or give them to someone who might be inspired by the words within them.
- Have students imagine themselves twenty-five years in the future. They are now parents, aunts, or uncles to kids in middle school. Have them compose letters encouraging those kids to be true to themselves, as Nancy Arroyo Ruffin did in *Letters to My Daughter*.

Uniqueness, Differences, and Respect

Read these quotes and think about what they say to you.

"There is a vitality, a life force, an energy, a quickening that is translated through you into action, and because there is only one of you in all of time, this expression is unique. And if you block it, it will never exist through any other medium and it will be lost. The world will not have it."
—Martha Graham

"Some students may be different or quirky and not everyone likes those traits in a person."
—8th-grade girl

"I have seen specific people in my grade be constantly picked on because of their differences."
—7th-grade girl

"People get picked on because of how they look, act, or even how they do in school. Anyone who stands out is easy to target."
—6th-grade boy

"People get teased because of their size, race, color."
—8th-grade boy

 From *Create a Culture of Kindness in Middle School* by Naomi Drew, M.A., with Christa M. Tinari, M.A., copyright © 2017. This page may be reproduced for individual, classroom, or small group work only. For all other uses, contact Free Spirit Publishing Inc. at www.freespirit.com/permissions.

Read the following quotes, then answer the questions that follow.

"Never forget that you are one of a kind. Never forget that if there weren't any need for you in all your uniqueness to be on this earth, you wouldn't be here in the first place."
—R. Buckminster Fuller

"Everybody deserves respect. No matter who you are or how you do things, you deserve respect!"
—9th-grade girl

"Do not be afraid to color outside the lines or to make mistakes. Take risks and do not be afraid to fail. Know that when the world knocks you down, the best revenge is to get up and continue forging ahead. Do not be afraid to be different or to stand up for what's right. Never quiet your voice to make someone else feel comfortable. No one remembers the person that fits in. It's the one who stands out that people will not be able to forget."
—Nancy Arroyo Ruffin in *Letters to My Daughter*

- What makes you the unique person that you are? Brainstorm a list of all your unique qualities. List as many as you can, and don't be afraid to list unusual traits, talents, or interests.

- Describe a time you or someone you know tried to act like everyone else in order to fit in and not seem different.

- Describe a time you silenced your voice in order to be accepted or liked by others. How did silencing yourself feel? What would you have said if you'd given yourself permission to speak up?

- If you're being mistreated because of a perceived difference, what can you do? Who can you go to for support?

- What can you do when you see someone being mistreated because of a perceived difference?

Remember, the things that make us different create our uniqueness. They're often the most special things about us. Even if you can't see it right now, your uniqueness is a valuable resource and one you can treasure.

From *Create a Culture of Kindness in Middle School* by Naomi Drew, M.A., with Christa M. Tinari, M.A., copyright © 2017. This page may be reproduced for individual, classroom, or small group work only. For all other uses, contact Free Spirit Publishing Inc. at www.freespirit.com/permissions.

Section 2

Fostering COURAGE, KINDNESS, AND EMPATHY

LESSON 13 Choosing Your Words

CHARACTER CONNECTIONS

kindness / compassion / personal responsibility

Lesson 13 asks students to consider the impact of "casual meanness," challenging them to come up with ways to prevent and counteract it.

Note: Be sure to do Lesson 6, "Words Can Change Your Brain" (page 38), before doing this one.

Students will

- review how angry, unkind, and mean words can affect the brain
- reflect on how we can counteract the presence of everyday unkindness
- role-play ways to promote kindness and reduce the effects of cruel words or actions

Materials

- student journals
- handout: "Stamp Out Mean Words" (page 69)

Preparation

On the board, write each of the following quotes:

> *"Before you speak, let your words pass through three gates.*
> *At the first gate, ask yourself, 'Is it true?'*
> *At the second ask, 'Is it necessary?'*
> *At the third gate ask, 'Is it kind?'"*
> *—Sufi saying*

> *"You never know who will start the chain reaction. We all have to try in our own ways."*
> *—Colin Beavan*

Introduction

Say: **We've already learned that words can change our brains. How do you feel when you hear mean words?** Accept a few responses. Ask: **What happens to your brain when you hear mean, critical, or angry words—especially when they're directed at you?** (Answers: The body releases stress-producing hormones, and the thinking part of the brain shuts down temporarily. We can find it hard to think straight, and we may experience uncomfortable feelings in the body.)

Ask: **Why is it never okay to direct hurtful or demeaning words at another person?** Invite responses and ask students to explain their answers. Stress that disagreeing with someone is different than attacking that person or calling him or her names, and that there are ways we can stand up for ourselves without using mean or disrespectful words. Let students know that they'll be learning a lot about these ideas from this lesson and others in this book.

Discussion and Activity

Talk with students about the power of words. Discuss that this power is why hate groups use words as their primary tool for spreading prejudice and provoking violence. (If necessary, define what hate groups are.) As of late 2016, there were 892 active hate groups in the United States, representing a 14 percent increase from 2014, and almost double the amount of hate groups existing in 1999.[29] This is another reason we have to work to reduce and prevent the use of hateful, prejudiced, and cruel words in our schools and in our society. (For more information, visit the Southern Poverty Law Center's site: splcenter.org.)

Distribute the "Stamp Out Mean Words" handout. Have a student read aloud the quote from a middle schooler at the top, starting with, "It's important for kids to be kind." Ask students for their reactions to this statement.

Now put students in pairs. Say: **These words come from middle schoolers who responded to a national survey.** Have partners take turns reading aloud the rest of the quotes on the handout and talk briefly about their thoughts, feelings, and reactions.

After several minutes, ask the whole group: **What can statements like the ones you just read do to the atmosphere of a classroom or school? How might they affect the people they're directed at?**

Say: **One student said he was called "gay." Why is it never okay to use the word *gay* as an insult?** If necessary for your group, offer a clear and concise definition of the word. Then help students understand that whenever the word gay is used to mean stupid or uncool, we demean those who are gay, or have friends or family members who are gay—even if we don't mean to be hurtful. The following words from Norma Baily, professor of middle level education at Central Michigan University, are an excellent way to respond when you hear a student using the word gay in a pejorative way: "I have a friend who is gay and it hurts me to see my friend hurt because I care about him. And, just like I wouldn't want anyone to say anything unkind about you because I care about you, I'm going to ask you not to say that again. OK?"[30] Talk about this.

Now read aloud the following quote from teacher Adam Sherman: ***"The hard part with kindness is that our collective society has made it easier to be mean. It is easier, and often more comfortable, to laugh at others, to judge them, to talk negatively behind their back."***

Ask: **What do you think this teacher meant by our society "has made it easier to be mean"?** Relate this back to the fact that it's common to hear cruel language. Ask: **Do you think it's easier to be mean or easier to be kind at our school? Why? How can we help each other be less mean and more kind? How can we be that way ourselves?**

Next have a volunteer read aloud the quote on the board from author Colin Beavan: *"You never know who will start the chain reaction. We all have to try in our own ways."*

Ask: **What choices can you personally make to counteract cruelty and meanness and start a chain reaction of kindness? For example, let's say some of your friends are putting someone down. What could you say or do?**

Have a volunteer read aloud the Three Gates quote from the board:

> *"Before you speak, let your words pass through three gates.*
> *At the first gate, ask yourself, 'Is it true?'*
> *At the second ask, 'Is it necessary?'*
> *At the third gate ask, 'Is it kind?'"*
> —Sufi saying

Talk about what students think this saying means. Say: **Imagine if everyone in our school practiced this. What might that be like?**

Say: **Let's try practicing the Three Gates now.** Choose two volunteers to come to the front of the room and role-play the following:

Students A and B are about to send a text about another student. Student A realizes that the text is unnecessary, unkind, and possibly untrue. Rather than continuing, Student A speaks up. Have Students A and B role-play the conversation that might follow.

Afterward have the group briefly discuss the pros and cons of doing this in real life.

Wrap-Up

Discuss what took place in the role-play. Ask students if they've ever realized after saying something that it was unkind. Did they do anything to make it better? Entertain responses. Next, have students look at the "Stamp Out Mean Words" handout and read the pledge at the bottom in unison: "I pledge not to use words, jokes, gestures, or gossip to hurt others or put them down in any way." Ask students to think seriously about the words of this pledge. Say: **How can we all honor the Kindness Pledge at school, at home, and in other areas of our lives?**

Follow-Up

- Have students answer the questions on the "Stamp Out Mean Words" handout. Tell them their answers will be confidential. Only you will get to see them. When you read students' answers, see if there's anyone you need to talk with. It's amazing what kids will reveal when given the opportunity. More than a few from our survey revealed suicidal thoughts, cutting, and feelings of despair. If that's the case with any of your kids, involve your school counselor (or other appropriate personnel) and be sure to follow up.
- Keep the Three Gates quote and the Colin Beavan quote at hand so you can refer to them when relevant.

Enrichment Activities

- Pose the following questions for students to answer in their journals: What can each of us do to start the chain reaction of kindness? At home? In school? In other places?
- Have students make artwork or writings inspired by the Three Gates quote. Invite them to share what they create with the group.
- Say: **How can we make the Kindness Pledge go viral? Come up with ideas to make this happen.** (For example, they might use online platforms, such as Instagram, Facebook, or Twitter, or start text or email campaigns.)

Stamp Out Mean Words

"It's important for kids to be kind because we all want to come into school happy and ready for the day, not to be sad and afraid to come here."
—7th-grade girl

We all want to be happy and feel safe at school, but sometimes that's not the reality. Here are some hurtful things middle schoolers report having heard:

"This kid always says, 'You're such a moron. You can't do anything right.'"

"They tell me I'm small and weak."

"He called me a worthless, ugly, anorexic."

"There were two boys in my class who kept teasing me about what I wore to school or what I liked to do or watch on TV. Every day they would tease me. It never stopped, not even when I told my parents and teachers."

"They called me a loser."

"I was being called a pig and I was being called fat and being cursed at."

"Kids always tell me, 'You are so weird!'"

"They call me gay."

"People call me 'emo' and tell me to kill myself."

- How do you feel when you read the words above?

- How do you feel when you hear people calling each other names? Why?

- If people make fun of you or call you names, describe how you feel when this happens.

- If you've called people names or put them down, how do you think your words affected them? If you're not sure, ask yourself how you would have felt if you were in their shoes.

- We all need to help start a chain reaction of kindness. How can you play a part?

REAL-LIFE CHALLENGE

» Take the Kindness Pledge!

I pledge not to use words, jokes, gestures, or gossip to hurt others or put them down in any way.

Promise yourself to live the Kindness Pledge every day for a week—at school, at home, and in all other places. Write in your journal about what happens as a result. Then make a commitment to *keep* following this pledge for even longer!

From *Create a Culture of Kindness in Middle School* by Naomi Drew, M.A., with Christa M. Tinari, M.A., copyright © 2017. This page may be reproduced for individual, classroom, or small group work only. For all other uses, contact Free Spirit Publishing Inc. at www.freespirit.com/permissions.

Strengthening Your Empathy Muscle

CHARACTER CONNECTIONS

acceptance / empathy / kindness / respect

Lesson 14 invites students to exercise their empathy muscles.

Students will

- understand the meaning of empathy
- assess the degree of empathy they have toward others
- exercise their empathy muscles by putting themselves in other people's shoes

Materials

- handouts: "Empathy Assessment" (pages 72–73) and "Bullying Incident at Ogemaw Heights High School" (pages 74–75)

»»» **Online Resource** »»»»»»»»»»»»

To show students an example of a message on empathy, have them view the short video "Empathy Can Change the World" made by eighth-grade students at Kalispell Middle School in Kalispell, Montana. Search YouTube for "Kalispell empathy can change" to see the video.

»»»»»»»»»»»»»»»»»»»»»»»»

Introduction

Say: **Today we're going to explore what it means to have empathy. What is empathy?** Take responses. Say: **Empathy is understanding and caring about someone else's feelings and experiences. Scientists who study empathy have determined that we're born with empathy, and we can strengthen our empathy muscles with practice.**[31] **Today's exercise will help you do just that.**

Discussion and Activity

Distribute the "Empathy Assessment" handout. Read the directions and give students five minutes to complete the ten assessment questions, and another few minutes to answer the questions for reflection and discussion. Afterward, briefly discuss students' responses. Say: **It's possible to strengthen our empathy skills. If this assessment revealed that you're a little low in empathy right now, don't worry. The lessons we do together will help you improve in this area. In fact, we're going to start right now.**

Note: If any of your students have disabilities or differences that make empathy difficult for them, offer additional assurance that strengthening empathy skills is possible for them.

Stress that empathy helps people understand each other and can help us get along better. Say: **We're going to do an exercise that will help you improve and practice your empathy skills.**

Distribute "Bullying Incident at Ogemaw Heights High School" and ask a volunteer to read the scenario aloud. Next, put students into groups of four or five. Have students in each group count off by a number. Have students look at the handout to find the person whose number corresponds with theirs. Say: **Your job is to put yourself completely into this person's shoes and imagine how he or she might have felt as a result of this incident.** Have students look at the questions at the bottom of the handout. If desired, have a student read the questions aloud.

- What did you think and feel when you heard students saying that Whitney's nomination to the Homecoming Court was a joke?
- What were your biggest concerns when you found out about what happened to Whitney?
- What would you like to see happen as a result of this incident?

Have students answer these questions as though they're the person whose number they got. Say: **Take several minutes to reread the story and imagine being this person. Silently reflect on feelings, thoughts, and concerns that come up when you're in his or her shoes.**

After a few minutes, say: **You have two jobs now. The first is to stay in the role you just imagined and write down your answers to the three questions on the handout. The second is to discuss your answers with your group and listen to everyone's point of view. Avoid getting into debates over people's responses. Instead, simply listen carefully to everyone's perspectives and try to understand them.**

Say: **Choose someone to begin. Each person will have about two minutes to speak.** Walk around and monitor the discussions, making sure students share from their assigned person's point of view. After ten minutes, have everyone conclude their discussions and rejoin the full group.

Wrap-Up

Ask: **What was it like to put yourself in someone else's shoes? What was challenging about it? What did you learn about yourself? Were you able to *feel* how the person you represented might have felt? That's what empathy is all about.** Take responses. Encourage students to try putting themselves in other people's shoes throughout the day.

Follow-Up

Talk with students about whether they're becoming more aware of their own empathy responses. What triggers their empathy? When do they find it more difficult to feel empathy for someone else?

Enrichment Activities

- Have students create a short public service announcement that encourages others to exercise their empathy muscles. Public service announcements and videos created by middle schoolers are available online. You can have students search for good examples.
- Have students look for a story in the news that triggers feelings of empathy. Ask them to talk or journal about aspects of the story that touched them most and explain why.

Empathy Assessment

Read the following statements and decide whether each one is just like you, somewhat like you, or not like you at all. Check your responses.

1. It's easy for me to see things from someone else's point of view.
- ☐ *Just like me*
- ☐ *Somewhat like me*
- ☐ *Not like me*

2. I often wonder how my family members might be feeling.
- ☐ *Just like me*
- ☐ *Somewhat like me*
- ☐ *Not like me*

3. When my friend is really happy, it makes me happy, too.
- ☐ *Just like me*
- ☐ *Somewhat like me*
- ☐ *Not like me*

4. When I see a tragedy on the news, I imagine what it must be like for the people who are affected.
- ☐ *Just like me*
- ☐ *Somewhat like me*
- ☐ *Not like me*

5. Sometimes I cry when I watch movies or TV shows, or when I read books that touch me.
- ☐ *Just like me*
- ☐ *Somewhat like me*
- ☐ *Not like me*

6. When I watch sports, I get riled up.
- ☐ *Just like me*
- ☐ *Somewhat like me*
- ☐ *Not like me*

7. It bothers me when I see someone being treated unkindly or disrespectfully, even if I don't know the person.
- ☐ *Just like me*
- ☐ *Somewhat like me*
- ☐ *Not like me*

8. I can tell a lot about how other people are feeling just by looking at their faces.
- ☐ *Just like me*
- ☐ *Somewhat like me*
- ☐ *Not like me*

9. I find it easy to understand why someone would react to a situation differently than I might.
- ☐ *Just like me*
- ☐ *Somewhat like me*
- ☐ *Not like me*

10. When I see someone who looks upset, I wonder what's bothering them.
- ☐ *Just like me*
- ☐ *Somewhat like me*
- ☐ *Not like me*

Now tally the number of times you checked each response:

Just like me:

Somewhat like me:

Not like me:

The higher the number you scored in the "just like me" category, the stronger your empathy muscle is.

From *Create a Culture of Kindness in Middle School* by Naomi Drew, M.A., with Christa M. Tinari, M.A., copyright © 2017. This page may be reproduced for individual, classroom, or small group work only. For all other uses, contact Free Spirit Publishing Inc. at www.freespirit.com/permissions.

- What did you learn from seeing your scores on this empathy assessment? Did anything surprise you? If so, what was it, and why was it surprising?

- What do you see as the upsides and downsides to having a lot of empathy?

- Do you wish you had more empathy? Why or why not? If you do want to have more empathy, what can you do to make that wish a reality?

REAL-LIFE CHALLENGE

» Paying attention to the feelings of others and imagining their point of view is a powerful way to strengthen your empathy muscle. Next time a friend or family member tells you about something that happened to him or her, listen carefully and observe the person's body language and facial expressions. What feelings do you think he or she is experiencing? Can you put yourself in this person's shoes without judging his or her feelings? What new insights have you gained from doing this? After putting yourself in this person's shoes, in what ways do you better understand him or her?

From *Create a Culture of Kindness in Middle School* by Naomi Drew, M.A., with Christa M. Tinari, M.A., copyright © 2017. This page may be reproduced for individual, classroom, or small group work only. For all other uses, contact Free Spirit Publishing Inc. at www.freespirit.com/permissions.

Bullying Incident at Ogemaw Heights High School

Read this true story and then do the activity that follows.

Whitney Kropp was a sophomore at Ogemaw Heights High School in West Branch, Michigan, when she was nominated to the Homecoming Court. When her nomination came in, Whitney was completely surprised. Usually, only the most popular girls in the school were nominated, and Whitney knew she wasn't one of them. She never expected to be part of the Homecoming Court and to be among the select group cheered by the entire school at the biggest football game of the year.

But within less than a day of her nomination, Whitney's surprise turned to dismay. The group of popular kids who nominated her told their friends they had done it as a joke. Word spread quickly. People started making fun of Whitney at school and online. Whitney felt humiliated to the core. "I felt like trash," she later told a CNN reporter. That night, Whitney contemplated ending her life.

When Whitney's mother and father, Bernice and Jason Kropp, found out what happened, they were shocked. They knew their daughter was a kind person who never picked on other kids. How could Whitney's classmates be so cruel?

Then, something wonderful happened. Word of the cruel prank started spreading beyond the walls of the school—and messages and offers of support started pouring in. Shannon Champagne, a local hair stylist, said that if Whitney took her place on the Homecoming Court, Shannon would do her hair for free. Another business owner in Whitney's town offered to pay for her homecoming dress. Another person volunteered to provide a free photo session. Jamie Kline, a former student at Ogemaw Heights High School, created a "Support Whitney Kropp" Facebook page. Jamie told a news reporter that she "wanted Whitney to know that she is loved, she is beautiful and it doesn't matter what anyone thinks." The Facebook page ended up with more than 100,000 supporters.

Before long, Whitney decided she *would* go to Homecoming—with her head held high. She gave reporters this message for other kids who were bullied: "Do not let them bring you down."

On the day of Homecoming, more than 1,000 students came out to support Whitney. Many of them wore orange T-shirts (Whitney's favorite color) that featured the slogan, "It's not cool to be cruel." When reporters asked Whitney where she got the courage to stand up proudly in front of the whole world after what had happened, she pointed to her heart and said, "Right here."

Since that day, Whitney's story has continued to give comfort to kids who've been bullied, and it's inspired thousands of people to speak out against bullying. Instead of allowing people's cruel actions to pull her down, she rose up, triumphed, and became a role model for others.

Form a group of four or five. Count off by number and circle your number in the list below. You'll be taking the role of the person whose number you got. For example, if you got number 2, imagine yourself being one of Whitney's parents.

1. Whitney Kropp, sophomore at Ogemaw Heights High School
2. Bernice Kropp or Jason Kropp, Whitney's parents
3. Duane Lyons, the school principal
4. A football player who was also nominated to Homecoming Court
5. Shannon Champagne, the hair stylist who volunteered to do Whitney's hair

From *Create a Culture of Kindness in Middle School* by Naomi Drew, M.A., with Christa M. Tinari, M.A., copyright © 2017. This page may be reproduced for individual, classroom, or small group work only. For all other uses, contact Free Spirit Publishing Inc. at www.freespirit.com/permissions.

Now answer the following questions from the perspective of the person whose shoes you're in.

- What did you think and feel when you heard students saying that Whitney's nomination to the Homecoming Court was a joke?

- What were your biggest concerns when you found out about what happened to Whitney?

- What would you like to see happen as a result of this incident?

From *Create a Culture of Kindness in Middle School* by Naomi Drew, M.A., with Christa M. Tinari, M.A., copyright © 2017. This page may be reproduced for individual, classroom, or small group work only. For all other uses, contact Free Spirit Publishing Inc. at www.freespirit.com/permissions.

LESSON 15 People Can Change

CHARACTER CONNECTIONS
kindness / compassion / acceptance / personal responsibility

Lesson 15 helps students understand that compassion can transform people, even those for whom change may seem impossible or completely unlikely. This lesson also challenges mindsets that can lead us to see people—including ourselves—as incapable of change.

Students will

- hear the story of Claiborne Paul Ellis, a KKK member who became a civil rights activist
- understand that even people who seem hateful or mean can change through the power of compassion
- consider the possibility that people in their own lives could change, too

Materials

- handout: "The Power of Compassion: A True Story" (page 78)

Preparation

Have a student prepare to read aloud "The Power of Compassion: A True Story" during this lesson. On the board, write the terms *segregation, integration, Ku Klux Klan,* and *civil rights movement.*

»»» **Online Resource** »»»»»»»»»»»»
For more detail on the story discussed in this lesson, listen to the portion of "All Things Considered" from November 8, 2005, of Ann Atwater talking about Claiborne Paul Ellis. You can find this recording at npr.org by searching for "C.P. Ellis."
»»»»»»»»»»»»»»»»»»»»»»»»»

Introduction

Ask: **Can you think of someone who seems or seemed so mean or hateful you thought they'd stay that way forever? This can be someone you know, someone in the news, or someone from a book or movie.** Entertain responses. Caution students not to use real names or identifying factors if talking about someone they know.

Ask: **Do you think it's possible for people like this to change? Why or why not?** Discuss briefly. Say: **Today you'll be hearing a powerful story from history. It may change the way you think about some of these ideas.**

Discussion and Activity

Say: **First, let's talk about some terms you'll hear in the story.** Point to the words you've written on the board: *segregation, integration, Ku Klux Clan, civil rights movement.* Ask students to talk about their understanding of each term. Here are definitions you can use to help guide the conversation and increase understanding:

- **segregation:** The enforced separation of different racial groups in a country, community, or establishment
- **integration:** The process of ending racial segregation

- **Ku Klux Klan:** A white supremacist hate group in the United States dedicated to committing violent acts against African Americans, Jews, Catholics, and foreign-born people
- **civil rights movement:** A movement in the United States intended to help African Americans achieve racial justice and equality, including fair housing, desegregated schools, and equal access to voting rights and jobs

Pass out "The Power of Compassion: A True Story." Have the student you chose as a reader come to the front of the room and read the story aloud.

Next, put students in pairs. For about three minutes, have them discuss their reactions to the story. Then have them answer and discuss each of the questions that follow the story.

Have the whole group reconvene and share responses, insights, and questions. Emphasize that people can indeed change, even those we may not believe are capable of it. Stress that compassion is a powerful force for changing people's attitudes and behaviors.

Wrap-Up

Ask students to pair up with their partners again and think about the people they thought of at the beginning of the lesson. Do they feel any differently about the possibility that this person could change? Why or why not? (Remind them not to use names if they're thinking of people in their lives.)

Say: **Compassion was sparked in Claiborne Paul Ellis when he heard children speak honestly about their pain. As a result of this experience, he changed. How have *you* changed as a result of the work we've been doing on respect, kindness, and compassion? How have your attitudes shifted?**

After about two minutes, take responses in the large group. Remind students to think of Ellis's example when they believe someone might be incapable of change.

Follow-Up

Have students journal about any insights, thoughts, questions, or feelings that arose from the discussion you've had today.

Enrichment Activities

- Ask students to consider what issues they care deeply about and wish other people cared more about (examples: hunger, homelessness, racism, global warming, war, poverty). If they could speak to a particular group and spark greater compassion about this issue, who would they speak to? What would they say? Guide them to think carefully about this and write essays expressing their thoughts.
- Have students research the civil rights movement to learn more about segregation. Or have them research current examples of racial discrimination and bias in the news.
- Have students research Claiborne Paul Ellis and Ann Atwater to learn more about their work together.
- Have students write essays based on their thoughts, concerns, and suggestions about the following questions: How does racism affect people's lives in our country and our community? What can we do to end racism?

The Power of Compassion: A True Story

Read this true story. Then write in your journal in response to the questions that follow.

Have you ever known someone who was so filled with hatred that you thought they could never change?

Well, that's the way many people felt about Claiborne Paul Ellis, a leader of the Ku Klux Klan (KKK) in Durham, North Carolina, in the 1960s. Ellis and other members of the KKK believed that anyone who wasn't white and Protestant should be hated—and in some instances, even killed. The murder of black Americans by lynching was common, and the Ku Klux Klan was behind many of these tragic incidents.

Racial prejudice was widespread beyond the Ku Klux Klan, as well, especially in the southern United States. Tension between blacks and whites was especially high in the 1960s and 1970s. The city of Durham wanted to address this issue, so they formed a Human Relations Commission where people of opposing views could work together toward racial harmony in the schools and beyond. Community leaders were asked to participate, and Ellis was one of them. So was a black civil rights activist named Ann Atwater.

At first, Ellis and Atwater hated each other. Ellis hated Atwater for being black, and Atwater hated Ellis for his racism. Ellis would show up at meetings with a gun in the trunk of his car. He'd once held a gun to the head of a twelve-year-old black child and threatened to kill him for taking fifteen cents from a white child. To Ann Atwater, finding common ground with Ellis seemed absolutely hopeless.

But one day everything changed. The meetings Atwater and Ellis attended each week always opened with a local children's choir performing. One day the children spoke to the adults about how much they'd been hurt by racial prejudice. They poured out their hearts.

As the kids spoke about the heartache they suffered because of racism, they touched Ellis's heart in a way he'd never experienced before. As he listened, he began to cry. So did Atwater. Compassion for the children took center stage, and at that moment both Ellis and Atwater knew they needed to put aside their differences and work together for the benefit of all kids who were victims of racial injustice in their community.

And that's exactly what they did. Ellis started working for civil rights. At one point, he stood before an audience of a thousand people and tore up his Ku Klux Klan card. He continued working for racial justice for the rest of his life. Here's what he eventually said: "I tell people there's a tremendous possibility in this country to stop wars, the battles, the struggles, the fights between people. Some people say: 'That's an impossible dream. You sound like Martin Luther King.' An ex-Klansman who sounds like Martin Luther King. I don't think it's an impossible dream. It's happened in my life."

- How did compassion change Claiborne Paul Ellis?
- How did kids play a central role in Ellis's transformation into a civil rights activist?
- After his transformation, what did Ellis do with his life? Why?
- Do you know anyone who seems so mean, unfriendly, or hateful that you believe they can never change? How do you feel after reading this story? Explain.
- What else can we learn from this story?

 From *Create a Culture of Kindness in Middle School* by Naomi Drew, M.A., with Christa M. Tinari, M.A., copyright © 2017. This page may be reproduced for individual, classroom, or small group work only. For all other uses, contact Free Spirit Publishing Inc. at www.freespirit.com/permissions.

Exclusion Hurts

CHARACTER CONNECTIONS

kindness / empathy / personal responsibility

Lesson 16 addresses exclusion and its effects and fosters empathy for those who have been excluded.

Students will

- reflect on the impact of exclusion
- consider ways to cope if they are excluded
- learn about an inspiring role model for inclusion

Materials

- student journals
- a notecard for each student
- handouts: "Exclusion" (page 81), "Coach Poggi's Golden Rule" (page 82), and "What to Do About Exclusion" (page 83)

Preparation

Choose two students who will read aloud a quote each from the handout "Exclusion" during this lesson. Give them a copy of "Exclusion" so they can prepare. Give a third student a copy of "Coach Poggi's Golden Rule" ahead of time so he or she is prepared to read it aloud to the group.

Also think of a time in your own life—perhaps from middle school—when you were excluded or when you excluded someone else. Prepare to tell your group about it during this lesson.

»»» **Online Resource** »»»»»»»»»»»

To prepare for this lesson, search online for "Delancey Place, the pain of exclusion" and read the excerpt.

»»»»»»»»»»»»»»»»»»»»»»»»»

Introduction

Have students take out their journals. Say: **In a little while we're going to be writing about something we all experience at one time or another: being excluded or excluding others.** Briefly share your personal story of exclusion. Share feelings you had during the experience and feelings you have about it now.

Ask: **Can you relate to the experience I just shared? Why does being excluded hurt so much?** Briefly discuss. Tell students there's a difference between being purposely excluded and inadvertently excluded. If they are sometimes excluded inadvertently, it's healthy to try not to take this too personally.

Discussion and Activity

Have one of the students you chose come to the front of the room and read aloud the first quote on the handout, "Exclusion." It begins with, "Our need to matter . . ."

Now have the second student come up and read the true story of a middle school boy who was excluded, beginning with, "I'm being bullied . . ."

Ask students what resonated with them most as they listened to each of the quotes. Discuss a few responses.

Then say: **Open your journals. We're going to do three minutes of automatic writing about a time when we were excluded or we excluded someone else. It could be a situation that took place in the past, or it could be happening right now. No one will see your writing but you, unless you choose to share it. When I say *begin*, I want you to pick up your pens and write for three minutes straight until I say**

stop. Neatness and spelling don't count here. What matters is letting thoughts spill out of your mind, through your pen, and onto the paper. We're going to be writing in complete silence. Please don't put down your pen until I say *stop*. If at any point you feel stuck, write about how being stuck feels. If you run out of things to say, write about that, too. The point is to just keep writing and see what comes out. You may discover thoughts you didn't even know you had. I'm going to be writing along with you.

See if students have any questions. Lead them in taking three slow, deep breaths. Then look at the clock and say: **Begin.**

As you and your students write, keep an eye on the clock and let them know when three minutes have passed. If any students want to keep writing for another minute or two, allow them to do so.

At the end of three minutes, pass out the notecards and ask students to each write down a word or phrase they think best describes the feeling of being excluded. Tell them not to put their names on the notecards. Let them know you'll be reading some of them aloud. After writing down their words or phrases, have students turn notecards face down. Walk through the room and collect them.

Bring the notecards to the front of the room and read several aloud. See if anyone wants to respond. Depending on your space and your group (or groups), you could also display some of the notecards with the title, "The Pain of Exclusion."

Tell students that we are not powerless when it comes to exclusion, even if it sometimes feels that way. Have the third student you recruited earlier come up and read "Coach Poggi's Golden Rule," the inspiring story of one person's drive to make sure all students are included.

Afterward, ask for responses to the story. Ask: **What do you think it would be like if every teacher or coach had the same rule as Coach Poggi?**

Wrap-Up

Pair up students and have them each share one thing they can do to follow Coach Poggi's example. Invite pairs to share a few responses with the whole group.

Pass out "What to Do About Exclusion." Instruct students to complete it at home and bring it back to school.

Follow-Up

- Next time you meet, review student responses to the "What to Do About Exclusion" handout. Ask: **What did you learn from completing this handout? As a group, how can we be more aware of exclusion? Are there any new agreements you think we should make as a group regarding exclusion?** If an agreement is suggested, ask how we can remind each other to honor it.
- Have students complete the journal questions on the "Exclusion" handout. See if anyone wants you to read what they've written and talk about it privately.

Enrichment Activities

- Keep encouraging students to live by Coach Poggi's rules. Have them create songs, poems, posters, or other creative expressions with Coach Poggi's message and related ideas. Ask how they can share Coach Poggi's message with others.
- Do the 10-Minute Time Cruncher "Being Excluded" on page 84.

Exclusion

Consider the quotes below. Then, in your journal, answer the questions that follow.

"Our need to matter and our need to belong are as fundamental as our need to eat and breathe. Therefore ostracism—rejection, silence, exclusion—is one of the most powerful punishments that one person can inflict on another. Brain scans have shown that this rejection is actually experienced as physical pain, and that this pain is experienced whether those that reject us are close friends or family or total strangers, and whether the act is overt exclusion or merely looking away."

—from the website Delanceyplace.com

- Recall a time when you experienced the pain of exclusion (that you haven't written about yet). Describe what happened, including your feelings, thoughts, and reactions.
- Was there someone who helped you? If so, how did this person help? If not, how did you handle the situation and the feelings that it caused?
- Is the problem still going on? If so, how are you doing? Would it help to talk to me or someone else about the situation?

"I'm being bullied. This new school I switched to doesn't have many kids who look like me. I'm mixed race. Plus, the kids here care a lot about what you wear and how much money you have. Since I've been here, I've been made fun of because of my name, my looks, and my clothes. Because the popular kids pick on me, no one else wants to talk to me or be seen with me at school. I think they think it will make them look bad. It would help if I was even included once, somehow. I'm feeling really alone and horrible about myself."

—7th-grade boy

- What could you do to help this boy? What might you say to him? How might you include him?
- How can you help kids who are new to our school?

From *Create a Culture of Kindness in Middle School* by Naomi Drew, M.A., with Christa M. Tinari, M.A., copyright © 2017. This page may be reproduced for individual, classroom, or small group work only. For all other uses, contact Free Spirit Publishing Inc. at www.freespirit.com/permissions.

Coach Poggi's Golden Rule

Coach Biff Poggi of Gilman High School in Baltimore, Maryland, has a rule for his winning football team that you'd probably never guess: Team members are not allowed to let any boys eat alone—including boys who aren't on the team. "Empathy and kindness for all" is what Coach Poggi demands—even more than winning. But win they do. Nationally, Poggi's team has ranked near the top several times.

Here's what Coach Poggi tells his team: "I expect greatness out of you. And the way we measure greatness is the impact you make on other people's lives."

Poggi cautions his team never to put people in boxes based on race, religion, the neighborhood they live in, the car they drive, athletic ability, level of education, or anything else. He says, "If you let that happen now, then you'll let it happen later." Poggi pushes his boys to break down stereotypes and to remember that every single person is special and has something to offer. He urges them all to do this:

"[If] you happen to see another boy off by himself, go sit with him or bring him over to sit with you and your friends. I don't care if you know him or not. I don't care if he's the best athlete in the school or the so-called nerd with his head always down in the books. You go get him and you make him feel wanted, you make him feel special."

Coach Poggi tells his players to live by one simple, central question for the rest of their lives: "What can I do for you?" He says, "Not what can I do for me. The only question that really matters is this: How can I help you today?"

He explains, "If we lose every game of the year, go oh-and-ten on the football field, as long as we try hard, I don't care. You learn these lessons, and we're ten-and-oh in the game of life."

After thinking about Coach Poggi's words, write your responses to the following questions.

- What did Coach Poggi say that inspired you the most?
- How can you be more like Coach Poggi in your daily life?
- How would our class and school be different if everyone lived by Coach Poggi's golden rule?
- How would your life be different if *you* lived this way?
- How would our world be different if everyone lived by these rules?

REAL-LIFE CHALLENGE

» **In seventh grade, Natalie Hampton sat alone at lunch every day. She felt lonely, excluded, and sad. After this experience, she decided she didn't want other kids to feel the way she had. So she created an app that would mean no other kid would ever have to sit alone and feel bullied or excluded. Her "Sit with Us" app helps kids find a welcoming table in the lunchroom, with the help of their classmates. What creative ideas can *you* come up with to reduce bullying and exclusion? Brainstorm about them in your journal.**

From *Create a Culture of Kindness in Middle School* by Naomi Drew, M.A., with Christa M. Tinari, M.A., copyright © 2017. This page may be reproduced for individual, classroom, or small group work only. For all other uses, contact Free Spirit Publishing Inc. at www.freespirit.com/permissions.

What to Do About Exclusion

If you're being excluded:

- Talk to someone who cares.
- Exercise or take a walk.
- Hang out with someone who likes you for who you are.
- Do a creative activity like art, music, or writing.
- Use positive self-talk to reassure and encourage yourself from the inside out.
- Help someone else. Studies have shown this is an immediate mood-lifter.

- Which of the above activities do you think would help you the most?

- What other ideas can you think of? Describe in detail several things you might do to help yourself feel better if you suffer the pain of exclusion. Include any healthy activities that aren't on the list above.

If you see someone being excluded:

- Ask yourself how the person might feel if you reached out to him or her. Then do it.
- Consider including the person in a group or an activity you're a part of.
- Do something kind for that person.

- Which of the above ideas would you like to try?

- What other ideas can you think of?

If you're thinking about excluding someone else:

- Ask yourself why you want to exclude this person. Is it for a legitimate reason? (For example, this person mistreats you or is a bad influence.) Or is the exclusion based on something more superficial? (For example, not seeming cool enough, not dressing the way you like, or coming from a different cultural background than you do.)
- Consider the possibility of including the person instead of excluding him or her. Think of the impact you could make on this person's life.

- What other ideas can you think of?

- What might stand in the way of including someone?

From *Create a Culture of Kindness in Middle School* by Naomi Drew, M.A., with Christa M. Tinari, M.A., copyright © 2017. This page may be reproduced for individual, classroom, or small group work only. For all other uses, contact Free Spirit Publishing Inc. at www.freespirit.com/permissions.

Being Excluded

CHARACTER CONNECTIONS
kindness / empathy / personal responsibility

This time cruncher coordinates with Lesson 16, "Exclusion Hurts" (page 79). It helps students reflect further on what it's like to be excluded, and why it's important to include others.

Materials

- handout: "Being Excluded" (page 85)

Directions

Distribute the handout to students and have them answer the questions. Take a few minutes to discuss their answers to the last two questions.

Being Excluded

"I'm being bullied. This new school I switched to doesn't have many kids who look like me. I'm mixed race. Plus, the kids here care a lot about what you wear and how much money you have. Since I've been here, I've been made fun of because of my name, my looks, and my clothes. Because the popular kids pick on me, no one else wants to talk to me or be seen with me at school. I think they think it will make them look bad. It would help if I was even included once, somehow. I'm feeling really alone and horrible about myself."

—7th-grade boy

Think about this student's words and answer the following questions:

- Why do you think this student is being excluded?
- How is being excluded affecting him?
- Have you ever been left out or excluded? If so, what happened? How did you feel and what did you do?
- Think of a time when you were *included* in a group of friends, club, or event. How did that feel?
- Imagine this student attended your school. What could you personally do to help him?
- What can people do to help kids feel included at your school?

From *Create a Culture of Kindness in Middle School* by Naomi Drew, M.A., with Christa M. Tinari, M.A., copyright © 2017. This page may be reproduced for individual, classroom, or small group work only. For all other uses, contact Free Spirit Publishing Inc. at www.freespirit.com/permissions.

The Courage to Be Kind

CHARACTER CONNECTIONS

kindness / compassion / personal responsibility / courage

Lesson 17 helps students consider ways to counteract unkind acts.

Note: Prior to doing this lesson, complete Lesson 9: "Your Actions Create Ripples" (page 49).

Students will

- reflect on ways unkind words and actions affect the atmosphere around us
- consider upstander actions they might take if they see someone being mistreated
- role-play responding supportively to someone who's been the target of unkind words

Materials

- student journals
- handouts: "On Kindness and Its Opposite" (page 88), "Considering Kindness" (page 89), and "Strengthen Your Courage Muscle" (page 90)

Preparation

On the board, write, *The Courage to Be Kind.*

Introduction

Say: **Today we're going to talk about a special kind of courage: the courage to be kind. Why does it sometimes take courage to be kind?** Accept answers.

Say: **As we've discussed before, every word we speak, every attitude we have, and every action we take sends out ripples affecting the people around us in either positive or negative ways. What examples have you seen of this?** Entertain responses.

Discussion and Activity

Distribute the "On Kindness and Its Opposite" handout. Ask for a volunteer to read the first quote where an eighth-grade boy describes the atmosphere at school, beginning with the words, "People make fun of you."

Ask: **What does this kind of talk do to the atmosphere around us?** Have students respond. Say: **Mean words and actions can cut deep and remain with us for a long time—even if the other people say they're just kidding. What are your feelings about this?**

Have students briefly respond, then have them take out their journals. Refer again to the handout. Have students do two minutes of automatic writing in response to the next statement on the handout: "When you call people names it can hurt them forever. Even if they say it is okay, some part of them might always stay hurt."

Say: **Write down whatever comes to mind when you consider these words.** Remind students that there's no right or wrong response, and they won't need to share what they wrote unless they want to. Write along with students.

Afterward, see if any students want to share what they wrote. If no one offers, share what you wrote. Ask: **Have you ever given support to someone who was put down or embarrassed by another person? What did you say or do?** Take a few responses.

Put students in pairs and ask: **What other supportive things can we say to someone who's been mistreated?** (Possible answers: "You didn't deserve that," "He had no right to say that," "I don't agree at all with what she said," or "It really bothers me when someone acts like that.") Give partners a few minutes to share and brainstorm, then ask for responses in the large group. Have a student list specific phrases and actions on the board under the title, "The Courage to Be Kind."

Ask: **Do you sometimes find it difficult to do what you just described? Why or why not?** Discuss responses and remind students that every time we show support for others, we strengthen the brain's neural pathways and foster our ability to display courage and kindness.

Say: **Sometimes we can show support and kindness through our actions, without having to say much at all. What are some things we can do?** (Possible answers: Invite the person to join you, stay with the person for a few minutes to make sure he or she is okay, walk him or her to class, or check in with him or her later.) Add students' ideas to the list on the board.

Next, have several students briefly role-play responding to a peer they have witnessed being put down or humiliated. ***Note:*** Don't have them role-play the humiliation part, just the aftermath and their response. Role-playing the negative behavior reinforces it.

Guide students to go over to the person who was hurt and say something kind or reassuring. Encourage them to invite the person to join them in some way. Have them also role-play texting or calling the person later to make sure he or she is okay. Say: **Research shows that including and encouraging someone who's been hurt is much more effective than saying something to the person who said the hurtful words.**

If you have time, repeat the role-play with a second group of kids. This time have them role-play having heard someone being put down for his or her clothing. The person looks sad and embarrassed. Again, don't have students role-play the put-down—just their role in being supportive.

Wrap-Up

Have partners talk about and then list in their journals three specific things they will do to counteract meanness and increase kindness. (Possible answers: Not join in, avoid doing anything to encourage the person who's acting mean.) Tell students you're going to check in with them to see how they're following through in and out of school. Stress how important it is for them to apply what they're learning to real-life situations.

Distribute both follow-up handouts ("Considering Kindness" and "Strengthen Your Courage Muscle") and go over the directions. Have students fill these out as homework.

Follow-Up

- Make time to talk about completed handouts with students. Discuss any insights students had.
- Have students visit the Random Acts of Kindness website (randomactsofkindness.org) and choose one kind act a day to do for others.
- Do the 10-Minute Time Cruncher "Shoes of Kindness" on page 91, which features an inspiring real-life story of compassion.

Enrichment Activities

- Have students do one or more of the activities at the bottom of the "On Kindness and Its Opposite" handout.
- Check in with students to see which random acts of kindness they've performed. Talk about how it felt to do what they did. What other acts of kindness do they want to perform in the future?
- Ask students to think about how they might form an "army of the kind," as referenced in the Cleveland Amory quote from the handout "On Kindness and Its Opposite." What would an "army of the kind" look like? What specific actions could they carry out?

On Kindness and Its Opposite

Cruel words and actions hurt. Read the following words from middle schoolers, and then read the quotes on kindness that follow. Next, take on the Real-Life Challenge at the end of the handout.

"People make fun of you for the smallest things. Some even call you names if you have a bad kick in kickball. They call people 'gay' or 'retarded.' I personally think that's rude and insulting because my best friend's parents are gay, and my cousin is mentally challenged. They call you things based on your weight or even the way you walk. Some people just look at others and full-out judge them from head to toe: 'Look at how fat she is.' 'Look at what she's wearing.' 'OMG, look at the way she walks.' It's awful." —8th-grade boy

"When you call people names it can hurt them forever. Even if they say it is okay, some part of them might always stay hurt." —6th-grade girl

"Everyone is a person, so you can't classify people into different groups for unkind reasons." —7th-grade girl

"I feel like there are many kids who act mean and disrespectful because they meet popular kids who do it and feel like if they want to be popular they have to be mean. I had a best friend who hung out with me every day for sixth and most of seventh grade. But he had a friend who was popular and I guess this friend's personality rubbed off on him a bit too much. Now my friend, who shall not be named, doesn't hang out with me anymore." —8th-grade boy

»»»»»»»»»»»»»»»»»»»»»»»»

"Astonish a mean world with your acts of kindness." —Maya Angelou

"What this world needs is a new kind of army—the army of the kind." —Cleveland Amory

"Three things in human life are important. The first is to be kind. The second is to be kind. And the third is to be kind." —Henry James

"A single act of kindness throws out roots in all directions, and the roots spring up and make new trees." —Amelia Earhart

"If you want to lift yourself up, lift up someone else." —Booker T. Washington

REAL-LIFE CHALLENGE

» After thinking about these quotes, take action to spread kindness in your school and beyond with the following ideas:

- After school, text or email your favorite kindness quote to at least three people and ask them to pass it on.
- Create a computer graphic, piece of artwork, song, or poem using at least one of the quotes on this handout. You can do this on your own, with a partner, or in a group. Share what you created with three or more people.
- Copy your favorite kindness quote or quotes onto colorful paper, decorate it, and hang it in your home for your family and visitors to see.
- If you're on Facebook, Instagram, Twitter, or some other platform, post your favorite kindness quotes from above, or seek out other kindness quotes that speak to you. Invite others to repost them or share their own favorites.

From *Create a Culture of Kindness in Middle School* by Naomi Drew, M.A., with Christa M. Tinari, M.A., copyright © 2017. This page may be reproduced for individual, classroom, or small group work only. For all other uses, contact Free Spirit Publishing Inc. at www.freespirit.com/permissions.

Considering Kindness

Before completing this handout, carry out at least one act of kindness. Then answer each question honestly. Use the back of this sheet or extra paper if you need more room.

- What act (or acts) of kindness did you perform? How did you feel afterward?
- How did the other person or people respond to your act of kindness?
- In general, how kind have you been in word and deed today? Think honestly about this and explain your answer.
- Did you do or say anything today that could have been interpreted as unkind—including through your facial expressions or body language?
- What acts of unkindness have you witnessed? (Be sure not to use real names.)
- How did you feel when you witnessed unkind acts?
- What did you do when you saw the unkind acts taking place? If you did something to support the person who was being mistreated, describe it here.
- If you did nothing to support someone who was being mistreated, what can you do next time?
- What other acts of kindness can you perform each day?

REAL-LIFE CHALLENGE

» **Team up with a friend and make a commitment to performing at least one kind act a day. Check in with your friend each night to encourage and support each other.**

From *Create a Culture of Kindness in Middle School* by Naomi Drew, M.A., with Christa M. Tinari, M.A., copyright © 2017. This page may be reproduced for individual, classroom, or small group work only. For all other uses, contact Free Spirit Publishing Inc. at www.freespirit.com/permissions.

Strengthen Your Courage Muscle

It takes courage to say or do something when you see someone being mistreated. But the more you do it, the more confident you'll feel. Take a look at the following ideas. All of them will help you strengthen your courage muscle.

- Before you go to bed each night, picture yourself filled with courage and kindness. Visualize standing tall in the face of meanness and being a support to others.
- Team up with a friend. Make an agreement to speak up when you see someone being mistreated. Together, practice what you're going to say.
- Write down a few things you can say to someone who's been mistreated. (Here are a few examples: "Are you ok?" "You didn't deserve that," "He had no right to say that," "I don't agree at all with what she said," or "It really bothers me when someone acts like that.") Pretend you're an actor and practice saying these words in the mirror. Stand tall, look yourself in the eye, and speak the words with confidence. Pretend you're saying them in real life.

REAL-LIFE CHALLENGE

» Practice all of the above ideas for a week. Then write in your journal about the experience.

» Create a written dialogue between yourself and someone who is being mistreated. Write out the compassionate words you would say to this person. Also write out his or her response. Start by describing the scenario, then write the dialogue that follows these events. For example: *Tony is standing alone by his locker. Two boys push him as they walk by and call him a mean name. He looks devastated.*

Me: ____________________

Tony: ____________________

Me: ____________________

Tony: ____________________

(Continue the dialogue for at least a page or so.)

 From *Create a Culture of Kindness in Middle School* by Naomi Drew, M.A., with Christa M. Tinari, M.A., copyright © 2017. This page may be reproduced for individual, classroom, or small group work only. For all other uses, contact Free Spirit Publishing Inc. at www.freespirit.com/permissions.

Shoes of Kindness

CHARACTER CONNECTIONS

kindness / compassion / personal responsibility / courage

This time cruncher coordinates with Lesson 17, "The Courage to Be Kind" (page 86). It invites students to consider a powerful example of kindness and empathy in action, and has them come up with kind acts they can carry out themselves.

Materials

- handout: "Shoes of Kindness" (page 92)

Directions

Search YouTube for "School hero Yaovi Mawuli." If possible, prepare to show students the video that goes with this story.

Distribute the "Shoes of Kindness" handout and read it aloud or have a student do so. Then, if possible, have students watch the video about the story.

After students hear the story or view the video, have them pair up or work in small groups to think of a person or group they would like to do an act of kindness for. Have them brainstorm kind acts and choose one to carry out within the next two weeks. Guide students to approach this challenge with altruism and humility rather than charity or condescension, stressing that every one of us can benefit from kind acts in one way or another.

Shoes of Kindness

When Yaovi Mawuli was a senior at Northeast Guilford High School in McLeansville, North Carolina, he witnessed other students bullying Jared Newby, a classmate whose sneakers were literally falling apart. Those sneakers were the only ones Jared ever seemed to wear. They were so worn out they hardly had any soles, and they hurt Jared's feet with every step he took. But instead of showing concern, kids in Jared's class made fun of him.

Yaovi himself had painful memories about being made fun of when he first moved to the United States. These memories loomed large as he watched Jared being bullied. Yaovi knew Jared was a good person and a good student. He wanted to help, but he wasn't sure how. Then he had an idea. He would give Jared a pair of shoes—not just regular shoes, but great shoes! Shoes he could be proud of: new Air Jordans. Yaovi had started his own business buying, selling, and trading shoes online. So he knew he could find a pair of Air Jordans that would be perfect for Jared.

But Yaovi didn't want to embarrass Jared with this gift. He didn't want Jared to think he felt sorry for him. And he understood what it was to have pride. So Yaovi messaged some friends on Facebook for advice. His friends advised him to do things privately. So he talked to the school guidance counselor and arranged to give Jared the new sneakers in her office.

Jared was extremely grateful for the gift of new sneakers, but he was even more grateful for the kindness behind it. In a news interview later, Jared said, "Sometimes with the dumb stuff that goes on in this world, the small little things that people will do for other people gives me a little bit more hope in the survival of humanity." In the same interview, Yaovi said, "Whenever you have a chance to give, just give to somebody else other than yourself."

Yaovi is a true upstander, and a person of deep kindness. He turned the pain he once suffered into compassion for others.

 From *Create a Culture of Kindness in Middle School* by Naomi Drew, M.A., with Christa M. Tinari, M.A., copyright © 2017. This page may be reproduced for individual, classroom, or small group work only. For all other uses, contact Free Spirit Publishing Inc. at www.freespirit.com/permissions.

The Dignity Stance

CHARACTER CONNECTIONS
courage / self-worth / assertiveness

Lesson 18 helps students stand tall and gain inner strength when faced with aggression, including meanness, put-downs, or anger.

Students will

- understand we can convey inner strength and assertiveness through our body language and facial expressions
- practice the Dignity Stance
- role-play using assertive words along with the Dignity Stance

Materials

- student journals
- handout: "The Dignity Stance" (page 96)

»»» **Online Resource** »»»»»»»»»»»»
You may want to suggest that students search online for "Your Body Language Shapes Who You Are Amy Cuddy" and watch Harvard social psychologist Amy Cuddy's TED Talk about how body language can increase our sense of personal power and affect the way people respond to us. Cuddy reports that doing this type of stance for two minutes results in a 20 percent increase in one's sense of personal power, and a 20 percent decrease in the stress hormone cortisol.
»»»»»»»»»»»»»»»»»»»»»»»»»

Introduction

Say: **As we know, when intentional meanness and aggressive put-downs are directed at us, it can feel pretty terrible. Being attacked can take away our energy and challenge our sense of self. Here's what one middle schooler had to say about this:** *"When someone is mean to me, I get emotional but hold it in, because I have been bullied my whole life."*

Say: **"Get emotional, but hold it in" . . . do** ***you*** **ever do that? What kinds of emotions do you think this person feels when someone's mean to him?** (Possible answers: Sadness, anger, powerlessness, shame.) Allow time for some responses.

Say: **Some of us get defensive and go on the attack when we feel that someone else has attacked us. What happens when we do that?** (Possible answers: Things escalate, we get attacked back, we end up making enemies.) Say: **On the other hand, some of us freeze when we're under attack and we can't think of anything to say. What can happen then?** (Possible answers: We feel ashamed or powerless; we send the signal that the person can keep being mean.)

Discussion and Activity

Say: **Today you're going to learn a strategy that will enhance your sense of personal power, self-worth, and dignity—no matter what. Personal power is the ability to stand tall and act with internal strength if you're being attacked or bullied—without being aggressive yourself.**

Note: If students ask why it's not okay to respond aggressively or disrespectfully even if someone's attacking us, turn the question back to them. Ask what happens when we meet disrespect with more disrespect, or meanness with meanness. (Possible answers: The problem escalates; nothing gets solved.) Then guide students to understand that by responding disrespectfully, we're allowing ourselves to be pulled down into the "basement" of ourselves—the lowest part, which is run by the reptilian brain. When we're in this place, we react without thinking. Instead, we can choose to go to "the balcony"—the highest part of ourselves, run by the neocortex. This enables us to choose an appropriate response. Then we can be both strong *and* respectful. When we go to the basement, we end up making the problem worse. The Dignity Stance helps students stay in the balcony, where they can think, choose, and have greater control.

Distribute the "Dignity Stance" handouts. Ask students to stand if they are able. Together, do each of the steps. Model each one as you teach it.

1. *Stand tall with your head held high, feet slightly apart, arms relaxed at your sides, and shoulders back proudly.*
   Remind students to rise up to their fullest height without stiffening their bodies or hunching.
   Guide students to keep their feet slightly apart. This is a power stance. Keeping feet close together doesn't convey as much strength. Arms need to be at the sides or linked in back, not crossed or linked in front. Linking hands in front can signify fear or timidity, while crossing arms can indicate aggression.
2. *Take slow, deep breaths.*
   Remind students that deep breathing will calm them and help them project a demeanor of confidence, even if they feel nervous inside.
3. *Keep your body language and facial expression neutral but strong.*
   Look around and assess what you see. Give feedback where needed. Remind students that the point of this is to look confident, not aggressive or threatening.
   Scan the room and notice if anyone has started to hunch or stiffen. If so, remind them to take another deep breath and use the calming statement they developed in Lesson 8.
4. *Make direct eye contact.*
   Demonstrate looking someone in the eye with confidence, not with fear or aggression. Partner up kids to try this together.
   Note: In some cultures, children are taught that looking someone in the eye is disrespectful. If you have students who were taught to avert their eyes, let them know it's okay to make direct eye contact in your school. Doing so can be an important way to communicate respect and confidence.
5. *Speak in a firm and steady yet nonaggressive tone of voice.*
   Demonstrate with the following statement: "That was disrespectful." Have students turn to their partners, stand tall, and take turns delivering this statement with full eye contact and a firm voice.
   Look around and see if students have crossed their arms or started to sink into themselves. Remind them to keep breathing and standing tall, arms at sides, *or* linking their hands behind their backs.
   Say: **Imagine that your partner has just called you a demeaning name. Take a deep breath, and repeat a calming statement in your head. Stand tall and strong, arms at your sides or behind your back. Then look directly into the person's eyes, and in a firm, level voice, say something strong but non-attacking, such as, "Don't talk to me that way."**
6. *Walk away tall and strong if the person continues to show disrespect.*
   Guide students to hold their heads up high as they do this. Say: **If someone attacks or humiliates us, we need to make an assertive statement, as in Step 5. If the person continues to act aggressively, then it's time to walk away, tall and strong—with full dignity.** Be clear that walking away tall and strong is very different than "running away" or being weak. Walking away tall and strong is a sign of strength, not weakness. Say: **Walking away tall and strong is your way of saying, "I'm not going to let you put me down. I have too much self-respect for that."**

Note: Let students know that they can use just the first five steps of the Dignity Stance when they're in situations that need to be talked out or if someone calls them a name in a non-bullying way. Walking away isn't always necessary in situations where the other person isn't on the attack. Also remind students that when it *is* necessary to walk away, it's important to know how to do so with pride and confidence, not fear or shame.

Next, have students imagine that their partners have just humiliated them in front of other people. (Don't have students role-play the humiliation—just the actions to take afterward.) Have them practice breathing deeply, repeating a calming statement, then walking away tall and strong. Circulate as they do this. If you see postures, gestures, or facial expressions that show aggression *or* passivity, help students make adjustments.

Wrap-Up

Reconvene the large group and ask students to suggest other circumstances where the Dignity Stance could give them the courage to speak up rather than withdraw or attack. (Possible answers: When you're in a conflict; if someone says something demeaning about a friend; if someone puts you down and then claims he or she was joking; if you witness someone being bullied.) Reiterate that if they're engaged in a conflict where they're *not* under personal attack, they should move on to talking out the problem as soon as they can. The steps of the Win/Win Guidelines from Lesson 31 (see page 156) can help them do this.

Follow-Up

Tell students to look for circumstances throughout the week where they can use the Dignity Stance. Then have them write in their journals about what happened. How did they feel doing this? How did the other person (or people) respond? After this lesson, continue to check in with students about their experiences using the Dignity Stance. Provide coaching where needed.

Enrichment Activities

- Have students create comic strips or booklets depicting each step of the Dignity Stance.
- Do role-plays from time to time that give students additional rehearsal in using the Dignity Stance. Have them help come up with scenarios to enact. Do the 10-Minute Time Cruncher "Practicing the Dignity Stance" on page 97 to give kids additional practice.

The Dignity Stance

1. Stand tall with your head held high, feet slightly apart, arms relaxed at your sides, and shoulders back proudly.
2. Take slow, deep breaths to help you feel calm and focused.
3. Keep your body language and facial expression neutral but strong.
4. Make direct eye contact.
5. Speak in a firm, steady, nonaggressive tone of voice.
6. Walk away tall and strong if the person continues to show disrespect.

REAL-LIFE CHALLENGE

» Practice the Dignity Stance in the mirror for several days. Think of someone you need to say something to. Say the words in your head or out loud as you continue practicing. Also write them down. This helps your brain remember and get comfortable with what you want to say. When you feel ready, try it in real life. Speak the words you've been rehearsing as you stand tall and strong before this person. And remember, you might not have to walk away. You might end up talking out what happened instead.

» In your journal, write down several things you could say to someone who's being disrespectful toward you. Also write down several things you could say if someone's trying to start an argument. Now say these replies in the mirror using the Dignity Stance.

» If someone is shouting at you because he or she is angry about something, try using the first five steps of the Dignity Stance and then saying something like, "Hey, I'm interested in what you have to say, but you're being super loud and it's distracting me from really listening to you."

 From *Create a Culture of Kindness in Middle School* by Naomi Drew, M.A., with Christa M. Tinari, M.A., copyright © 2017. This page may be reproduced for individual, classroom, or small group work only. For all other uses, contact Free Spirit Publishing Inc. at www.freespirit.com/permissions.

Practicing the Dignity Stance

CHARACTER CONNECTIONS
courage / self-worth / assertiveness

This time cruncher coordinates with Lesson 18, "The Dignity Stance" (page 93). It gives students additional practice using the Dignity Stance.

Materials

- handout: "The Dignity Stance" (page 96) *(optional)*

Directions

Choose several students to role-play the following scenarios in front of the group using the Dignity Stance. ***Note:*** Each role-play should start with the *response* to the negative behavior, not the negative behavior itself.

- Someone just made fun of your new shoes. You stand tall and deliver a statement that's firm but respectful, such as, "I like my shoes. They're just right for me and I don't appreciate your comments." If you feel the need to walk away afterward, do so with your head held high.
- At lunch, someone just called your friend a name and tried to get other kids to laugh. You stand tall by your friend's side and say something kind to him or her that takes the power away from the put-down and shows you're not going to watch silently as a bystander. Then you and your friend walk away together.
- Every time you walk into homeroom, the same person tries to put you down or embarrass you. This time you stand tall, look the person in the eye, and say, "I'm not going to let you talk to me like that." Then, with your head held high and your posture strong, you proudly walk away.

Invite the group to give feedback on role-players' actions. Was the stance tall and proud in each role-play? Were the words spoken with strength and pride, not aggression? Did body language and facial expression convey self-respect? If necessary, have role-players make adjustments and try again.

The Courage to Stand Up: Malala Yousafzai

CHARACTER CONNECTIONS

courage / compassion / personal responsibility / integrity

Lesson 19 provides an inspiring example of what it is to be an upstander of the highest order.

Students will

- learn about one of the world's greatest living upstanders, Malala Yousafzai
- expand the meaning of upstander to include standing up for the rights and safety of others
- learn more about how to be an upstander on personal as well as humanitarian levels

Materials

- student journals
- handouts: "The Dignity Stance" (page 96), "Malala's Story" (page 100), and "Making Your Courage Bigger than Your Fear" (page 101)

Preparation

Prior to this lesson, distribute Malala's story and have students read it.

Introduction

On the board write *upstander* and *Malala Yousafzai*. Say: **Malala is one of the most inspiring upstanders ever. After reading her story, what does the word *upstander* mean to you?** Entertain students' responses. Tell them that we can be upstanders for individual people when we see someone being mistreated, or we can be upstanders for groups of people who are being oppressed. Ask which kind of upstander Malala is. Remind students that both ways of being an upstander are very important and both take enormous courage.

Ask: **How old was Malala when she started speaking out?** (Answer: About twelve.) **What thoughts ran through your head as you read her story?** Discuss briefly.

Discussion and Activity

Say: **Being an upstander can be scary. The situations you face may not be as dangerous as Malala's, but they can still be frightening in very real ways. Malala was able to be an upstander of this magnitude by allowing her courage to be larger than her fear. If *you* let your courage be larger than your fear, what might you do when you see someone being mistreated?** Accept a few answers and discuss.

Say: **Malala believes that each of us can change the world—no matter how young or old we are. Do you agree? Why or why not?** Tell students that Malala isn't the only young person changing the world. On the board, write the following name: *Craig Kielburger*. Tell students that Craig is another amazing upstander. At the age of twelve he started helping kids who were forced into child labor in life-threatening conditions. Craig has saved many of these children's lives. Let students know they'll be learning more about Craig after this lesson.

Say: **Changing the world starts with how we treat each other right here in our school. The steps you're about to read will help you start building the courage to be an upstander. Let Malala's story inspire you to be an upstander for one person, or for many.**

Pass out the "Making Your Courage Bigger than Your Fear" handout. Either go over it as a full group, or put students into groups of four or five to read and discuss.

Allow about ten minutes for going over the handout. After discussing the steps, ask for a few examples of what kids can say if their friends say or do mean things to another person. Guide them to start with "I," not "you." (For example, "I feel uncomfortable seeing someone being hurt.") Acknowledge that doing this can be hard, especially if we've never done it before, but that's how we build courage.

Next, choose four students to role-play the following scenario:

You're in the lunchroom with two friends. They've just said something mean to another person at the table. You can tell that person is hurt. What are you going to do?

Make sure students don't role-play the mean behavior itself, but only what they do to help afterward. Again caution them not to start with "you" when they speak. Using "you" puts people on the defensive. Here are some phrases they can use instead: "Let's not do this, okay?" Or, "Come on, let's stop." Or, "I feel bad seeing someone hurt." Coach the upstander to say or do something supportive for the person who was hurt, such as checking in with that person later, asking if he or she is okay, or privately expressing regret for what happened.

If time allows, choose three more students to do a second role-play:

You see a student looking crushed after being humiliated by several kids. You want to help, but you're nervous. You decide to ask a friend to join you in going over to that person. You say something supportive, like, "Are you okay?" or, "They don't know what they're talking about." Then you ask if he or she would like some company walking to class.

Wrap-Up

Have students each choose one upstander action to take in the coming days if they see others being mistreated. Have students write down the actions they've chosen in their journals. Ask them to also consider what might stand in the way of doing this, and then have them write down a solution to this obstacle. For example, a student might write:

Obstacle: I might be afraid to do this in real life.

Solution: I could rehearse it first and talk to friends ahead of time to see if they'll join me in being an upstander. Or, I could talk to a trusted adult in my life and get some advice. Or, I could read about other upstanders and follow their lead.

Remind students that, regardless of age, we all can make the world better.

Follow-Up

- Check in with students in the coming days to see how they've put the ideas in this lesson into real-life action. Acknowledge those who have, and encourage those who haven't. Try doing this in your own life and give students examples of words you spoke and actions you took.
- Have students look up Craig Kielburger online, learn about his work, and write about something they might be inspired to do to make a difference in the lives of others, whether on a small or large scale.

Enrichment Activities

- Invite students to research how Malala continues to stand up for her rights and the rights of others. Suggest that students read more about her work and the impact it's been making. Have them journal about how they might follow her example in some way, large or small.
- Have students create songs, poems, or other creative expressions about anything that inspired them in this lesson's stories.

Malala's Story

Malala Yousafzai is an upstander of the highest order. As a result of her courageous deeds, she was awarded the Nobel Peace Prize in 2014 at the age of seventeen. She is the youngest person ever to receive this prize. In April 2015, a NASA astronomer named a galaxy after her. It's called "Malala 316201." She came in second place for *Time* magazine's person of the year in 2015 and was on *Time*'s list of the "100 Most Influential People in the World" in 2013, 2014, and 2015. Here is her story.

When Malala was ten years old, she lived in a beautiful village named Mingora in the Swat Valley of Pakistan. Her father ran the local school. But everything changed when Malala's village and many other villages were taken over by the Taliban, a group of extremists who use violent tactics to gain power.

One of the Taliban's goals was to take away rights from women and girls. They made it a crime for girls to go to school. Malala dreamed of becoming a doctor, and education was one of the most important things in her life. Other girls she knew had dreams, too. Malala decided that she could not allow the Taliban to stop them from going to school. She started blogging and speaking out on behalf of every girl's right to an education. She was determined not to be bullied into silence, even when the Taliban started threatening her.

Before long, the Taliban began bombing schools. Malala continued speaking out even though she was scared. Television stations learned of her bravery and started asking for interviews. Although she knew this publicity would put her life in even more danger, her courage was greater than her fear. "How dare the Taliban take away my right to education?" she said in an interview. In another she said, "They cannot stop me. Our challenge to the world around us is: Save our school, save our Pakistan."

One day when Malala was fifteen and on her way to school, armed Taliban members forced her bus to stop. "Which one of you is Malala?" one of them asked. Before anyone had a chance to speak, the man spotted Malala. He raised a pistol and shot her in the face. Amazingly, she survived.

Malala was flown to a hospital where she endured eight hours of surgery. She fully recovered—and she went right back to speaking out for the rights of girls (and all people) to an education. She said, "When the whole world is silent, even one voice becomes powerful."

Malala believes that education, not violence, is the key to a better future. She said, "Let us pick up our books and pens. They are the most powerful weapons. One child, one teacher, one book, and one pen can change the world." Malala's message has spread far and wide, inspiring others to stand up, speak out, and allow courage to be stronger than fear.

Let Malala's powerful message inspire you to speak up, too. Here are more of her words:

"I speak not for myself but so those without a voice can be heard . . . their right to live in peace, their right to be treated with dignity, their right to equality of opportunity, their right to be educated."

"I truly believe the only way we can create global peace is through not only educating our minds, but our hearts and our souls."

"I think that the best way to solve problems . . . is through dialogue, is through peaceful ways."

"You must not treat others with cruelty."

"We were scared, but our fear was not as strong as our courage."

"We can change this whole world."

 From *Create a Culture of Kindness in Middle School* by Naomi Drew, M.A., with Christa M. Tinari, M.A., copyright © 2017. This page may be reproduced for individual, classroom, or small group work only. For all other uses, contact Free Spirit Publishing Inc. at www.freespirit.com/permissions.

Making Your Courage Bigger than Your Fear

The following actions will help you make your courage bigger than your fear when you see kids being picked on or excluded.

Start small. Use your voice. Speak up about something relatively nonthreatening you might ordinarily remain silent on. For example, you might have always remained silent when friends have "bashed" a teacher you really like behind his or her back. You find this unfair and uncomfortable, but you've stayed silent because you didn't want to seem like the odd person out. Try speaking your real thoughts. Say something like, "I disagree. I think Mr. Peretti is a really good teacher, even if he gives too much homework."

Speak up when your friends say mean things about people who aren't around instead of joining in or remaining silent. Try saying something like, "I don't like hearing mean things about people. Can we just let it go?" It can be hard to speak up, especially if you're worried about getting on your friends' bad sides. But doing it anyway will build your courage muscle. You may be surprised when some friends end up agreeing with you and tell you that they're glad you spoke up.

Team up with a friend and make an agreement to say something kind to someone who's been hurt or excluded. Or invite that person to join or sit with you.

Rehearse what you're going to say ahead of time if you want to speak up in support of someone who's being picked on. Practice in the mirror or with someone you know.

Stand by the side of someone who's being picked on. Even if you don't say a word, your presence alone will help. Check in with the person later to make sure he or she is okay.

REAL-LIFE CHALLENGE

» Get inspired by reading about two more people who let their courage be bigger than their fear. Search online for the following terms to learn about the amazing things these people did as kids:

- Biography of Craig Kielburger
- Camille Paddock: Dare to Be Different

» Choose at least one of the actions listed on this handout and perform it this week. Then write about the experience in your journal. Every day, remind yourself to let your courage be bigger than your fear.

From *Create a Culture of Kindness in Middle School* by Naomi Drew, M.A., with Christa M. Tinari, M.A., copyright © 2017. This page may be reproduced for individual, classroom, or small group work only. For all other uses, contact Free Spirit Publishing Inc. at www.freespirit.com/permissions.

Why Be an Upstander?

CHARACTER CONNECTIONS

personal responsibility / compassion / respect

Lesson 20 helps students understand the responsibility we all have to be upstanders.

Students will

- identify the risks and rewards of being an upstander
- reflect on the impact of being an upstander
- determine reasons they would choose to be upstanders

Materials

- handouts: "Standing Up for Dee Andrews" (page 104) and "Why I Would Be an Upstander" (page 105)

Preparation

On the board, write the following quote:

> *"Do your little bit of good where you are; it's those little bits of good put together that overwhelm the world." —Archbishop Desmond Tutu*

»»» **Online Resource** »»»»»»»»»»»»»

If desired, search huffingtonpost.com for "A Cheerleader with Down Syndrome Was Bullied" to watch a video about Dee Andrews in preparation for this lesson or to share it with students.

»»»»»»»»»»»»»»»»»»»»»»»»»

Introduction

Direct students' attention to the quote on the board. Ask: **What does this quote mean to you? How can you relate it to standing up for others in bullying situations?** Take a few responses. Say: **An upstander can be someone who takes a risk to help a target of bullying or persecution. What risks might be involved in being an upstander?** Take student responses.

Say: **In some situations, being an upstander can be very risky. People like Malala Yousafzai, Martin Luther King Jr., Cesar Chavez, and Aung San Suu Kyi stood up for others and risked their lives at the same time.** Briefly discuss the contributions of these or other upstanders depending on your group and the time you have available. Say: **But most of the time, being an upstander is challenging but does not put our lives as risk. Today, we're going to talk about reasons for being an upstander in situations where you're not in grave danger, but where someone's being harmed emotionally or physically.**

Discussion and Activity

Say: **Here's a great example of kids your age being upstanders for someone who was being picked on.** Distribute the "Standing Up for Dee Andrews" handout and give students a few minutes to read the story.

Ask the following questions from the bottom of the handout: **Do you think you would have taken the opportunity to be an upstander in this situation?** Ask for a show of hands. Ask: **What might have stood in your way?** Take responses. Ask: **What risks did the basketball players take by standing up for Dee? What were the benefits of being upstanders?**

Say: **A lot of middle schoolers report that they want to help kids who are being bullied, but they're also worried about the risks. In a survey of over 1,000 middle schoolers, many said they don't report bullying because they're afraid they'll be targeted next. Do these concerns sound familiar to you?** Discuss.

Say: **Although it's not easy to be an upstander, most of the time it is worth the risk. There are many reasons to stand up for what is right.**

Give students the handout "Why I Would Be an Upstander." Read the choices on the handout together as a group. Say: **Consider which reasons resonate the most with you. Circle the reasons you would choose to be an upstander.** Give students five to six minutes to complete the handout.

Put students into pairs or small groups. Say: **With your partner, talk about the reasons you chose.** Give students about five minutes for discussion.

Wrap-Up

Ask a few students to share their reasons why they would be upstanders. Say: **Let's consider some advice from two middle schoolers.** Have two volunteers read the quotes toward the bottom of the "Why I Would Be an Upstander" handout (under "Think About It").

Say: **Being an upstander is difficult, but there are a lot of reasons why it's the right thing to do. Even just one upstander can make a big difference in the life of someone who needs help. Let it be you!**

Follow-Up

- Have students look for news articles, social media posts, and other material featuring people (of any age) who acted as upstanders. Have them summarize the material they choose in a short paragraph and share it with the group.
- Ask students to use the search term "upstander" online to explore more facts and information about upstanders. Ask students to each find three points of information they can share with their classmates.

Enrichment Activities

- Have students ask their parents or other family adults to share a story about a time when someone stood up for them. What kind of impact did this have? Invite students to also seek out stories about times when family members stood up for others. What motivated them to be upstanders in these situations? How did their actions impact the people they stood up for?
- Invite students to research the life of Martin Niemöller and to read and consider his poem that begins "First they came . . ." Ask students to compose essays exploring the following questions: Who are "they" in the poem? What is meant by "speak out"? What does this poem suggest about the importance of speaking out or standing up for others in the face of injustice? When did Martin Niemöller live? In what ways was he an upstander? In what ways did he fail to be an upstander? What were Niemöller's regrets? What can we all learn from his experience?

Standing Up for Dee Andrews

Read this true story and answer the questions that follow.

Desiree Andrews, known as Dee, was a seventh-grade student cheerleader at Lincoln Middle School in Kenosha, Wisconsin. During a boys' basketball game, some students in the stands started making fun of her because she has Down syndrome and she was stepping to her own beat. When several basketball players noticed what was going on, they decided to take action. During a time out, they walked off the court and approached the offending students. They asked them to stop their insensitive behavior and said, "Cut that out. It's not right." Afterward, the players were recognized by their school and the news media for being upstanders. Feeling supported by her classmates helped Dee happily continue in her role as cheerleader.

- Do you think you would have taken the opportunity to be an upstander in this situation?

- What might have stood in your way?

- What risks did the basketball players take by standing up for Dee?

- What were the benefits of being an upstander?

REAL-LIFE CHALLENGE

» Keep your eyes and ears open for kids who might be getting picked on or teased. Think of an action you could take that would show kindness and support toward that person. If you're not sure what to do, talk this over with an adult in your life.

 From *Create a Culture of Kindness in Middle School* by Naomi Drew, M.A., with Christa M. Tinari, M.A., copyright © 2017. This page may be reproduced for individual, classroom, or small group work only. For all other uses, contact Free Spirit Publishing Inc. at www.freespirit.com/permissions.

Why I Would Be an Upstander

Make a check mark next to the reasons that describe why you would be an upstander.

I would choose to be an upstander because:

- ☐ It's the right thing to do.
- ☐ It feels good to help other people.
- ☐ I want school to be a safe place.
- ☐ I believe that all people deserve to be treated with respect.
- ☐ It helps me practice my leadership skills.
- ☐ Someone stood up for me once, so I know how it feels.
- ☐ I believe each person can make a difference.
- ☐ I would want someone to do the same for me.
- ☐ It would encourage others to do the same.
- ☐ Being an upstander can put an end to bullying episodes.
- ☐ I want to feel proud of my actions.
- ☐ Other:
- ☐ Other:
- ☐ Other:

Think about these quotes and write your responses to them in your journal:

"Stop bullying people and stand up for people who get picked on.
It's that simple. Don't be mean to people.
Treat people how you want to be treated."
—7th-grade boy

"Let the people being bullied know you have their back.
Just ask if they are okay and say something to make them smile.
Someone did that for me and it made a big difference."
—6th-grade girl

REAL-LIFE CHALLENGE

» Be an upstander when you see someone being picked on, teased, harassed, or bullied. Say something, check in with the person afterward, or just stand by his or her side. If you're not sure the situation is safe, or if you don't know what to do, GET HELP. Talk to someone you trust.

From *Create a Culture of Kindness in Middle School* by Naomi Drew, M.A., with Christa M. Tinari, M.A., copyright © 2017. This page may be reproduced for individual, classroom, or small group work only. For all other uses, contact Free Spirit Publishing Inc. at www.freespirit.com/permissions.

Redefining Cool

CHARACTER CONNECTIONS

respect / kindness / compassion / personal responsibility

Lesson 21 guides students to redefine their concept of "cool," encouraging them to include in its definition the qualities of courage, compassion, and respect.

Students will

- reflect on their attitudes about what it means to be cool and if it's possible to be both cool and kind
- explore the concept that it's cooler to be kind
- create a new definition of cool that includes kindness, courage, and respect

Materials

- student journals

Introduction

Say: **Today we're going to talk about what it means to be cool.** Read aloud these quotes from middle schoolers: *"Kids are mean to each other 'cause they want to be cool." "Mean doesn't equal cool, and being picked on stinks." "Some people act mean to seem cool in front of their friends."*

Ask: **What qualities do *you* associate with coolness? If someone's cool, what does that mean? Describe someone who others see as cool (but don't use the person's name).** Briefly discuss. Talk with students about the pressure they may feel to be cool, and ask them to consider how they think popularity or coolness in middle school might affect—or not affect—their lives later on.

Discussion and Activity

Have students open their journals and write "Cool people are . . ." at the top of a new page. Give them a minute or so to quickly brainstorm every word or phrase they associate with "cool people."

After time is up, invite students to come up and write on the board a word or phrase they just listed. Afterward, ask the group to consider the words on the board. Did anyone include qualities such as kind, caring, respectful, inclusive, and brave? Did anyone mention integrity? Why or why not?

Now reread this student quote aloud, sharing the rest of it: ***"Kids are mean to each other because they want to be cool. They need to know it's cooler to be kind."***

Invite students to respond. Ask: **Do you agree or disagree with this statement? Why?** Say: **Now think of someone you really respect and admire—someone you want to be like.** Put students in pairs and have them tell their partners about this person, explaining why they respect and admire him or her.

After a few minutes, have students open to a new page in their journals. At the top have them write the name of the person they just talked about with their partners, followed by the word "is." (For example, "Aunt Mia is . . .") Have them list at least five admirable qualities this person possesses.

Have students reconvene with their partners. Have pairs compare the qualities of "cool people" listed on the board with those of the people they admire and respect.

Ask: **What did you notice? Are there overlaps, or are these lists completely different? If so, what does this say about our concept of what it means to be cool? Is it possible to be both cool and**

compassionate? Cool and respectful? Cool and kind? Take responses.

Ask: **Would our school and neighborhood be different if everyone tried to be cool in a kind, compassionate way? How so? Do you think it takes more courage to be cool in this way? Why or why not?**

Direct students' attention back to the "Cool people are . . ." list on the board. Ask: **Are there any new words you want to add to this list? Are there any you want to eliminate?** Invite kids to come back to the board to make changes.

Wrap-Up

Say: **With your partner, create a new definition of cool. Write it in your journals.** Ask several pairs to share what they came up with.

Follow-Up

Have kids create visuals representing or illustrating their expanded definitions of cool. Have them post what they create online or share it in other ways.

Enrichment Activities

- In their journals, have students reflect on how they can spread new definitions of cool. Consider implementing some of the ideas they come up with. For example, someone may have come up with a great slogan or graphic that you'd like to see go viral. Consider helping them create a video, website, or other digital platform to spread the word. Or, refer students to someone with tech skills to help make this happen.
- Contact a local journalist or radio station and invite him or her to interview kids about their new definition of cool and why it's important to adopt this definition.
- Do the 10-Minute Time Cruncher "How Cool Is This?" on page 108.

How Cool Is This?

CHARACTER CONNECTIONS

respect / kindness / compassion / personal responsibility

This time cruncher coordinates with Lesson 21, "Redefining Cool" (page 106). It gives students an inspiring real-life example of extraordinary kindness and challenges them to come up with their own ways to follow suit.

Materials

- handout: "How Cool Is This?" (page 109)

Directions

Distribute the handout. Have students read it and answer the questions at the end. Discuss their responses to the story and the questions.

How Cool Is This?

Before Konner Sauve graduated from East Valley High School in Yakima, Washington, he did something extraordinary. Over the course of eleven months, he made more than 600 anonymous Instagram posts complimenting his classmates and offering sincere words of kindness. Before doing this, Konner had taken the time to meet every single student in the sophomore, junior, and senior classes. He looked for distinctly positive qualities in each person and then brought attention to these qualities through his Instagram account.

Throughout the year, no one at school knew who was sending the uplifting messages. Finally on graduation day, Konner went to the podium as valedictorian of his class and revealed that he was the person who'd sent everyone these messages. The entire senior class rose and gave Konner a standing ovation. They were touched that someone would actually take the time to notice something positive about each and every one of them, *and* compose a personal message of affirmation!

So, why did Konner do this? Here's what he told ABC News: "Everyone makes mistakes and I wanted to focus on the better aspects of people." He also explained his motivation: "To shed a positive light on each individual, make them feel appreciated, and to know that someone cares." He added, "I hope that even with high school rumors and drama, that [students] can look at people . . . and be able to view them without being too judgmental."

Dottie Say, principal of East Valley High School, praised Konner's actions, saying, "It was very positive to raise the morale and address the negativity of social media."

To see some messages of kindness that Konner posted, you can visit his Instagram account at instagram.com/thebenevolentone3.

- What do you find most inspiring about Konner Sauve's story? Why did this affect you the way it did?

- Konner was inspired by "benevolence," the desire to do good for others. What does being benevolent mean to you? How can you spread benevolence in your school?

- What specific kind acts can you perform for others? How can you inspire kindness in others?

REAL-LIFE CHALLENGE

» Spend one whole day looking for the good in people. Consider writing notes, emails, texts, Instagram posts, tweets, or Facebook messages affirming others for their positive qualities. Try doing this at school and at home.

From *Create a Culture of Kindness in Middle School* by Naomi Drew, M.A., with Christa M. Tinari, M.A., copyright © 2017. This page may be reproduced for individual, classroom, or small group work only. For all other uses, contact Free Spirit Publishing Inc. at www.freespirit.com/permissions.

LESSON 22

Living Kindness

CHARACTER CONNECTIONS

kindness / compassion / personal responsibility

Lesson 22 invites students to brainstorm concrete ways they can "live kindness"—making it an integral part of their actions and lives every day.

Students will	Materials
• reflect on the impact of simple kindnesses in their lives • brainstorm a list of simple kind acts they can perform • commit to implementing some kind acts they came up with to "live kindness" every day	• student journals

Preparation

Think of a simple act of kindness that either changed your life or touched it in an important way. We've all had them. Think back to teachers you've had throughout your life. Did any of their words of encouragement, support, or acknowledgment touch you? Be prepared to share briefly about your experience of kindness.

Introduction

This lesson benefits from using deep breathing to begin. Have students close their eyes or look down. Say: **Let's start by doing some deep breathing to calm our minds and bodies.** Lead the group in several rounds of deep breathing, having students breathe in all the way down to the lower abdomen, imagining a balloon there that they can fill with each inhalation. Guide them to breathe in slowly and hold, then breathe out even more slowly. Remind them that each breath should be silent, deep, and gentle. Breathe with them.

Discussion and Activity

After several rounds of breathing, ask students to keep their eyes closed or lowered and focus on the words you are about to say. Now say: **Kindness has the capacity to touch our lives more than anything else. I'm going to share a personal experience with a simple act of kindness that touched my life.** Share your story, then ask students to think about a way kindness has touched them and made a difference in their lives or in the quality of a day. Remind them that even something as small as a smile from a stranger can make a huge difference when you're feeling down. Encourage students to think about simple kind acts that made an impact on them. If they can't think of something that happened to them personally, have them think of a kindness they heard or read about that touched them deeply.

After several minutes of silence, have students open their eyes and take out their journals. Have them do two to three minutes of automatic writing about their memory of kindness. Remind them that no act is too small to be significant. Have them write about how the simple act of kindness made them feel and how it touched their lives. Have them consider any ripples that resulted from this act.

After several minutes, have students stop writing. (Those who want to can continue for another minute or so.) Partner up your students and have them share their stories with each other. They can either read their writing or simply retell their stories. After a few more minutes, remind students to switch so everyone has a chance to share.

Reconvene as a large group and ask who'd like to share their story of kindness. This can be via retelling or by reading what they've written.

Now have partners come back together, this time joining with another pair to form groups of four. Have one student be the recorder. That student can take notes in his or her journal. Give groups the following challenge: **See if you can come up with twenty simple, kind acts that anyone can do.** Have them think of things that can easily be done throughout the day. Say: **These acts can be small, but they are ways that we can "live kindness" each and every day. Examples might include saying hi to someone you don't know, smiling instead of frowning, offering to help someone carry something, giving someone a snack, leaving a nice note for someone, thanking someone for doing something nice, saying nothing rather than saying something mean, asking someone how her day is going or how she is doing, or simply listening to what someone else has to say even if it doesn't interest you.**

Tell students they're going to have four minutes to come up with twenty acts, so they need to let the ideas flow and not judge, criticize, or self-censor. Tell students that getting out their ideas is more important than deciding which ones are best.

Have groups sit so all four members are facing one another. Make sure the group recorders have journals open and pens in hand. Tell them that spelling and neatness aren't important. What *is* important is making sure they record every idea. Tell groups to make sure everyone has a turn. More vocal members should encourage more reserved members to contribute.

When groups are ready, say: **Begin.** Circulate as students brainstorm. Let them know when they have one minute left. Then say: **Stop.**

Have groups count up their ideas. See how many each group came up with. Now have each group choose their ten best ideas. They can do this by voting or through discussion. At the end of four minutes, have each recorder circle the ten ideas the group chose.

Ask the recorder in each group to read aloud the circled ideas. On the board, jot down each "living kindness" idea as it's read. Only list new ones. If duplicates are named, do not write them again, but place check marks next to ideas that are brought up multiple times. After each group has shared, ask the large group which ideas appeal to them most. Circle them. See if you can arrive at twenty-five or thirty ideas in all. Copy down this final list by hand or create a computer document. Give copies of this list to your students. If it's possible, post a copy in the room as well.

Wrap-Up

Ask students to jot down in their journals three kind acts they will do right away. Briefly discuss. Ask them what they hope the impact of their kind acts will be. Remind them, however, that performing these kind acts is what's most important—even if they never know what the impact is.

Follow-Up

Give each student a copy of the list. Check in with the group on subsequent days to see what happens as they continue performing kind acts. Add more ideas to the list if desired. Encourage students to observe the changes they feel or see as they perform these kind acts.

Enrichment Activities

- Encourage your students to "live kindness" in all areas of their lives and do kind acts at home, in after-school activities, for teachers, in the community, and for people they don't know. Continue checking in to see how these kind acts are changing their relationships with others—and with themselves.
- Have your students write letters of kindness. In these letters, students can thank others for things they've done, offer sincere words of affirmation, acknowledge others for qualities the students respect or admire, or offer words of encouragement and support. Encourage students to share these letters with the people to whom they are addressed. Afterward, talk about the impact the letters made—on the receivers and on the givers. See if students would like to do this again. How many lives can they touch through simple kindnesses?

SECTION 3

CELEBRATING UNIQUENESS AND ACCEPTING DIFFERENCES

LESSON 23 Accepting Differences

CHARACTER CONNECTIONS
acceptance / compassion / kindness

Lesson 23 helps students see that we all have many similarities, regardless of differences.

Students will

- understand that they may have things in common with people they see as different from themselves
- reflect on how their lives and school might be if people were more accepting of others
- practice getting to know people who are different from themselves

Materials

- student journals
- handout: "Thinking About Differences" (page 116)

Preparation

Write the following quotes on the board:

> *"Everyone is different. We can't pick on someone because of a difference. If we do, it means that we don't appreciate what they have to offer. Everyone has something to offer, no matter how small." —7th-grade boy*
>
> *"Our most basic common link is that we all inhabit this small planet. We all breathe the same air." —John F. Kennedy*
>
> *"I am another you." —Mayan saying*
>
> *"People should get to know each other better and not generalize based on physical appearance or rumors. This way they'll get to know how nice some people really are." —8th-grade girl*

Introduction

Ask: **How many of you tend to hang out with people who are a lot like you? Think of a time you assumed you wouldn't have much in common with someone who appeared to be different from you. What happened? What would have happened if you hadn't made that assumption?** Discuss.

Ask: **Do you think kids often assume that people who don't look like them must be very different than they are? Why or why not?** Entertain responses. Ask: **Have you ever gotten to know someone you thought was different from you and discovered that you had things in common?** Ask for examples, reminding students not to use real names.

Discussion and Activity

Say: **Today we're going to have an opportunity to discover unexpected things we have in common with others.** Refer to the quotes on the board. Ask for a volunteer to read the first one, beginning with, *"Everyone is different."* Invite students to share their responses.

Next, have students move their desks so the center of the room is empty. Ask them to stand in a large circle. Say: **Step inside the circle if . . .** Go through the following list one item at a time, having students step back to the perimeter after each item.

- you like pizza
- your favorite color is red
- your favorite color is blue
- your favorite color is green
- you have some other favorite color
- you love hot sauce

- you hate hot sauce
- you like to watch [name a popular TV show]
- you spend a lot of time online
- you like to play a musical instrument
- you like to paint or draw
- you love animals
- you like working with computers
- you like [name a regional sports team]
- you like [name a rival of the team above]
- you play soccer
- you do gymnastics
- you wish you could sleep later on school days
- you love your family and friends

Afterward, have everyone sit in a circle on the floor. Ask the following questions and allow a few minutes to discuss students' responses:

- What did you learn through this activity?
- What surprised you?
- Why is it important to be open to people we perceive as different?
- What are some basic things that all people have in common?
- What do you think our school would be like if people were more accepting of other people's differences and unique qualities? What do you think our world might be like?

Direct students' attention back to the four quotes on the board. Ask for volunteers to read aloud each of the three remaining quotes. Then ask students which quote had the most meaning for them and why. Discuss.

Wrap-Up

Have students reassemble in their seats and do about two minutes of automatic writing in their journals about any insights that were revealed to them during this lesson. Distribute the handout and go over it as a group.

Follow-Up

- Make time with students to go over insights that emerged from their journal reflections and from the "I am another you" exercise on the handout.
- Ask students what changes they might want to make regarding how they treat people who they perceive as different from themselves. How might they initiate those changes in real life?

Enrichment Activities

- Pair up students, matching them with partners they might not usually hang out with. Have pairs create and design a visual of their choice on accepting differences. It can be via video, computer graphics, or hard copy using illustrations, words, or some combination. Have pairs disseminate what they've created within your school, and possibly beyond.
- Introduce the "Join Me Challenge." Encourage students to invite someone they perceive as different from themselves to join them for lunch, a study session, or another activity. Afterward, have them write in their journals about what the experience was like and what they learned from it.

Thinking About Differences

- What does the following quote mean to you?

  "Recognize yourself in he and she who are not like you and me." —Carlos Fuentes

- Think of someone you see as very different from yourself. In what way might you be a little bit like this person? What part of yourself can you recognize in him or her?

- Read this quote to yourself three times: *"I am another you." —Mayan saying*

  Now, picture the person you thought about in the question above—the person you see as different from you. Imagine actually *being* him or her. Then write about what your life might be like. What would it be like to be at school each day as this person? How might you feel?

- What are some ways in which you could be more open-minded? What are some specific things you could do to be more welcoming and accepting toward people you see as different? What could you do to encourage others to be more open-minded and less likely to shut out or ignore people they see as different? Why is it important to do this?

 From *Create a Culture of Kindness in Middle School* by Naomi Drew, M.A., with Christa M. Tinari, M.A., copyright © 2017. This page may be reproduced for individual, classroom, or small group work only. For all other uses, contact Free Spirit Publishing Inc. at www.freespirit.com/permissions.

Different and Alike

CHARACTER CONNECTIONS

acceptance / compassion / respect

Lesson 24 helps students find things in common with people they may have once perceived as different.

Note: Prior to this lesson, have students conduct "Different and Alike" interviews. See the handout on page 119.

Students will

- interview fellow students they perceive as different from themselves
- discover at least one thing they have in common with the people they interview
- reflect on the fact that similarities exist among us even alongside real or perceived differences

Materials

- student journals
- handout: "Different and Alike Interviews" (pages 119–120)

Preparation

Distribute the "Different and Alike Interviews" handout several days before this lesson. Arrange a time when students can conduct their interviews at school. You might want to team up with another teacher, counselor, or staff member in your building and plan to have students interview each other.

Introduction

Have students take out their interview handouts. Ask someone to read aloud the quote at the top, beginning, "It is not our differences that divide us." Have students respond to the quote. Ask: **Do you feel any differently about this quote now that you've completed your interviews?** Have students explain their answers.

Discussion and Activity

Put students in pairs. Ask them to talk with their partners about the experience of completing the interviews and what they discovered. In the large group, have students share some of their insights.

Now go through the four questions at the end of the "Different and Alike Interviews" handout:

What did you learn about this person that surprised you? Why did it surprise you?
Encourage students not only to refer to the specific interview questions from the handout, but also to talk about any qualities of the person they interviewed that they might have noticed for the first time, such as a sense of humor, kindness, a great smile, or the ability to listen really well.

Did you discover anything that you didn't realize you had in common with this person? If so, what was it? (If you discovered multiple things you had in common, list them all.)
Encourage students to share any shared trait or circumstance that was revealed, including things that weren't on the handout, such as "we both have dogs we love" or "we both have sisters who pester us."

Was there something you learned that you liked, admired, or respected about the other person that you didn't know about before? If so, what was it? (Again, if you have multiple answers, share them all.)
Encourage students to really think about this one. Encourage them to look at qualities like warmth, intelligence, compassion, courage, or talents in areas they were previously unaware of.

Imagine that the person you interviewed is here right now. What could you say to acknowledge the things you appreciate in him or her?
Encourage students to think of sincere statements. Then ask for a few volunteers to share them aloud.

Following this discussion, have students write notes to the people they interviewed, recognizing and affirming them for any positive qualities revealed during their interviews. Guide them to include their answers to question 3: "Was there something you learned that you liked, admired, or respected about the other person that you didn't know about before? If so, what was it?"

Wrap-Up

Have students think of another person they perceive as different from themselves. Encourage them to learn more about that person. In journals, have them jot down the person's name along with something they can do to get to know him or her a little better. Some examples are:

- Ask the person to join you for lunch.
- Ask him or her to join you in an activity or sport.
- Suggest working on a homework assignment together.

If time allows, see the first enrichment activity for a way to take this a step further.

Follow-Up

- Have students complete the "Different and Alike Interviews" again with new interview subjects, perhaps people who don't go to their school. Have students add some new questions they would like to ask, and revise the questions that are not relevant to their interviewees.
- Encourage students to include people they see as different in activities—in and out of school. Urge them to learn more about others and what positive and interesting qualities they can discover.

Enrichment Activities

- As an extension to the "Wrap-Up" section, have students create Venn diagrams of two intersecting circles (as in the model below) with their name above one circle and the name of the person they're getting to know better above the other. Make sure students leave plenty of room in the space where the two circles intersect. Have them list each of their unique differences—qualities that are not in common with the other person—in the portion of the circle below their names, and commonalities in the middle where the circles intersect. Encourage them to find at least six things in common.

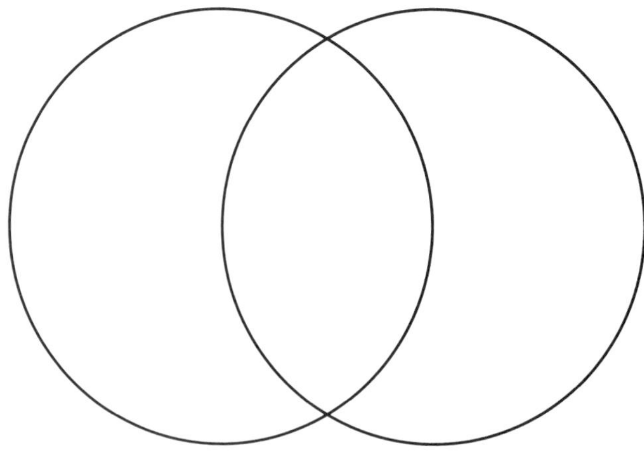

- Encourage students to spend a whole day actively noticing when they perceive someone as different. Then guide them to make an effort to talk to each person and try to learn at least two or three things about him or her. Have students note the unexpected commonalities they share, while also taking an interest in the differences and what they can learn from these differences. Have students journal about what they discovered about themselves by engaging in this activity. What new insights and understandings did they gain by taking the time to get to know someone they otherwise might not? How might the world be different if more people did this?
- Do the 10-Minute Time Cruncher "Cultural Backgrounds" on page 121.

Different and Alike Interviews

"It is not our differences that divide us. It is our inability to recognize, accept, and celebrate those differences."
—Audre Lorde

Choose a fellow student that you don't hang out with regularly and that you perceive to be different from yourself in some way. Ask that person if you can interview him or her. If the person says yes, ask the following questions and write down the answers.

- What are some of your favorite songs?
- What are some favorite movies? TV shows? Videos?
- What do you most like to do when you're not at school?
- What's your favorite subject in school? Why?
- What's something you're really good at?
- What would you like to get better at?
- What do you worry about?
- What makes you feel happy?
- What makes you feel sad?
- What makes you feel angry?
- Who do you really admire, and why?
- What or whom do you care about most in the entire world?
- What's something about you that you think would surprise me?

From *Create a Culture of Kindness in Middle School* by Naomi Drew, M.A., with Christa M. Tinari, M.A., copyright © 2017. This page may be reproduced for individual, classroom, or small group work only. For all other uses, contact Free Spirit Publishing Inc. at www.freespirit.com/permissions.

After the interview is over, answer the questions below:

- What did you learn about this person that surprised you? Why did it surprise you?

- Did you discover anything that you didn't realize you had in common with this person? If so, what was it? (If you discovered multiple things in common, list them all.)

- Was there something you learned that you liked, admired, or respected about the other person that you didn't know about before? If so, what was it? (Again, if you have multiple answers, share them all.)

- Imagine that the person you interviewed is here right now. What could you say to acknowledge the things you appreciate in him or her?

 From *Create a Culture of Kindness in Middle School* by Naomi Drew, M.A., with Christa M. Tinari, M.A., copyright © 2017. This page may be reproduced for individual, classroom, or small group work only. For all other uses, contact Free Spirit Publishing Inc. at www.freespirit.com/permissions.

Cultural Backgrounds

CHARACTER CONNECTIONS

acceptance / compassion / respect

This time cruncher coordinates with Lesson 24, "Different and Alike" (page 117). It gives students an opportunity to share what they know about their cultural backgrounds.

Materials

- handout: "My Cultural Background" (page 122)

Directions

Distribute the "My Cultural Background" handout. Read the instructions and provide students with several minutes to jot down their answers to the questions. Then have students pair up and discuss their responses. Circulate among the pairs to monitor for respectful communication. After students have discussed their responses for a few minutes, ask: **What did you find out about your partner?** Take responses from a few pairs. Ask: **What is the benefit of learning about people's cultural backgrounds—our own *and* those of other people?**

My Cultural Background

Your cultural background is a combination of many things: your language, race, religion, gender identity, ethnicity, customs, values you were raised with, and more. Read and answer the following questions about your cultural background, which you will be discussing with a partner.

- What do you know about your own cultural background, or the cultural background of the family who is raising you? If you're not sure, is there a way to find out more?

- Does your first or last name have any meaning or translation of which you are aware? If so, what?

- What more would you like to learn about your cultural background?

- If you could travel to another place and learn about another culture, where would you go? Explain what interests you about that culture.

 From *Create a Culture of Kindness in Middle School* by Naomi Drew, M.A., with Christa M. Tinari, M.A., copyright © 2017. This page may be reproduced for individual, classroom, or small group work only. For all other uses, contact Free Spirit Publishing Inc. at www.freespirit.com/permissions.

Assumptions and Stereotyping

CHARACTER CONNECTIONS
acceptance / tolerance / personal responsibility / respect

Lesson 25 helps students recognize assumptions and understand the impact of stereotyping.

Students will

- define assumptions and stereotyping
- reflect on the impact of assumptions and stereotyping
- consider ways to prevent or decrease stereotyping

Materials

- paper and markers
- handouts: "Assumptions and Stereotyping" (page 125) and "Assumptions and Stereotyping: Digging Deeper" (page 126)

Introduction

Say: **Let's play a quick guessing game. I'm going to ask you to make some guesses about me. I'm wondering if you think my desk at home is messy and disorganized, or tidy and organized? Raise your hand if you think it is messy. Now raise your hand if you think it's clean. Why did you guess the way you did?** Entertain responses.

Say: **Okay, here's another one. Do you think I'm generally a night owl (like to stay up late), or an early bird (prefer to rise early)? Raise your hand for night owl. Now raise your hand if your guess is early bird. Here's one more: What do you think is my favorite ____________? (Fill in the blank with a category of your choosing such as food, music, or color.)**

Accept guesses from a few students and ask why they chose the responses they did. Ask: **What are you basing your assumptions on?** Play devil's advocate. For example, a student might assume that your desk at home is very tidy because you keep your desk at school very tidy. You could ask: **Isn't it possible that I might keep my work desk tidy, but have a much messier desk at home?** Then share the real answers to the questions you asked. (Students will likely enjoy noting when they were correct in their assumptions).

Discussion and Activity

Say: **An assumption is a conclusion we make about something or someone based on limited information. Our assumptions are just as likely to be wrong as they are likely to be right! People don't often fit into the neat boxes we may want to create for them.**

Ask: **Has anyone ever made an incorrect assumption about you? What was that experience like? How did you feel?** Take some responses. Say: **Sometimes people base their incorrect assumptions on stereotypes. What does *stereotyping* mean?**

Make sure students understand that stereotyping is when people have fixed ideas (often incorrect) about a particular group of people and its members based on the way they look, dress, talk, or act, or because of their religion, ethnicity, gender, sexual orientation, neighborhood, socioeconomic group, or other characteristics. These ideas may apply to *some* individuals in that group, but not all. Stereotypes are based on assumptions about an entire group, rather than on facts about individual people. (For example: *All* girls like to shop; *all* boys like to watch sports.)

For the next activity, place students in small groups of three or four, divided by gender identity. Provide each group with paper and some markers. Say: **You will have seven minutes to brainstorm stereotypes you've heard about girls (assigned to**

the groups of girls) or boys (assigned to the groups of boys). List these stereotypes on your papers. You may want to start your stereotype examples with "All girls . . ." or "All boys . . ." Then we'll share together to see what you came up with.

When time is up, have students share their lists (or a few items from them, depending on your time constraints) with the whole group. During this time, you may hear some chatter about the stereotypes that are being shared, such as, "But that one is true!" Challenge students to think about whether or not something is necessarily true for *all* boys or *all* girls. Ask: **What impact does stereotyping have on boys? On girls? How can stereotyping limit the ways we express ourselves? How can it keep us from really getting to know one another?**

Ask: **What can each of us do to challenge stereotypes?** Take several responses. (Possible answers: Catch ourselves making assumptions about people and question those assumptions; remind ourselves when our assumptions about others have been wrong; remind ourselves that we don't like being stereotyped and that others are likely to feel the same way.)

Say: **Most of us feel that the stereotypes other people believe about *us* are not true. If that's the case, then is it possible the stereotypes we believe about *others* are also not true?** Discuss. Ask: **How can stereotyping be harmful?** (Possible answers: It can lead us to believe inaccurate information; it may deter us from getting to know people as individuals; it can cause divisions and conflicts.)

Say: **It's easy to fall back on assumptions and stereotypes when we don't know much about people who are different from us. What can we do instead of relying on assumptions and stereotypes?** (Possible answer: We can keep an open mind and allow people the opportunity to show us who they really are.) Discuss.

Wrap-Up

Write these two sentences on the board so students can copy them into their journals: *People assume that I __________ because I __________. But the truth is that I __________.* Give students a few minutes to fill in the blanks. End the lesson by inviting some students to share their completed sentences if they're comfortable doing so. Distribute the "Assumptions and Stereotyping" and "Assumptions and Stereotyping: Digging Deeper" handouts for students to do as homework.

Follow-Up

Review student responses to the "Assumptions and Stereotyping: Digging Deeper" handout.

Assumptions and Stereotyping

assumption: A conclusion about something or someone based on limited information. (Example: Your desk at home must be neat because your desk at school is neat.)

stereotyping: Having a fixed (and often incorrect or unfair) idea about a particular person based on the way they look, dress, talk, or act, or because of their religion, ethnicity, gender, sexual orientation, neighborhood, or other characteristics. (Example: *All* girls like X; *all* boys like Y.)

Fill in the blanks below with stereotypes you have heard, seen, or read.

Girls are

Boys are

Men are

Women are

Americans are

Athletes are

Teachers are

Scientists are

- Do you believe that every single person who falls into each of these categories fits the stereotype you wrote in the blanks? Why or why not?

- Why is it unfair to stereotype?

- How does stereotyping cause pain or conflict in our society and our world?

REAL-LIFE CHALLENGE

» Notice when you are making assumptions based on partial information about people you meet. Instead of automatically believing your assumption is true, remind yourself that you might not have all the facts. Whenever possible, ask questions to find out true facts about the person or situation. For example, you might meet a friend's brother who is in college. He's very tall and looks athletic. You start to assume he plays basketball, but then you catch yourself. Instead of asking, "Do you play basketball?" you could ask, "What's something you like to do in your free time?"

From *Create a Culture of Kindness in Middle School* by Naomi Drew, M.A., with Christa M. Tinari, M.A., copyright © 2017. This page may be reproduced for individual, classroom, or small group work only. For all other uses, contact Free Spirit Publishing Inc. at www.freespirit.com/permissions.

Assumptions and Stereotyping: Digging Deeper

Find a stereotyped character in a TV show, movie, online video, or video game. Then answer the following questions.

- Describe the character. Explain what factors or characteristics lead you to conclude that this character is being presented in a stereotyped way.

- Why do you think the people who created the character chose to present him or her this way?

- Do any of the other characters challenge or question the stereotype being presented? If so, how?

- If *you* were a character in this story or scenario, how could *you* challenge the stereotype?

- Do you think stereotyped characters in TV shows and movies cause or reinforce stereotyping in real life? Why or why not? Explain your reasoning.

 From *Create a Culture of Kindness in Middle School* by Naomi Drew, M.A., with Christa M. Tinari, M.A., copyright © 2017. This page may be reproduced for individual, classroom, or small group work only. For all other uses, contact Free Spirit Publishing Inc. at www.freespirit.com/permissions.

Challenging Prejudice and Discrimination

CHARACTER CONNECTIONS

courage / acceptance / tolerance / personal responsibility / kindness / respect

Lesson 26 helps students understand prejudice and discrimination and learn skills for challenging them.

Note: Before doing this lesson, complete Lesson 25, "Assumptions and Stereotyping" (page 123).

Students will

- define prejudice and discrimination
- reflect on the impact of prejudice and discrimination
- consider ways to challenge prejudice

Materials

- handouts: "Challenging Prejudice and Discrimination: What Would You Do?" (page 129), "Words that Challenge Prejudice and Discrimination" (page 130), and "Prejudice and Discrimination: Digging Deeper" (page 131)

Introduction

Ask: **What impact does stereotyping have on us? On other people? Have you ever been stereotyped? If so, how?** Take several responses. Say: **Today we're going to learn about prejudice and discrimination.**

Discussion and Activity

Say: **Eckhart Tolle has said, "Prejudice of any kind . . . means you don't see the other human being anymore, but only your own concept of that human being."** Ask for students to share reactions to this quote.

Say: **Prejudice means holding a negative feeling or opinion about a person or group of people that is not based on reality or experience. The word *prejudice* comes from "prae," meaning "before," and "judicium," meaning "judgment." So, prejudice can also mean judging a person before knowing him or her.** Ask: **How can prejudice lead to unfair treatment?**

Ask: **What is discrimination?** Take responses, then say: **Discrimination is unfair treatment based on prejudice against a group that a person belongs to. Many people face discrimination. This can damage their emotional and physical health, limit their ability to make a living, and much more.** Ask: **What examples of discrimination do you know about from the news or history?** Take responses.

Say: **Prejudice and discrimination will continue unless we challenge them. What can each of us do to challenge prejudice and discrimination?** Discuss responses.

Say: **Knowing appropriate responses to prejudice and discrimination can help us counter them.** Distribute the "Words that Challenge Prejudice and Discrimination" handout. Go over it and discuss.

Put students into small groups. Pass out the "Challenging Prejudice and Discrimination: What Would You Do?" handout. Review the directions. Give groups ten minutes to read the scenarios and brainstorm possible responses.

Tell students to record responses in their journals to share with the big group later. Remind them that answering disrespect with disrespect is never the best course of action. Encourage them to rise higher, rather than go lower, with their responses.

After small groups have discussed the scenarios and their responses, ask for representatives from each group to share their group's responses to questions 4 and 5.

Ask: **Would you feel comfortable using these actions or words to challenge discrimination?** Take responses. If students express their hesitancy to challenge discrimination, brainstorm additional ways they might get support in doing so. For example, they may want to partner with a friend or reach out to an adult for advice.

Say: **Prejudice and discrimination are never okay. Here's what one middle schooler had to say on the subject:** ***"I think we should definitely just accept people for who they are and who they choose to be. I do not think it's fair that people are picked on because of sexual orientation or how much money their family has. That's just not right at all! Sooner or later we will eventually have to get along somehow."***

Wrap-Up

Provide students with time to respond in their journals to these two questions:

- How do you feel about prejudice and discrimination?
- What actions can you take to challenge prejudice and discrimination when you see it happening?

Distribute the "Prejudice and Discrimination: Digging Deeper" handout for students to do as homework.

Follow-Up

Review responses to the "Prejudice and Discrimination: Digging Deeper" handout.

Challenging Prejudice and Discrimination: What Would You Do?

prejudice: A preconceived negative feeling or opinion about a person or group of people, not based on reality or experience.

discrimination: Unfair treatment based on prejudice against a group, class, or category that a person belongs to, rather than on individual merit.

Consider the following scenarios, then answer the questions below each one.

A girl at school is wearing a headscarf. She enters the library and two kids make a remark about terrorists. The girl lowers her head and goes to a far corner of the library to sit by herself.

Why is this girl being discriminated against? What is the prejudice underneath the kids' remarks? What can you do to counteract this act of prejudice? What can you do to support this girl?

A student who looks like a boy and likes to wear eyeliner walks into the cafeteria. Two boys whistle at him and start to laugh at him as he walks by.

Why is this student being discriminated against? What is the prejudice underneath the boys' disrespectful actions? What can you do to counteract this act of prejudice? What can you do to support this student?

A Latina student raises her hand to answer a question in history class. Someone in the back of the room whispers, "Why don't you go back to the country you came from? You don't belong here."

Why is this girl being discriminated against? What is the prejudice underneath the disrespectful words that were said? What can you do to counteract this act of prejudice? What can you do to support this girl?

- Describe a time when you, your family, or someone you know was discriminated against.
- What other acts of discrimination are you aware of?
- Why is it up to each of us to counter acts of prejudice and discrimination?
- What do you think our world would be like if prejudice and discrimination no longer existed?
- What can we each do to make that happen?

From *Create a Culture of Kindness in Middle School* by Naomi Drew, M.A., with Christa M. Tinari, M.A., copyright © 2017. This page may be reproduced for individual, classroom, or small group work only. For all other uses, contact Free Spirit Publishing Inc. at www.freespirit.com/permissions.

Words that Challenge Prejudice and Discrimination

It's not always easy to know what to say when you witness someone being discriminated against. However, it's important to challenge discrimination so others understand that any behavior based on prejudice is unacceptable. Challenging discrimination also provides support to those who are targeted. This support can make a big difference to anyone who feels rejected, embarrassed, helpless, or angry because of the discrimination directed at them.

Below are some examples of words you can use to challenge discrimination. Consider these words and then answer the questions that follow.

> *"It's not okay to treat someone disrespectfully based on his or her [looks/race/religion/sexual identity]."*
>
> *"Being mean to someone because he or she is different from you shows a lack of confidence. After all, everyone is different and unique. That's what makes our world interesting."*
>
> *"There's no one way to be a girl or a boy. Making fun of someone because of how he or she looks isn't right. We each get to choose what kinds of things we like and don't like. No one gets to choose for us."*
>
> *"It's wrong to tell people they don't belong here because of their race or ethnicity. Every person has the right to be a member of our community."*
>
> *"The names you're calling that person are untrue and hurtful. They're based on prejudice, which is never acceptable. If you really got to know that person as an individual you might feel differently than you do now."*

- Which of these statements might you feel comfortable saying?

- What other statements can you come up with to challenge prejudice and discrimination?

- In what kind of situations would it be fitting to use any of these statements?

- Can you think of another way of letting your peers know that you don't approve of prejudice and discrimination of any kind, including in jokes?

 From *Create a Culture of Kindness in Middle School* by Naomi Drew, M.A., with Christa M. Tinari, M.A., copyright © 2017. This page may be reproduced for individual, classroom, or small group work only. For all other uses, contact Free Spirit Publishing Inc. at www.freespirit.com/permissions.

Prejudice and Discrimination: Digging Deeper

Look through a newspaper or the online news to find an example of prejudice or discrimination. Then do the following.

- Provide the name of the news source and the title and date of the article you chose.
- Provide a brief summary of the news story.
- What prejudices can you identify in this story?
- Did that prejudice lead to discrimination? If so, how?
- In what ways might the outcome of the story be different if the people involved were not influenced by prejudice?
- Did anyone in this story challenge the prejudice or discrimination? If so, how?
- What else could be done in this situation to challenge the prejudice or end the discrimination? Describe at least two ideas.

From *Create a Culture of Kindness in Middle School* by Naomi Drew, M.A., with Christa M. Tinari, M.A., copyright © 2017. This page may be reproduced for individual, classroom, or small group work only. For all other uses, contact Free Spirit Publishing Inc. at www.freespirit.com/permissions.

The Power of Conscience

CHARACTER CONNECTIONS

respect / decency / integrity / personal responsibility / thoughtfulness

Lesson 27 guides students to listen to the voice of their conscience and make choices accordingly.

Note: This lesson pairs with Lesson 28, "Gossip, Rumors, and Conscience" (page 137). Try to do them back-to-back.

Students will

- understand that wrong is wrong—even if "everyone's doing it"
- reflect on situations when they didn't listen to their conscience
- tune into their conscience and imagine how they'd handle several different situations

Materials

- handouts: "What Does Your Conscience Tell You to Do?" (page 135) and "Thinking About Conscience" (page 136)

Preparation

On the board, write the following definition and quote:

> *conscience: a feeling or knowledge of right and wrong that guides us to do what we know or believe is right*
>
> *"Wrong does not cease to be wrong because the majority share in it." —Leo Tolstoy*

»»» **Online Resource** »»»»»»»»»»»»

Take a look at a study revealing how humans are prone to justifying and excusing unethical acts: "Memories of unethical actions become obfuscated over time" by Maryam Kouchaki and Francesca Gino at pnas.org/content/113/22/6166.full.

»»»»»»»»»»»»»»»»»»»»»»»»

Introduction

Say: **What does the word *conscience* mean to you personally?** Discuss responses briefly, then ask a student to read the definition of conscience on the board. Share a time when you personally struggled with your conscience as a young person, particularly when it came to going along with the crowd.

Ask: **What are some signals your conscience gives you when you're faced with a decision between right and wrong?** (Possible answers: A wrenching or sick feeling in the stomach; a sharp or heavy feeling in the chest; flashes of ideas or images about what you should do.) Have students put one hand on the area of the heart, and the other on the abdomen. Remind them that physical sensations signaling the voice of our conscience often show up in these areas, sometimes for only a moment. Say: **It's really important to tune in to these sensations and what they're telling us. They can help us listen to our conscience.**

Say: **Now think of a time when *you* struggled with your conscience. Have you ever done something to go along with your friends, even though you knew you shouldn't? Or has there been a time when you knew you *should* do something, like stand up for someone who was being picked on, but you remained silent?** Ask for a couple volunteers to share their experiences, cautioning against the use of real names. Acknowledge kids for their honesty.

Discussion and Activity

Ask a student to read aloud the Tolstoy quote: *"Wrong does not cease to be wrong because the majority share in it."* Ask: **What does this quote mean to you? How do these words relate to your life? Are there certain things you see kids doing that you question in terms of right and wrong?** (Possible answers: Cheating, lying, gossiping, putting other people down, bullying, or looking the other way when someone's being mistreated.)

Ask: **When we do things we know we shouldn't, how do we sometimes try to justify our actions?** (Possible answers: Tell ourselves everyone else does it, tell ourselves that if no one knows we're doing it it's okay, convince ourselves that it's really not a big deal, tell ourselves that if it's not hurting anyone else it's okay to do.) Ask: **Does being able to justify an action make it right?** Take responses.

Say: **Listen to these words from a girl in seventh grade: *"I'm always supposed to spy for this person, or trick someone into saying something mean to someone else."***

Now do the following improvisational role-play with two people. One plays the girl who said the words above, and the other plays the voice of her conscience:

The girl who's been doing the spying is at home at the end of another day where she's done something she knows is wrong. She starts ruminating aloud, and suddenly the voice of her conscience starts speaking to her. They engage in a dialogue about what's been going on.

Note: To fully engage both boys and girls in this process, you could do this role-play twice—once with two girls and once with two boys.

Have students talk about the role-play afterward. What ideas and understandings emerged for them? (If it doesn't come up, raise the possibility that the girl might have been bullied into doing what she's been doing. If so, what could she have done?)

Now put students in pairs. Have them tune into their conscience and answer the following questions:

- What would you do if you were in this girl's situation?
- What could you do to get some support? Who could you turn to?
- Would you tell an adult? Why or why not?
- How could you make amends to the people you've hurt? This is important even if you were forced into doing what you did.

Have students share responses with the large group. Stress that we all do "wrong" things from time to time. That doesn't mean that we're bad people. And tuning in to our conscience helps us make better choices the next time.

Note: Help students see that seeking an adult's help when someone's being harmed, including them, can stop further harm, and can prevent future bullying situations.

Wrap-Up

Distribute both handouts. Tell students to fill them out as honestly as possible and bring them to the next lesson. (Assure them that you will be the only one who will see these handouts.)

Remind students to always check in with their conscience when they're facing difficult decisions or questions of right and wrong. Stress that the voice of their conscience is always there, sometimes in the form of the physical sensations you talked about earlier. These are our "gut feelings."

Follow-Up

Have students bring both completed handouts next time you meet. Discuss any questions, concerns, insights, or dilemmas that arose from reflecting on the content. Guide students to keep tuning in closely to the voice of their conscience. Suggest they talk with trusted adults about questions they need or want to explore further.

Note: During this session and the next, let students know you're available to talk to them one-on-one if they have concerns or questions that are private in nature. Issues of conscience can tap into more complicated issues such as reporting abuse. Sometimes there's a taboo against "telling." Be aware of this as you conduct these lessons.

Enrichment Activities

- In pairs or small groups, have students write short skits that illustrate dilemmas in which someone must tune in to the voice of his or her conscience. Encourage students to show the struggle people can have when the voice of their conscience differs from the direction they want to take—or the direction others are pushing them to take. If time allows, have students put on these skits for each other.

- Have students journal about real-life situations involving issues of conscience. Some examples might be: Incidents where racist, sexist, or homophobic slurs were used; seeing someone being mistreated but being afraid to speak up; being faced with a dilemma like being pressured to smoke or drink. Have students write about what their consciences might tell them to do in each situation, and why it might be hard to listen.

What Does Your Conscience Tell You to Do?

"Wrong does not cease to be wrong because the majority share in it."
—Leo Tolstoy

Consider the following three scenarios and write your honest response to each. Don't give the answer you think you *should* give. Give the answer that's true for you.

- You're with your friends. They're picking on this younger kid named Alex. Alex is kind of small and doesn't have a lot of confidence. Everyone's laughing. You feel bad for Alex. *What does your conscience tell you to do?* What are other voices in your head telling you? How do you think your friends might react if you follow your conscience? Will you do it anyway? Why or why not?

- You and your friends are at Jessie's house for the afternoon. Jessie's parents aren't there. Jessie suggests watching an R-rated movie that your parents have said you are not allowed to see. Everyone in the group is excited. When you hesitate, they tell you to stop acting like a baby. *What does your conscience tell you to do?* What are the other voices in your head telling you? Which one will you listen to? Why?

- You're eating lunch in the cafeteria when Riley asks to join you and your friends. You think Riley's a nice person and you're about to say yes. But Jamie, the leader of the group, says, "Sorry, there's no room here," even though there's an open spot. Riley starts turning away. You want to say, "Sit here, Riley. There's plenty of room." But when you see Jamie looking at you, you stop. *What does your conscience tell you to do?* What are the other voices in your head saying? How do you think your friends would react if you offer Riley a seat? Which voice will you listen to? Why?

REAL-LIFE CHALLENGE

» **When you're home with your family, notice when the voice of your conscience tries to speak. Even if it's just a whisper, listen to what it has to say. Then, pay attention to what your conscience is telling you. For example, your mom might be calling from another room, reminding you to start your homework. You really feel like ignoring her and telling her later that you didn't hear what she said—but your conscience is telling you otherwise. Follow your conscience and see what happens.**

From *Create a Culture of Kindness in Middle School* by Naomi Drew, M.A., with Christa M. Tinari, M.A., copyright © 2017. This page may be reproduced for individual, classroom, or small group work only. For all other uses, contact Free Spirit Publishing Inc. at www.freespirit.com/permissions.

Thinking About Conscience

"You should never let your fears prevent you from doing what you know is right."
—Aung San Suu Kyi

- Describe a time when you were faced with a decision between right and wrong, and you listened to your conscience. How did things work out? Were you happy with the decision you made? Why or why not? What might you do differently if you faced the same situation now?

- Describe a time when you *didn't* listen to your conscience. What happened? How do you feel about the choice you made? How did things turn out? Looking back, what might you change about the choice you made?

- When you see someone being bullied or picked on, what does your conscience tell you to do? Are you able to follow the voice of your conscience? If not, what stands in the way? How can your conscience help you do what is right?

- Describe a time when someone tried to get you to do something you knew was wrong. What did the voice of your conscience tell you to do? What did the other voices in your head tell you to do? What did you end up doing? Explain why you did what you did.

 From *Create a Culture of Kindness in Middle School* by Naomi Drew, M.A., with Christa M. Tinari, M.A., copyright © 2017. This page may be reproduced for individual, classroom, or small group work only. For all other uses, contact Free Spirit Publishing Inc. at www.freespirit.com/permissions.

Gossip, Rumors, and Conscience

CHARACTER CONNECTIONS

personal responsibility / integrity / compassion / conscience / respect

Lesson 28 helps students tune in to the voice of their conscience and consider what they can say and do to stop the spread of rumors and gossip.

Note: This lesson is part two of a two-lesson series with Lesson 27: "The Power of Conscience" (page 132). Try to do these two lessons back-to-back.

Students will

- reflect on times when they have struggled with conscience
- consider the impact of rumors and gossip
- role-play a situation in which someone listens to the voice of conscience and acts accordingly

Materials

- completed student handouts from Lesson 27
- student journals
- handout: "Gossip, Rumors, and Conscience" (page 139)

Preparation

Before doing this lesson, choose a student to play the role of Gabrielle from the "Gossip, Rumors, and Conscience" handout. Choose someone who can improvise in front of the group. Give this student the handout in advance to prepare.

Write the definition and Tolstoy quote from Lesson 27 on the board:

> conscience: *a feeling or knowledge of right and wrong that guides us to do what we know or believe is right*
>
> *"Wrong does not cease to be wrong because the majority share in it." —Leo Tolstoy*

Introduction

Review the meaning of conscience, and ask a student to read aloud the Tolstoy quote. Ask what new insights students have had about these words since the last lesson.

Discussion and Activity

Have students take out their completed handouts from Lesson 27: "What Does Your Conscience Tell You to Do?" and "Thinking About Conscience." Ask students what they learned about themselves as they answered the questions. Ask if they might respond differently now or in the future to situations similar to those they wrote about. Why or why not? Collect all handouts so you can review them to see if there's anyone you need to follow up with.

Say: **Today we're going to look at another situation that requires you to listen to your conscience: responding to rumors and gossip.**

Share the following facts with students: In a national survey of middle schoolers, 60 percent said rumors and gossip were among the top conflict starters in their schools. In addition, 46 percent said rumors and gossip are spread around school every single day.

Read aloud the following quotes from middle schoolers and ask students to respond to them:

"Sometimes people will intentionally spread rumors to get even with kids who get them mad."

"I think people really need to stop gossiping about each other! And stop spreading stupid rumors!"

Ask: **How can rumors and gossip hurt people? How do they affect the atmosphere at school? What does your conscience tell you to do if someone's spreading gossip or rumors?** Ask students what the other voices in their heads might be telling them (such as voices of rationalization, self-justification, or peer pressure). Ask why it can sometimes be hard to do what they feel is right.

Distribute the "Gossip, Rumors, and Conscience" handout. Ask a volunteer to read the "Background" section aloud. Then say: **Now you're going to meet Gabrielle. She's going to tell you how rumors affected her.**

Bring up the volunteer you chose to improvise the part of Gabrielle. Have her take two or three minutes to tell the group why she was so devastated by the rumors that were spread about her. Have her describe how she felt physically and emotionally.

After "Gabrielle" finishes speaking, say: **This is what happened two weeks later.**

Choose three students to do a dramatic reading of the conversation titled "Confronting Rumors." The parts are Maria, Corrine, and John.

When the reading is complete, ask: **Why did Maria listen to her conscience this time? What did Maria do to show she wasn't going to take part in spreading more rumors? How did Maria's words affect the other kids? What did Maria do when Corrine tried to argue with her? How did Maria deflect further arguments from Corrine?** (Answer: She changed the subject.) Tell students that tactfully changing the subject can be an effective way of deflecting or defusing arguments. Ask: **What are some other things you could say or do in similar situations?**

In their journals, have students write down three things they can say or do if they are faced with rumors and gossip. Have them pair up and practice speaking the words they come up with.

Wrap-Up

Revisit some of the signals our conscience might give us when we're faced with a decision between right and wrong. (For example, a wrenching or sick feeling in the stomach; a sharp or heavy feeling in the chest; flashes of ideas or images about what you should do.) As you did in Lesson 27, have students put one hand on the area of the heart, the other on the lower abdomen, then breathe. Remind them that the signals that come from these places can help guide them.

Follow-Up

Give students a real-life challenge. Say: **The next time you hear rumors and gossip being spread, listen to your conscience and speak up. Use the words you just wrote down or others that are appropriate to the situation.** Have students report back on how it went. Talk about challenges they may face—including a sense of confusion—in trying to listen to the voice of their conscience.

Enrichment Activities

- Invite students to create their own dramatic scenarios relating to the "Rumors, Gossip, and Conscience" handout. They can perform them for your group or another group.
- Have students create public service announcements around the theme of preventing or stopping rumors and gossip. Depending on the format they choose, they can share these announcements on social media or in other ways.

Gossip, Rumors, and Conscience

"A clear conscience is more valuable than wealth."
—Filipino proverb

Let's imagine that a student named Maria is the person who said, "I think people really need to stop gossiping about each other! And stop spreading stupid rumors!" She feels this way because of something that happened to Gabrielle.

A couple of weeks ago, Maria and her friends spread a rumor that Gabrielle was flirting with someone when her boyfriend wasn't around. Lots of kids texted the rumor to friends and it ended up going viral. Gabrielle's boyfriend broke up with her. But the rumor was false. To make matters worse, Gabrielle's boyfriend's buddies are now bad-mouthing her. Everywhere Gabrielle goes, kids are talking about her and giving her looks. Gabrielle is devastated. She stayed home from school for a few days and didn't leave the house all weekend. It also turns out that her parents are going through a divorce. The impact of the rumor has been too much for her to handle.

When Maria discovers how this situation has affected Gabrielle, she feels awful. She realizes she could have tried to stop the rumor instead of spreading it. Maria promises herself that she'll speak up the next time a rumor starts.

Shortly after learning about Gabrielle's reaction, Maria has the following conversation with two of her friends.

Corrine: Take a look at this text! Leo and Jacob got into a fight behind the school and their parents got called in! I bet they got suspended.

John (reading the text): Whoa! Forward it to me. There's someone I want to send it to.

Maria: Wait a minute, guys.

Corrine: Hang on, just let me forward the text.

Maria: No, please don't.

Corrine: Why not?

Maria: First of all, how do we know it's true? And even if it is, why spread it around?

Corrine: Oh, come on, Maria. What's the big deal?

Maria: I don't want us to be part of making anyone feel bad again. Especially after what happened with Gabrielle.

Corinne: You never even liked Gabrielle! And you don't really know the kids who got in the fight. So why should you even care?

Maria: After what happened with Gabrielle, I promised myself I wouldn't get involved in spreading rumors—ever again.

John: You're taking this way too seriously, Maria. It's just a text.

Maria: It *is* serious. We caused Gabrielle a lot of pain, and I don't want to be part of doing that to someone else.

Corinne: Hey, it's not like we were the only ones doing it!

Maria: That doesn't make it right. What if people were spreading rumors about one of *you*?

John: Okay, you've got a point . . .

Corinne: Well, I don't think it's that big of a deal.

Maria: It's a big deal to the people rumors are spread about.

John: That's true. I remember when some pretty bad rumors were being spread about my sister. She was upset for a long, long time.

Corinne: Yeah, but . . .

Maria: Hey, does anyone want to grab a snack? I'm hungry. Let's go to the vending machine.

John: Sounds good. Let's go.

Maria: Come on, Corinne, I'll split some pretzels with you. Hey, did you see that new video?

REAL-LIFE CHALLENGE

» **What can you do to follow Maria's lead next time you're in a situation like this one? What might stand in your way? Think carefully about this. Now ask an adult you trust about his or her ideas for finding the courage to speak the voice of your conscience, even in the face of fear and doubt. Make a plan to use these ideas next time you're faced with a sticky situation.**

From *Create a Culture of Kindness in Middle School* by Naomi Drew, M.A., with Christa M. Tinari, M.A., copyright © 2017. This page may be reproduced for individual, classroom, or small group work only. For all other uses, contact Free Spirit Publishing Inc. at www.freespirit.com/permissions.

LESSON 29

Social Power and Personal Power

CHARACTER CONNECTIONS

self-worth / personal responsibility / integrity

Lesson 29 helps students understand how to claim their personal power, as well as understanding social power structures and their influence.

Note: Prior to this lesson, complete Lesson 18: "The Dignity Stance" (page 93).

Students will

- understand the meanings of social power and personal power
- role-play responding to situations involving social power
- learn specific ways to claim their personal power and be less susceptible to negative social power

Materials

- student journals
- handouts: "The Dignity Stance" (page 96), "Seven Steps to Claiming Your Personal Power" (pages 142–143), and "Personal Power and Social Power" (page 144)

Preparation

On the board, write the following quote:

> *"I will not feel less than you, even if you try to make me feel that way." —8th-grade girl*

Introduction

Say: **Today we're going to talk about social power and personal power.** Ask: **What do you think social power is?** Take a few responses and then offer this definition: **Social power is the ability to have influence or control over others.** Ask: **What does social power look like in middle school?** Take responses. (Possible answers: cliques, the social pecking order, in-groups and out-groups.)

Ask: **What is personal power?** Discuss briefly, then give the following definition: **Personal power is about believing in yourself—knowing that you have the ability to solve problems, work out conflicts, assert yourself, and *be* yourself. It's power within yourself, not power over others.**

Discussion and Activity

Say: **Social power can often be positive.** Ask for some examples of positive social power. (Possible answers: Leadership, contributing to the common good, or standing up for people who are mistreated.) Say: **Social power can also be used in negative ways. In school, what are some harmful or hurtful ways kids use social power?** (Possible answers: Excluding others, putting down other people, looking down on others, applying negative peer pressure.)

Discuss peer pressure as an example of negative social power. Say: **Sometimes kids follow the lead of peers even if they know the behavior is wrong. What are some examples of this? What are some things you can say to someone who's trying to pressure you into doing something you don't feel right about?** Write some suggested phrases on the board.

Ask for two volunteers to role-play an example of standing up to negative social power. Have one of the volunteers effectively resist the other person's attempt to pressure him or her into something he or she doesn't want to do.

Ask: **How do people gain social power?** Take responses and emphasize that the social power held by a person or group becomes stronger when others follow or go along with them. Stress that people cannot have power over us unless we allow them to.

Say: **When we're confident and strong in our personal power, it's easier to stand up to social power.** To reinforce this idea, read aloud the quote on the board from a middle school girl: "I will not feel less than you, even if you try to make me feel that way." Discuss. Say: **Just because someone tries to make you feel "less than," you don't have to let them succeed.**

Refer to the "Dignity Stance" handout and remind students to use this posture in situations where someone tries to make them feel less than they are. Reiterate that assuming the Dignity Stance helps increase confidence and can be used at any time. Have students stand, face the front of the room, and assume the Dignity Stance. Have them read aloud the quote on the board.

Pass out the "Seven Steps to Claiming Your Personal Power" handout. Say: **Using these steps again and again will strengthen neural pathways that help you claim your power. The more you practice, the more quickly these neural pathways will grow.**

Ask a student to read aloud the quote at the top of the handout that begins, "You are not your mistakes . . ." Ask students what this quote means to them, then ask for a volunteer to read aloud each step. When you reach Step 4, take a few moments to guide your students through the envisioning process it outlines. Similarly, after a volunteer reads aloud Step 5, have students brainstorm in their journals some personal power statements. Remind them that these statements should be framed positively. For example, instead of, "I won't let anyone put me down," try, "I stand tall and proud everywhere I go, and I'm filled with self-respect."

It's important to tell students that they don't have to believe the statement for it to work. Our power statements help us imagine a self that might not exist in this moment and help us work on making that self a reality.

Continue to have volunteers read aloud each remaining step. Briefly discuss each one before moving on to the next.

Wrap-Up

Refer students to Steps 4 and 5 on the handout. Put students in pairs and have them each choose one or both to practice every night for a week. (If they choose Step 5, encourage them to repeat their personal power statements silently throughout each day.) Have them put a star by the step they chose and explain to their partner what they hope to gain by practicing it.

Follow-Up

After a week, check in with students about how they're doing with the step they chose. Emphasize that it's perfectly natural for voices of self-doubt to come up as they do this. Guide students to refocus on their positive vision or statement rather than empower the voice of self-criticism. If possible, offer to meet individually with students who need additional support. For example, some students might find it difficult to create a positive self-image. If that's the case, help them challenge voices of self-criticism or self-doubt that may arise.

Enrichment Activities

- The "Personal Power and Social Power" handout gives students an opportunity to reflect on maintaining their personal power. With a partner, have them read the handout, talk about it, and answer the questions together. Encourage them to discuss situations when they might give their power away and succumb to following others or letting others put them down. Have them talk about ways to overcome this.
- Do the 10-Minute Time Cruncher "Defining Your Personal Power and Using It for Good" on page 145.

Seven Steps to Claiming Your Personal Power

"You are not your mistakes, you are not your struggles, and you are here NOW with the power to shape your day and your future."
—Steve Maraboli, author of *Unapologetically You*

"If you realized how powerful your thoughts are, you would never think a negative thought."
—Peace Pilgrim

"I will *not* feel less than you, even if you try to make me feel that way."
—8th-grade girl

1. **Do things that make you feel happy, confident, and engaged.** Exercise your talents and interests. Do things you enjoy that exercise your body, too. The following tasks will help you identify these activities:
   - Write down one or two specific activities that make you feel happy and excited.
   - Write down one or two interests that capture your imagination and fully absorb you.
   - Write down one or two physical activities that make you feel strong and energized.

2. **Never allow anyone to make you feel less than you are.** If someone tries, do one or all of the activities above. You can also use one of the following phrases to address the person:
   - "I'm not going to let you talk to me that way."
   - "That was disrespectful."
   - "I'm just as good as you are."

3. **Remember that you have the power to change your brain.** Each time you envision yourself filled with personal power, confidence, and happiness, your brain will get better at perceiving you that way. Action follows thought, so keep doing the things that make you *feel* this way every single day.

4. **Envision yourself filled with personal power, confidence, and happiness.** Close your eyes and picture yourself walking into school with this feeling and maintaining it throughout the day. If a negative image of yourself arises, let it pass, and refocus on the positive self-image you've just envisioned. Do this every night before you go to sleep and every morning when you wake up.

 From *Create a Culture of Kindness in Middle School* by Naomi Drew, M.A., with Christa M. Tinari, M.A., copyright © 2017. This page may be reproduced for individual, classroom, or small group work only. For all other uses, contact Free Spirit Publishing Inc. at www.freespirit.com/permissions.

5. **Create a personal power statement and write it down. Hang it in a place where you will see it every day. Memorize it and repeat it throughout the day.** You can come up with your own original statement, or use one of these:
   - "I am an amazing person, and I can do whatever I set my mind to."
   - "I am smart, strong, and capable."
   - "I am worthy of respect, happiness, and love."
   - "Only the best is in store for me."
   - "I can create whatever I envision."
   - "I am a unique and wonderful human being."

6. **Ask for support when you need it.** If you're having a rough time, don't try to go it alone. Who are two trusted people you can talk to? Write their names on this sheet or in your journal. Talking to them will help you remember the power you have inside, even if you forget it's there. If it's hard to think of someone, talk to a teacher or school counselor.

7. **Use the Dignity Stance.** Don't just use this stance when you face conflict or bullying. Use it anywhere or anytime you need to connect to your personal power.

REAL-LIFE CHALLENGE

» Take the two-month challenge. Choose one activity you wrote about in Step 1—something that makes you feel happy, confident, and excited. Write it down on a notecard or large sticky note, and hang it in a place where you will see it daily. Set a goal of doing this activity every day for two months. That's how long it typically takes to form a new habit. At the end of two months, write in your journal about the experience. What has changed since you began? How do you feel? How confident are you in your personal power?

From *Create a Culture of Kindness in Middle School* by Naomi Drew, M.A., with Christa M. Tinari, M.A., copyright © 2017. This page may be reproduced for individual, classroom, or small group work only. For all other uses, contact Free Spirit Publishing Inc. at www.freespirit.com/permissions.

Personal Power and Social Power

These two quotes from students are examples of personal power in the face of social power. Reflect on each one, and then answer the questions that follow.

> *"I'm not in a particular group. I have many different kinds of friends and I want to keep it that way. Being in one group can limit you." —9th-grade boy*

> *"The kids with the biggest influence over our grade are too comfortable in their positions to do anything to jeopardize their spot at the top of the social ladder. The kids who do want change don't think they have the power to make it happen. To be quite honest, I'm comfortable where I am. I know who my true friends are and don't have to deal with drama. And most people who aren't my friends still respect me." —8th-grade girl*

- How do you feel about what the ninth-grade boy said? Do you agree or disagree with his sentiments? Explain your answer as honestly as you can.

- Write down your thoughts about the quote from the eighth-grade girl. In what ways are you similar to this girl? In what ways are you different?

- What can you do if you realize a group you're in is no longer good for you? How can you create a new group or make new friends?

- How can you strengthen your personal power when dealing with challenging situations, such as starting a new school or joining a team where you don't know anyone? Look at the "Seven Steps to Claiming Your Personal Power" handout for some ideas. Write down one or two that you'll try.

 From *Create a Culture of Kindness in Middle School* by Naomi Drew, M.A., with Christa M. Tinari, M.A., copyright © 2017. This page may be reproduced for individual, classroom, or small group work only. For all other uses, contact Free Spirit Publishing Inc. at www.freespirit.com/permissions.

Defining Your Personal Power and Using It for Good

CHARACTER CONNECTIONS
self-worth / personal responsibility / integrity

This time cruncher coordinates with Lesson 29, "Social Power and Personal Power" (page 140). It helps students further define their personal power by looking at character strengths, and invites them to consider how they can use these strengths to make a positive impact on others.

Materials

- handout: "Defining My Personal Power and Using It for Good" (page 146)

Directions

Distribute the handout and give students a few minutes to read the character strengths listed. Have them circle the strengths that contribute to their personal power. Ask a few students to share the character strengths they chose. Then provide students with five minutes of quiet writing time to complete their responses to the second question.

Defining My Personal Power and Using It for Good

We each have our own unique mode of personal power. Your character strengths contribute in important ways to the type of personal power you possess, especially when you use your strengths to benefit others.

- Read the character strengths below and check the ones you feel you possess.

  - ☐ courage
  - ☐ creativity
  - ☐ determination
  - ☐ empathy
  - ☐ forgiveness
  - ☐ perseverance
  - ☐ teamwork
  - ☐ honesty
  - ☐ kindness
  - ☐ leadership
  - ☐ respect
  - ☐ self-control
  - ☐ fairness
  - ☐ ability to get along with others

- Write a paragraph about how you can use one or more of your character strengths to make a positive impact on others. Begin by completing this topic sentence: I can use my character strength of ______________________ to ______________________________________.

 From *Create a Culture of Kindness in Middle School* by Naomi Drew, M.A., with Christa M. Tinari, M.A., copyright © 2017. This page may be reproduced for individual, classroom, or small group work only. For all other uses, contact Free Spirit Publishing Inc. at www.freespirit.com/permissions.

Social Groups and Cliques

CHARACTER CONNECTIONS

acceptance / empathy / kindness / respect

Lesson 30 helps students understand the differences between social groups and cliques and consider the upsides and downsides of each.

Students will

- understand some of the reasons people form social groups and cliques
- reflect on the differences between social groups and cliques
- identify the positives and negatives of social groups and cliques

Materials

- handouts: "Social Group or Clique?" (page 149) and "Thinking About Cliques and Social Groups" (page 150)

Preparation

On the board write one header that says *Clique* and another that says *Social Group*. You'll be asking students to stand by these titles later, so be sure there's enough room by each for students to gather.

Introduction

Put students into pairs for the following brief warm-up so you can discover how they define social groups. Later you will be giving them the correct definition. Say: **Share with your partner your answer to these questions: What do you think a social group is? What social groups are you a part of? What do you like about the groups, and what don't you like?**

Discussion and Activity

After pairs have shared for two to three minutes, discuss their responses to the questions. Ask: **What are some reasons people hang out in social groups?** Entertain responses. Let students know that a social group is a group of people linked by similar characteristics, interests, or goals, or by friendship. Ask: **What kinds of social groups exist at school?** Ask for two volunteers to write student responses on the board. Encourage students to list as many social groups as they can. (Possible answers: Band kids, jocks, rich kids, popular kids, geeks, nerds.) Make note of social group names that seem disparaging. Ask: **Who determines the names of these social groups? How might a disparaging name impact the way kids in the group feel about themselves and the way they are viewed by others?** Accept and discuss a few answers.

Ask: **How many of you have heard the word *clique* used in reference to certain kinds of groups?** Point to the "Clique" heading on the board. Ask: **What does this word mean to you?** Briefly entertain responses, then say: **Turn back to your partner and talk about the differences between a clique and a social group.**

After a minute or two, ask a few students to define the differences between a clique and a social group. Then say: **Now listen to the following scenario and stand by the sign that you think best describes it: A group of students who are all involved in drama club sit together during lunch every day. When someone who isn't in the club sits at the same table, they say hi, but otherwise don't interact with him or her.** Ask: **Does this group seem like a social group or a clique?** Have students stand by the sign that matches their answer. Then ask several students to share their reasoning. Listen carefully to responses without expressing judgments about what students say. Your goal is to prompt reflection and clarify their thinking around this idea.

Provide another scenario and have students once again stand next to the "Social Group" or "Clique" heading to express their response. Say: **Five eighth-grade students go to school dances and other social events together, and always wear similar types of clothing. They often ignore people who try to make conversation with them. Do you think this group is a social group or a clique? Choose the name that you think best describes them.** Again, briefly discuss how a few students answered and why.

Have students return to their seats. Ask: **What do you think differentiates a clique from a social group?** Entertain some responses. Say: **It's natural for students who have similar interests to spend time with one another, but when they start excluding people, their social group may have turned into a clique. Cliques don't easily allow kids to join them—or, sometimes, to leave them. In addition, kids may be pressured into doing things to get into a clique, and once they're in, they may be discouraged from expressing their individuality. What else have you noticed about cliques?** Address the idea that kids in cliques might look down on those who aren't part of their group.

Distribute the "Social Group or Clique?" handout and ask a student to read aloud the first list on the handout, which focuses on social groups. Discuss the list and invite students to share related examples or anecdotes (without using real names). Then ask another student to read the list on the handout describing cliques, and discuss that list as well.

Refer to the questions on the handout and discuss students' responses to them.

Wrap-Up

Say: **Unfortunately, while social groups can help people feel comfortable and accepted, cliques can cause people to feel excluded, make our school seem unwelcoming, and exclude students who want to be friends with a variety of different people.**

Invite responses from several students to the following prompt: "Describe something you can do to avoid being cliquey and instead keep social groups positive."

Distribute the "Thinking About Cliques and Social Groups" handout and have students complete it at home. Make time to go over it in the coming days.

Follow-Up

Discuss students' responses to the "Thinking About Cliques and Social Groups" handout. Use the discussion questions to help students reflect on the ways they can have positive social interactions without excluding or disparaging others.

Enrichment Activity

Have students ask family adults about their experiences with social groups and cliques. What social groups are they now part of? Have they ever experienced being in or out of cliques? What did they learn from their experiences? Ask students to journal about insights that emerged out of their talks with family adults. Are there any parallels to their own lives? What new understandings were revealed?

Social Group or Clique?

Social Group	Clique
People in social groups usually: ▪ share some similar interests ▪ enjoy each others' company ▪ are given the freedom to be themselves ▪ support one another ▪ accept differences within the group ▪ spend time together doing things they enjoy ▪ are open to welcoming new people into the group ▪ are members of several different groups	*People in cliques often:* ▪ share some similar interests ▪ are encouraged to act the same as others in the clique ▪ place a high value on popularity and social power ▪ are discouraged from expressing individuality ▪ may feel pressured to do things to join (or stay in) the group ▪ exclude other students ▪ limit interactions with people in other groups

- How do social groups affect your experience at school?

- How do cliques impact your experience at school?

- Think about the groups you are involved with in and out of school. Reread the lists above to review the characteristics of social groups and cliques. Do any groups you're involved with function like a clique? If so, what could you do to turn the clique into a positive social group?

From *Create a Culture of Kindness in Middle School* by Naomi Drew, M.A., with Christa M. Tinari, M.A., copyright © 2017. This page may be reproduced for individual, classroom, or small group work only. For all other uses, contact Free Spirit Publishing Inc. at www.freespirit.com/permissions.

Thinking About Cliques and Social Groups

Consider this quote from a middle schooler about her experience with a group of kids at school. Then answer the questions that follow.

> *"They usually make fun of the clothes I wear and ignore me while I am trying to get to know them. They roll their eyes at me and turn away to face their other friends. They also walk away and go to their group of friends whenever they see me come near them, even if I'm not actually planning to go talk to them. Or sometimes they will talk to me when they're not together in a group, but then ignore me later when their friends are around." —7th-grade girl*

- Take a look at the "Social Group or Clique?" handout. Do you think this "group of friends" is a social group or a clique? What makes you think that?

- How do you think this student is feeling?

- How would you feel if you were treated this way?

- What advice would you give this student?

REAL-LIFE CHALLENGE

» Pay attention to the behaviors of your own social group (or groups). How welcoming are you to students who might want to join your group? Invite someone who is not in your social group to join your group for lunch or an activity. Journal about your experience.

From *Create a Culture of Kindness in Middle School* by Naomi Drew, M.A., with Christa M. Tinari, M.A., copyright © 2017. This page may be reproduced for individual, classroom, or small group work only. For all other uses, contact Free Spirit Publishing Inc. at www.freespirit.com/permissions.

Section 4

Dealing with CONFLICT

Resolving Conflicts

CHARACTER CONNECTIONS

respect / personal responsibility / conflict resolution

Lesson 31 introduces the Win/Win Guidelines for resolving conflicts.

Note: Before doing this lesson, have students complete the "Conflict Self-Assessment" (page 155) and bring it with them to the lesson.

Students will

- understand that it's possible to resolve conflicts peacefully through communication and compromise
- learn how to use each step of the Win/Win Guidelines
- role-play the resolution of conflicts using the Win/Win Guidelines

Materials

- handouts: "Conflict Self-Assessment" (page 155), "Using the Win/Win Guidelines for Working Out Conflicts" (page 156), and "Observing Conflict" (page 157)

Preparation

Prior to this lesson, distribute copies of the "Conflict Self-Assessment" and "Using the Win/Win Guidelines for Working Out Conflicts" handouts. On the board, write the following quotes and definitions:

> *"I'm glad I understand that while language is a gift, listening is a responsibility."*
> *—Nikki Giovanni*
>
> *"When you talk, you are only repeating what you already know; but when you listen, you may learn something new." —the Dalai Lama*
>
> ***conflict:*** *a fight or disagreement*
>
> ***win/win:*** *a way of handling conflicts that leads to a positive solution acceptable to all parties*

Introduction

Say: **Today we're going to learn to use a tool that will change the way we handle conflict.** Ask: **As you filled out the "Conflict Self-Assessment" sheet, what did you notice about how you typically handle conflict? Do you usually try to "win," or are you more likely to try to understand the other person's point of view so you can work things out fairly? What kind of results have you been getting from your usual methods?** Ask students to describe what tends to happen when they simply try to win an argument rather than trying to resolve a conflict.

Share the following quote from a middle school girl, then ask how many kids can relate to it. *"There's always some kind of conflict going on. It drives me crazy and makes it hard to concentrate in class."*

Share the following quote from a middle school boy. If you like, mention that sometimes insecurities and painful emotions are especially difficult for boys to handle, since they may believe that it's not okay for them to have them. Stress that all human beings have difficult emotions from time to time, and it's perfectly normal—regardless of gender. In fact, people who can acknowledge painful emotions and find healthy ways to handle them often end up stronger and more resilient. *"If everyone was respectful to each other we wouldn't have all this disgusting conflict and so many kids being insecure. I'm a boy, for crying out loud! I shouldn't have to care about stuff like this, but after a conflict with one popular kid, I lost two of my best friends, and other people started to resent me. If we just all respected each other, school would be a better place."*

Discussion and Activity

Refer to the definitions of the terms *conflict* and *win/win*. Briefly discuss these ideas and answer any questions that arise. Ask: **What kinds of negative things can occur as a result of angry conflicts?** (Possible answers: Hurt feelings, lingering anger, lost friendships, or friends taking sides.) **How might results be different if we worked things out in a respectful way?**

Direct students' attention to the "Using the Win/Win Guidelines for Working Out Conflicts" handout and focus on the guidelines section. Tell students that these steps will help them work out conflicts they face. Ask a student to read the first step: "Take time to cool off." Ask: **What generally happens if we try to talk out a conflict when both parties are still mad?** (Possible answers: Blaming, escalation of the conflict, hurt feelings, name-calling.)

Ask: **What can we do to cool off *before* we start talking?** Invite ideas from students and list a few on the board. (Possible answers: Get a drink of water; take some deep breaths; walk away from each other for a while.) Give students this phrase to use during conflict: "I need to take a minute." Have students picture themselves walking away for a minute to cool down, then returning to handle the conflict in a calmer, more rational state.

Have another student read Step 2 aloud: "Talk it over starting with 'I,' not 'you.'" Give an example of an I-statement, such as, "I have something on my mind—I heard you were talking about me." Or, "I disagree with your call on that play." Explore how these statements are in contrast to accusatory "you" statements such as, "You're mean!" Ask students to come up with I-statements for conflict scenarios, such as in a situation where someone else gossiped about them. Take responses.

Have a student read aloud Step 3: "Listen with an open mind." Direct students' attention to the two quotes on the board and choose volunteers to read them aloud. Invite reflection on these quotes. Then ask: **How does the willingness to hear out the other person help us resolve conflicts? How does *not* listening make conflicts worse?** Discuss briefly.

Continue having students read each step of the Win/Win Guidelines, giving clarification where needed. Stress that in nearly all conflicts, both people involved are at least partially responsible for the conflict beginning or continuing. Have them think of a recent conflict in their lives. Ask: **Can you think of a way you were even *a little bit responsible* for that conflict starting, continuing, or growing?** Entertain responses. Stress that taking responsibility for even a small thing is one of the most powerful steps toward resolving any conflict.

Ask for two volunteers. Help them role-play resolving the following conflict (or another of your own choosing) using the Win/Win Guidelines. Stress that their goal is to reach a resolution, not to role-play having an argument: *Every day at school, Anthony teases Grace about her hair. Whenever Grace tells him to stop, Anthony tells her to lighten up. Grace wants to make him stop once and for all. She decides to talk it out using the Win/Win Guidelines.* Background: *Grace sometimes teases Anthony about his braces.*

Wrap-Up

Discuss together how the role-play went. Did the role-players hear each other out? Were they willing to compromise? Were they respectful? Did they each take responsibility for their part in the conflict, or did they try to blame each other?

Say: **When we take the lead in working out conflicts respectfully, the other person will often follow. And each time we use the steps we just learned, we slowly help our brains adopt a more effective way of dealing with conflict. Over time, moving through the steps becomes easier and more automatic, even if it feels awkward at first. Like any new skill, it gets easier the more we practice.**

Follow-Up

- Send the guidelines home with your students so they can try applying them in family conflicts. Send home additional copies to family adults with a brief note explaining that these guidelines are used in school and will also help at home.

- Distribute the "Observing Conflict" handout and have students complete it as homework. Set aside time at a later date to go over student responses.

Enrichment Activities

- If you're able to find five extra minutes now and then, have students practice additional role-plays using the Win/Win Guidelines. See the 10-Minute Time Cruncher "Conflict Resolution Role-Playing" on page 158 for guidelines. You may want to invite students to suggest scenarios based on real conflicts, but make sure they don't use real names or identifying factors. Each time students work out conflicts through role-play, it gets easier to do it in real life.
- Check in with students periodically and ask how they're using the Win/Win Guidelines with friends, family, teammates, and others. Help them make this a living practice.
- Have students role-play resolving conflicts for another group of students, preferably composed of younger kids. Have them copy the "Using the Win/Win Guidelines for Working Out Conflicts" handout and distribute it to the students they role-play for.

Conflict Self-Assessment

We all have conflicts, and we all have many ways of reacting to them. Take a look at this list of responses and put check marks next to the items that are usually or often true for you. If you can't honestly pick any, that's okay. Before long, you'll be able to.

- ☐ I try to calm down before I react.
- ☐ I try to focus on seeking solutions rather than "winning" the argument.
- ☐ I avoid using sarcasm and put-downs.
- ☐ I avoid using negative body language.
- ☐ I say what's on my mind but do so respectfully.
- ☐ I listen openly to what the other person has to say.
- ☐ I avoid blaming the other person.
- ☐ I try to avoid judging the other person as right or wrong and focus instead on attempting to understand his or her point of view.
- ☐ I look for ways I might be responsible for some part of the conflict.
- ☐ I try to put myself in the other person's place to understand where he or she is coming from.
- ☐ I try to work with the other person to seek solutions.
- ☐ I know how to be assertive without being attacking.
- ☐ I know how to stay strong inside and not let myself be put down—without going on the attack or withdrawing.
- ☐ I try my best to avoid "you statements."
- ☐ I'm willing to compromise.

- What items on the list do you need to work on more?
- What items are you able to do already?
- Who do you often have conflicts with?
- Think of a recent conflict you were involved in. How do you think you're at least *a little bit responsible* for this conflict starting or continuing?
- What's one negative conflict habit you can work on changing now?

Remember: Resolving conflicts is a skill that anyone can learn—and having this skill can change your life forever.

From *Create a Culture of Kindness in Middle School* by Naomi Drew, M.A., with Christa M. Tinari, M.A., copyright © 2017. This page may be reproduced for individual, classroom, or small group work only. For all other uses, contact Free Spirit Publishing Inc. at www.freespirit.com/permissions.

Using the Win/Win Guidelines for Working Out Conflicts

"I'm glad I understand that while language is a gift, listening is a responsibility."
—Nikki Giovanni

The Win/Win Guidelines

1. Take time to cool off.
2. Talk it over starting with "I," not "you."
3. Listen with an open mind.
4. Take responsibility for at least one small part of the conflict.
5. Come up with a fair solution together.
6. Affirm, forgive, thank, or apologize.

Rules for Using the Win/Win Guidelines

1. Treat each other with respect. Don't blame the other person or use put-downs.
2. Attack the problem, not the person.
3. Refrain from interrupting, making negative faces, or using negative body language.
4. Be willing to compromise.
5. Tell the truth, but do it respectfully.

Using these steps to handle and resolve conflicts will make your life better. The more you practice them, the easier it will become to deal with conflict.

 From *Create a Culture of Kindness in Middle School* by Naomi Drew, M.A., with Christa M. Tinari, M.A., copyright © 2017. This page may be reproduced for individual, classroom, or small group work only. For all other uses, contact Free Spirit Publishing Inc. at www.freespirit.com/permissions.

Observing Conflict

"When you talk, you are only repeating what you already know;
but when you listen, you may learn something new."
—the Dalai Lama

Throughout the coming week, observe conflicts you see taking place—yours and other people's. Notice how these conflicts are handled, then answer the following questions.

- In conflicts you observed, what did people do that made the conflicts worse?

- In conflicts you had with others, what did you do, if anything, that made the conflict worse? What did you do that made it better? Explain.

- What positive choices did you observe—things that helped conflicts get worked out fairly?

- Describe in detail one positive way of handling conflict that you observed and would like to apply in your life.

- Describe some better ways people could have handled some of the conflicts you saw.

- Describe some better ways you could have handled a conflict that you had.

- In the future, what do you want to do differently when it comes to handling conflict?

From *Create a Culture of Kindness in Middle School* by Naomi Drew, M.A., with Christa M. Tinari, M.A., copyright © 2017. This page may be reproduced for individual, classroom, or small group work only. For all other uses, contact Free Spirit Publishing Inc. at www.freespirit.com/permissions.

Conflict Resolution Role-Playing

CHARACTER CONNECTIONS

respect / personal responsibility / conflict resolution

This time cruncher coordinates with Lesson 31, "Resolving Conflicts" (page 152). It gives students a chance to practice using the Win/Win Guidelines to resolve conflicts and assess their effectiveness in doing so.

Materials

- handouts: "Using the Win/Win Guidelines for Working Out Conflicts" (page 156) and "Maintaining a Win/Win Mode" (page 159)

Directions

Pass out both handouts and briefly go over each one. Put students into groups of three. Read aloud the conflict scenario that follows. In each group, choose a Student A and a Student B to role-play resolution of the conflict using the Win/Win Guidelines. The third student will actively observe the process, checking off related items on the checklist, "Maintaining a Win/Win Mode." When the role-play is complete, the observer will give feedback to the role-players. Together groups will answer the two questions at the end of the handout. Circulate among groups and give guidance as they role-play and debrief.

Conflict Scenario

Student A borrowed Student B's library book and didn't return it on time. Now the book is overdue and there's a fine. Student B is annoyed and thinks Student A should pay the fine. Student A was overwhelmed with homework and family obligations and thinks Student B should be more understanding. Student B calls Student A selfish and irresponsible. Now Student A feels insulted.

Maintaining a Win/Win Mode

To resolve conflicts in a Win/Win way, focus on the following:

- neutral body language
- neutral tone of voice
- neutral facial expression
- good eye contact
- overcoming the urge to interrupt or argue
- a willingness to hear out the other person
- a willingness to take responsibility for your role in the conflict
- resisting the urge to make excuses or blame others
- a commitment to working toward a fair solution

- In the conflict role-play, what did you do that worked well?

- What do you still need to improve upon?

From *Create a Culture of Kindness in Middle School* by Naomi Drew, M.A., with Christa M. Tinari, M.A., copyright © 2017. This page may be reproduced for individual, classroom, or small group work only. For all other uses, contact Free Spirit Publishing Inc. at www.freespirit.com/permissions.

Responsibility vs. Blame

CHARACTER CONNECTIONS

personal responsibility / compassion / conflict resolution / integrity

Lesson 32 helps students take responsibility for their role in conflicts and brings them face-to-face with a long-term conflict that persisted due to blaming rather than taking responsibility.

Students will

- understand that when conflicts occur, all people involved are often responsible in some way
- understand that assigning blame makes conflicts worse, while taking responsibility helps conflicts get resolved
- role-play a conflict that took a long time to resolve because people blamed each other rather than taking responsibility

Materials

- handouts: "The True Story of a Three-Year Conflict" (page 162) and "Responsibility vs. Blame" (page 163)

Preparation

Write the following quotes on the board:

> *"The first to apologize is the bravest, the first to forgive is the strongest, the first to forget is the happiest." —Unknown*

> *"Placing the blame or judgment on someone else leaves you powerless to change your experience; taking responsibility for your beliefs and judgments gives you the power to change them." —Byron Katie*

Introduction

Say: **Today we're going to talk about responsibility versus blame. When people get into conflicts, what do they tend to do—blame the other person or take responsibility?** Have students respond. Ask: **When we blame, what usually happens?** (Possible answers: Conflicts escalate, we can lose friends, people get mad at us.)

Discussion and Activity

Ask for two volunteers to role-play a conflict where neither person takes responsibility and both people blame each other. (Before they begin, give students a few minutes to make up a specific scenario and plan their role-play.) After the role-play, ask: **Did the conflict get solved? Why or why not?**

Ask: **Why can it be difficult to take responsibility for our part in a conflict?** (Possible answers: We want to be right and see the other person as wrong; we don't want to get in trouble; we might be afraid to admit what we did; we haven't developed the habit of taking responsibility.) Discuss, then emphasize that even though it can be hard to take responsibility, we pay too great a price when we blame. Say: **When we take responsibility, many good things happen. What might some of them be?** (Possible answers: Conflicts get resolved, people respect us more, we respect ourselves more, people see us as mature, people admire our courage and honesty.)

Direct students' attention to the quotes on the board. Have a volunteer read the first quote aloud: *"The first to apologize is the bravest, the first to forgive is the strongest, the first to forget is the happiest."*

Ask: **What do these words mean to you?** Briefly discuss this quote. Then ask another student to read the other quote on the board: *"Placing the blame or judgment on someone else leaves you powerless to change your experience; taking responsibility for your beliefs and judgments gives you the power to change them."*

Ask: **What do you think this quote means? What happens when we assign blame rather than taking responsibility?** Briefly discuss.

Pass out "The True Story of a Three-Year Conflict" handout. Tell students this true story is a classic example of what can happen when blame takes center stage. Ask for volunteers to read alternating paragraphs of the story. Afterward, ask the following questions:

- What did the girl in this story finally realize?
- If she had stopped blaming the other girl sooner, what might have changed?
- Describe a time you kept a conflict going by blaming rather than taking responsibility. What was the result? What might you do differently now?

Discuss students' responses briefly. Then say: **Let's role-play the part of the story where the principal helps the girls talk things out.** Ask for two volunteers to play the girls. Take the role of the principal yourself.

At the end of the role-play, have students give feedback. Ask the role-players how it felt to take responsibility. Ask: **Do you think it's possible to resolve a conflict if just one person takes responsibility?** Let students know that when one person takes responsibility, this can be the turning point that leads to resolution. Taking responsibility can give the other person (or people) the courage to do the same.

Ask students how unresolved conflicts affect people's lives.

Wrap-Up

Ask students to think of a situation where they could take responsibility right now. Home is a good place to start. Give them this real-life challenge. Say: **When you go home today, take responsibility for something you did that you shouldn't have done.** (For example, talking back to a parent, not listening, or being mean to a sibling.) Say: **Admit your mistake and offer an apology. Then write in your journal about what happened.**

Follow-Up

Have students read and complete the "Responsibility vs. Blame" handout. Make time to discuss it in the coming days.

Enrichment Activities

- Have students keep a "Responsibility Log" in their journals. Have them note when they resort to blame and what results they get. Have them describe what happens each time they take responsibility.
- Ask students to interview adults about a conflict in which they wished they'd taken responsibility rather than blaming. Have students ask, "What were the results of this conflict? What would you do differently now?"

The True Story of a Three-Year Conflict

Read this real-life story and answer the questions that follow.

It started in third grade and continued into sixth. This new girl came to our school. My best friend was in her class. The new girl became good friends with the boys, and I was friendlier with the girls. The boy she started hanging out with was really rude to me. Then the girl made a comment that hurt me a lot. I started crying and I said something mean back. I only said it because I was so hurt. That's when her friends started turning on me.

The conflict continued into fourth grade. By fifth grade things had calmed down a little, but the problems didn't completely go away. When we went to middle school for sixth grade, things were still tense, but kids started acting kind of normal to me again. I was still nervous, though, because I didn't know what would happen next.

Eventually the girl and I ended up having another fight, and things got bad again. I'd be hanging out with a friend and she'd come over and interrupt and say things in a way that always made me look bad. My friends would get uninvolved with me and all involved with her. I tried hard to get my friends to understand what was really going on. The problem was, the girl would talk to everyone. She accused me of doing horrible things to her, and people believed her!

My parents said to just ignore it. But it got to the point that I was so upset I didn't want to go to school. Finally, I went the principal. He brought us both into his office and had us talk it out. He made us listen to each other without interrupting. That was when I realized that I was contributing to the problem, too: I was giving her looks whenever she passed by and saying mean things back when she hurt my feelings. I never realized how much this bothered her. She thought I was just as mean as I thought she was.

Now that we're getting along I see that she's really a good person. She's actually very caring. We were *both* doing things to make the problem worse. I wish I'd been able to see this sooner. The last three years of our lives—and the start of middle school—could have been so much better.

- How did this girl play a role in continuing the conflict?

- How might this girl's life have been different if she'd understood earlier how she was also contributing to the conflict?

- Why is it important to take responsibility for our role in conflicts rather than blaming others?

 From *Create a Culture of Kindness in Middle School* by Naomi Drew, M.A., with Christa M. Tinari, M.A., copyright © 2017. This page may be reproduced for individual, classroom, or small group work only. For all other uses, contact Free Spirit Publishing Inc. at www.freespirit.com/permissions.

Responsibility vs. Blame

"Placing the blame or judgment on someone else leaves you powerless to change your experience; taking responsibility for your beliefs and judgments gives you the power to change them."
—Byron Katie

In nearly all conflicts, *both* people are at least a little bit responsible. Both people usually did something to make the conflict start, get worse, or keep going—even if what they did was small.

Blaming almost always causes conflicts to escalate. But when even one person takes responsibility, the conflict often begins moving toward a solution. When *both* people take responsibility, the conflict is almost guaranteed to get resolved. Taking responsibility is one of the most important things you can do in every area of your life.

Think of a conflict you've had. Was there a way you were *even a little bit* responsible? For example, even if you didn't say anything negative to the other person, did you communicate hostility or dislike through your facial expression or body language? How was your tone of voice when you spoke? Displaying negative body language and facial expressions can escalate conflicts. So can using a sarcastic or edgy tone of voice. Did any of these things worsen the conflict you're thinking of?

When you take responsibility for your actions and your words, your personal power grows. This is true in all areas of your life, not just in conflict. Here are some of the many benefits of taking responsibility:

- You respect yourself more.
- You have healthier relationships.
- People respect and admire you more.
- You get along better with your friends, classmates, teachers, and family members.
- People trust you more.
- You trust yourself more.
- You end up having fewer conflicts, and the conflicts you do have get resolved faster.
- You spend less time drained by conflicts and have more time to focus on things that make you happy.
- You train your brain in a pattern that will help you for the rest of your life.

Taking responsibility is a sign of strength and maturity. It's a habit that will help you throughout your entire life.

REAL-LIFE CHALLENGE

» Think about a conflict you were involved in recently. Did you take responsibility or did you blame? Recall what you said and did. Did the conflict get resolved? Why or why not? Can you think of one way you were even a little bit responsible? Talk to the person you had the conflict with and take responsibility for something you did. Then see what happens. Write about it in your journal.

» Be responsible for the nonverbal messages you communicate. Look in the mirror and pretend you're talking to someone you're mad at. How does your face look? How are you holding your body? Be aware of your facial expression and body language next time you get angry, and try not to send negative nonverbal messages.

From *Create a Culture of Kindness in Middle School* by Naomi Drew, M.A., with Christa M. Tinari, M.A., copyright © 2017. This page may be reproduced for individual, classroom, or small group work only. For all other uses, contact Free Spirit Publishing Inc. at www.freespirit.com/permissions.

Perceptions and Perceptual Filters

CHARACTER CONNECTIONS

personal responsibility / respect / conflict resolution

Lesson 33 helps students understand how our perceptions and perceptual filters influence the way we interpret things. Students also learn how respectful listening can help us avoid creating conflicts when our perceptions differ from someone else's.

Students will

- understand that we all see things through the lens of our perceptual filters
- consider the importance of accepting differences in people's perceptions
- practice respectful listening with someone who might perceive things differently than they do

Materials

- an image of Pablo Picasso's "Three Musicians"
- a pair of sunglasses
- handout: "Perceptual Filters" (page 166)

Preparation

Search online for Pablo Picasso's painting "Three Musicians" for an image that you can project on a screen or display in some other way.

Introduction

Ask students what *perceptions* means. Make sure they understand that perceptions are how we see things and that our individual perceptions are influenced by who we are—our experiences, age, ethnicity, gender, social group, and more. These are our perceptual filters, and they influence everything we experience.

Invite a student to come to the front of the room. Say: **Please take a look at the group. Just look around and say what you see.** After the student has done this, have him or her put on the sunglasses. Ask the student to look at the group again. Ask: **Can you describe how things look to you now?** Give the student a moment to answer. Make sure he or she points out the difference between the first look and the second. Then say: **This is how perceptual filters work. We see everything through the lens of whatever filters we have, from age to gender identity to race and more."** Briefly discuss, pointing out that we often don't even realize we have these filters.

Discussion and Activity

Let students know that the activity they're about to engage in will bring out their different perceptions. Stress that it's critical to practice respectful listening when differences arise. Remind students to listen with an open mind, refrain from interrupting, and try to understand and learn from other people's points of view.

Ask: **Who is Pablo Picasso?** Invite students to share what they know about him. If it isn't mentioned, let students know that Picasso is regarded as a genius and one of the greatest artists who ever lived.

Show the image of Picasso's "Three Musicians." Ask: **What do you think of this painting?** Entertain responses. Ask: **What do you see in this painting? How much do you think this painting should be worth, and why? Do you think this painting should be worth millions of dollars? Why or why not?** After the last question, tell students that another Picasso painting sold for $179 million in 2015, and this one could easily be sold for a similar amount. After students have had a chance to respond, ask what they noticed about other people's reactions to this painting. Ask: **Why are there differences of opinion?** Discuss the fact that our opinions differ because we each have varying perceptions and experiences. Say: **It's like wearing those sunglasses. Each person sees through his or her own perceptual filters.**

Ask: **When it comes to conflict, how do you think differences in perception play a role? What happens when people get stuck in their own perceptions, believing they're right and the other person is wrong? Why is it important to try to see things from the other person's point of view? Why can this be hard to do?** Entertain responses.

Demonstrate this concept with a volunteer. Ask your partner if he or she thinks this Picasso painting should be worth millions of dollars. Maintain good eye contact as you listen to your partner's response, and paraphrase the main points you heard. Ask if you got it right. If not, have your partner repeat his or her main points and try again. Switch roles and repeat the process. Ask why it can be counterproductive to argue with someone else's opinion and see yourself as right and the other person as wrong.

Now have students partner up. Tell them they will do the same process you just demonstrated. Say: **Remember, when it's your turn to listen, focus on what your partner is saying and try to understand his or her point of view. Then paraphrase the main idea of what you heard. Check in to see if you got it right. Resist the urge to jump in before it's your turn to speak.**

Direct students' attention back to the Picasso painting and have them share their perceptions of it with their partners. Caution them not to argue with their partner's perceptions and opinions, or to try to convince them to see things another way. After a minute or two, have partners switch, so each one gets a turn. Remind them to check in at the end of their paraphrase to see if they got it right.

Wrap-Up

Ask: **How many of you had partners whose opinion about or perception of the painting was different from your own? Were you still able to listen respectfully and say back what you heard? What did you discover as you did this? Did anyone have a partner who expressed disagreement through their body language or facial expression? How did that feel? What message did it communicate?** Discuss.

Ask: **How difficult was it to stop yourself from judging or arguing with what your partner said?** Many kids will probably say they discovered how hard it is to hold back and just listen to the other person, especially if they disagreed with what the person said. Emphasize that the ability to simply listen—especially when opinions differ—can enable us to get along better with people whose perceptions and views are not the same as our own.

Ask: **How might our world change if people of differing opinions and perceptions learned to listen to each other rather than fight over differences?**

Distribute the "Perceptual Filters" handout. Go over it, making sure students fully understand the definition of *perceptual filters*. Ask several students to name some perceptual filters they possess. (Possible answers: Age, gender, where we live, or ethnicity.)

Follow-Up

To help students practice respectful listening, take five minutes at a time during future meetings to pair up students and pose questions that will draw out differing perceptions and opinions. Remind students that their challenge will once again be to listen respectfully. After they listen to what the other person has to say, have them paraphrase what they heard, resisting the urge to argue, persuade, or denigrate.

Perceptual Filters

Many different factors influence our perceptions and affect how we see and experience the world. These are our "perceptual filters." These filters tend to limit our vision and shape what we see. The most common perceptual filters are:

- culture, race, and ethnicity
- gender and sexuality
- previous experiences
- age
- peer group
- level of education
- economic status or background
- where you live or grew up

Our past experiences also act as powerful perceptual filters. Here's an example of how perceptions based on past experience can lead to conflict and misunderstanding:

John's mother is someone who cries easily and shows lots of emotion. His sister is the same way. Therefore, John developed a perceptual filter through which he sees girls and women as overly emotional and overly sensitive. This belief is a perceptual filter, not a fact.

John's girlfriend, Lisa, had a father who rarely showed emotion and didn't offer much empathy when she was upset. Because of this experience, Lisa developed a perceptual filter through which she views men and boys as emotionally detached and lacking in empathy. This isn't a fact either. It's a perceptual filter based on Lisa's past experience.

John and Lisa have lots of arguments over issues triggered by these perceptual filters. Instead of realizing they can find solutions to their conflicts, John and Lisa stay stuck in their perceptual filters, each believing that the other has some unchangeable flaws. As a result, they never work out their conflicts with each other.

What do you think about this story? Can you relate? **Check in with yourself and then respond to the following questions.**

- What are three of your perceptual filters?

- Which perceptual filters of yours are based on negative past experiences?

- Describe a conflict you've had because of perceptual filters.

- Describe a time you judged a person or a group of people based on your perceptual filters.

- Our perceptual filters can limit us. What can we do to see beyond them?

 From *Create a Culture of Kindness in Middle School* by Naomi Drew, M.A., with Christa M. Tinari, M.A., copyright © 2017. This page may be reproduced for individual, classroom, or small group work only. For all other uses, contact Free Spirit Publishing Inc. at www.freespirit.com/permissions.

Perceptions, Conflict, and Ripples

CHARACTER CONNECTIONS

personal responsibility / respect / conflict resolution

Lesson 34 expands students' understanding of how perceptions can lead to blame and conflict, and the outward ripples that can affect others as a result.

Note: Complete Lesson 32: "Responsibility vs. Blame" (page 160) and Lesson 33: "Perceptions and Perceptual Filters" (page 164) prior to doing this one.

Students will

- review the meaning of perceptual filters and consider how their filters can lead to conflict
- understand how blame can intensify conflict and how their conflicts can affect the people around them
- practice respectful listening with someone whose perceptions may be different from their own

Materials

- students' completed "Perceptual Filters" handout from Lesson 33
- handout: "Perceptions, Blame, Conflict, and Ripples" (page 169)

Preparation

Before doing this lesson, review "The True Story of a Three-Year Conflict" from Lesson 32.

Introduction

Review the meaning of perceptual filters and go over students' completed "Perceptual Filters" handouts. Ask students to think of one way perceptual filters affect the way they see others and the way others see them. Ask for an example of how the filters of age, gender, or race can be significant. For example, how might someone older view middle school students? How might this lead to misunderstanding or conflict?

Discussion and Activity

Say: **Our past experiences create powerful perceptual filters. They influence how we view life and handle conflicts. For example, if blame has always played a part in your past experiences with conflict, how might it play a part in a new conflict you face?** (Possible answer: You might automatically blame others or work to avoid being blamed.)

Say: **Remember the part that blame played in the three-year conflict we talked about in Lesson 32?** Have students briefly recap. Say: **Remember how the girl at the center of the conflict was stuck in her perception that someone else was completely to blame? What resulted from her unwillingness to let go of this perception?** Discuss.

Say: **Everything we do has a ripple effect. Often other people are affected by the things we do. Now you're going to hear how other people perceived that three-year conflict, and how it impacted their lives.**

Distribute the handout and ask for a volunteer to read aloud the story from a sixth-grade girl who was in the same class as the girls involved in the three-year conflict. Entertain a few reactions to this story. Then put students in pairs and have them discuss the following questions: "If someone always blames the other person when conflicts arise, do you think it's possible for that person to change? Why or why not?"

(If students need help remembering the questions, write them on the board.)

Have pairs start with one student asking the question and listening to the partner's response using respectful listening. The first listener should then paraphrase what he or she heard, and check in to see if he or she got it right. Then have students switch roles and repeat the process.

Caution students to listen with an open mind, trying to see things through their partners' eyes and allowing their partners to complete their thought uninterrupted.

Afterward, ask how the process went. Did each person feel heard? Ask: **What was it like to hold back if your partner perceived things differently from you? What did you learn by doing this?**

Wrap-Up

Ask: **How can the act of truly listening to and being respectful of someone's differing perceptions lead to greater understanding? How might this help us get along with family adults, siblings, friends, and anyone who perceives things differently from us? How might our world be better if all people could truly listen to one another?**

Follow-Up

Assign the following journal activity on perceptual filters: Imagine being a different race or gender. How might you perceive others differently? How might others perceive you? How might this lead to misunderstandings? What can we do to understand each other more fully?

Perceptions, Blame, Conflict, and Ripples

Think back to the three-year conflict we talked about in Lesson 32. Remember how the girl was stuck in her perception that the other person was completely to blame? Now read this story to see how this conflict affected others, and answer the questions that follow.

For a long time there were two girls in our school who weren't getting along. They drew us all into their conflict. It went on forever and ended up affecting everyone. Each girl would try to get people to side with her. They both thought they were right and the other person was wrong, but the truth is, they were both wrong. If you sided with one you couldn't be friends with the other. It was extremely stressful. They would watch to see who you were talking to. Kids started reporting on each other. Sometimes I would go home and worry about what to do. A lot of kids did. It became a major problem for everyone.

After a while I couldn't focus on my schoolwork. Both girls would come to me separately and try to get me to side with them. If there was a birthday party, kids would be left out if they sided with the wrong person. It created stress in the entire sixth grade and it divided all of us.

Finally the sixth-grade teachers got us all together to talk about it. We learned that when there's a conflict, each person should stand back and ask if he or she is doing something wrong, too. The girls at the center of this conflict couldn't see their role in it. They were so stuck on how they saw things, they couldn't see that they were both making the conflict worse. They had no idea how much this affected everyone else. If they had only worked it out sooner, sixth grade would have been different for all of us.

- Think of a conflict where you were stuck in your own perceptions and couldn't see the other person's point of view. Describe what happened.

- Describe a conflict you've been in where blame played a part.

- Think of a conflict that rippled out and affected other people. What happened?

REAL-LIFE CHALLENGE

» Next time someone has a different perception from yours, try to listen with an open mind to what that person has to say. Rather than arguing, say back what you heard. (This works well with parents!) If you feel the urge to jump in and voice an opposing opinion, take a few deep breaths and remind yourself to keep hearing out the other person. Afterward, try saying something like, "Even though we see things differently, I care about what you have to say." Notice what happens next.

» Imagine that a younger student or sibling asks you how to deal with a friend who perceives an issue differently from him or her. What advice could you give? What might you say about respectful listening? What might you say about the value of trying to understand the other person's point of view? Write a letter outlining your best advice. Then try applying it to your own life.

From *Create a Culture of Kindness in Middle School* by Naomi Drew, M.A., with Christa M. Tinari, M.A., copyright © 2017. This page may be reproduced for individual, classroom, or small group work only. For all other uses, contact Free Spirit Publishing Inc. at www.freespirit.com/permissions.

Positive and Negative Choices in Conflict

CHARACTER CONNECTIONS

conflict resolution / critical thinking / personal responsibility / respect

Lesson 35 helps students distinguish between positive and negative choices in conflicts, recognizing that they have the power to choose positive responses.

Students will

- understand that they have choices about how to handle conflicts
- reflect on outcomes of positive and negative choices
- practice evaluating positive and negative choices when dealing with conflicts

Materials

- student journals
- handouts: "What Middle Schoolers Have to Say About Making Choices in Conflict" (page 172) and "Positive Responses to Conflict" (page 173)

Introduction

Say: **I'd like you to imagine you are in a conflict with someone you don't get along with. Imagine this conflict being over which band or sports team is the best one. Since this conflict is with someone you don't like, think of how you might react if this person said your opinion was wrong and his or hers was right. I'm looking for an honest answer, not the one you think you "should" say. Take out your journals and jot down real ways you might react. We'll do this for about three minutes.**

After the allotted time, invite a few students to share their responses. Ask students who respond to consider whether the way they handled this conflict might be positive, negative, or dependent on the circumstances. Encourage students to think critically and consider multiple points of view.

Say: **Now imagine having the same kind of conflict with a close friend. Would you respond differently than you did with the person you don't get along with?** Take responses. Your objective in this part of the lesson is to learn more about where your students are coming from, what their motivations are, and how they think.

Discussion and Activity

Now distribute the "What Middle Schoolers Have to Say About Making Choices in Conflict" handout and ask for a volunteer to read aloud the first student quote, beginning, "I ignore the person."

Say: **Please give me a thumbs-up if you think this is a positive choice, a thumbs-down if you think it's a negative choice, or a thumb to the side if you think it depends on the specific situation.** Ask a few students to explain their responses.

Now repeat the process with each quote on the handout, asking the following questions where appropriate: "What makes this a positive or negative choice?" "When do you think it might depend on the details of the conflict?" Encourage students to consider the possible outcomes of each action to determine how positive or negative the choices are.

Next, put students in groups of four and read the following scenario aloud: **You and a friend made plans to hang out last weekend. You texted your friend several times to coordinate getting together, but you didn't get a reply. Later you saw a picture online that showed your friend having fun doing activities with other people. You're feeling ignored and hurt because your friend didn't respond to you.**

You feel like you've been blown off. You approach your friend to resolve the conflict.

In each group of four, have two students role-play as the two friends and the other two students act as observers. Say: **Actors, your job is to interact with one another in a realistic way, demonstrating how you would respond to this conflict. Observers, your job is to watch the role-play and notice the specific ways in which each person handles the conflict.**

Note: If you feel your students might not stay on task in small groups, have two volunteers role-play the conflict in front of the group. In this case, the rest of the students will act as observers.

After students have completed the role-play, distribute the "Positive Responses to Conflict" handout. Have observers offer responses. Ask: **Which responses helped the conflict get resolved? If the conflict didn't get resolved, which words or actions got in the way of resolution?** (Guide students to name specifics such as blaming, name-calling, interrupting, or showing disrespect for the other person.) **How do you think the choices the role-players made could impact their friendship?** Then ask: **How would *you* have responded to this conflict? Why would you have made the choices you did?**

Ask: **When we choose negative responses to conflicts, what are some of the repercussions?** (Possible answers: Lost relationships, escalation of the original conflict, long-term animosities, loss of someone's respect.) Ask: **What are some of the more positive responses we can make when we're in conflicts—things that could help lead to a fair resolution?** (Possible answers: Cool off first, think about what to say before you say it, resist name-calling or blaming.)

Wrap-Up

Say: **We have lots of choices about how to handle conflicts. When is it difficult to make a positive choice?** (You may want to share an example from your own life.) Student responses might include, "When I'm really mad at someone," "When someone has hurt me," "When I don't like the person," or "When I really want something my way." Remind students that even though it can be difficult, choosing a positive response is likely to yield a positive result. Stress that learning how to resolve conflicts now can set them on a lifelong path to healthier, more harmonious relationships.

Follow-Up

Throughout the coming days or weeks, discuss conflict scenarios that come up in your curriculum, in the news, or in life. Ask: **What choices did people have in this situation? What choices did they make? What were the consequences of their choices? Were their choices positive or negative?** Invite responses and discussion.

Enrichment Activities

- Invite students to work in groups to create short public service announcements stressing the importance of thinking about the consequences of our choices—positive or negative—when faced with conflict.
- Have students journal their responses to the questions on the "Positive Responses to Conflict" handout. Place students in pairs and have them discuss their answers with their partners.

What Middle Schoolers Have to Say About Making Choices in Conflict

In a survey of more than 1,000 middle schoolers, students wrote about the choices they make during conflicts. Here are some of their responses. Do you think each action is a positive or negative response to conflict, or do you think it depends on the situation? Check the box that matches your answer.

"I ignore the person who is making me upset. I don't like to get into it with people."	☐ positive	☐ negative	☐ it depends
"I try to find out why the person is mad at me."	☐ positive	☐ negative	☐ it depends
"I tell the person how I'm feeling and see if we can come to a compromise."	☐ positive	☐ negative	☐ it depends
"I usually end the friendship because I don't need drama."	☐ positive	☐ negative	☐ it depends
"I try to understand the other person's point of view."	☐ positive	☐ negative	☐ it depends
"I talk to a friend to get advice."	☐ positive	☐ negative	☐ it depends
"I get into a fight, either yelling or physically fighting."	☐ positive	☐ negative	☐ it depends
"I try to get the person to agree with me or give in to what I want."	☐ positive	☐ negative	☐ it depends

- What other *positive* responses can you think of? List them here:

 From *Create a Culture of Kindness in Middle School* by Naomi Drew, M.A., with Christa M. Tinari, M.A., copyright © 2017. This page may be reproduced for individual, classroom, or small group work only. For all other uses, contact Free Spirit Publishing Inc. at www.freespirit.com/permissions.

Positive Reponses to Conflict

The following ways of responding to conflicts are positive and productive. Take a look at these responses and then answer the questions that follow.

- Talk it out.
- Put yourself in the other person's shoes.
- Imagine some ways you could reach a resolution.
- Get advice from a trustworthy friend.
- Think about the pros and cons of reaching a solution.
- Compromise: Give a little, get a little.
- Use a friendly, nonjudgmental tone of voice.
- Ask for a mediator.
- Take a break and talk about it when you're not as upset.
- Listen to what the other person has to say.
- Brainstorm a few solutions with the other person.
- Try looking at the conflict from a different perspective and see if that sparks ideas for resolving it.
- Reevaluate how important the conflict is to you.
- Give respect to get respect!
- Practice what you would like to say before saying it.
- Notice your body language, facial expression, and tone of voice. Ask yourself if any of these could be sending negative messages.
- Be flexible and open, rather than stuck in your own position.

- Think of a time when you chose a negative way to handle a conflict. What were some of the negative things you did? Be specific. How did your choice affect your relationship with the other person?

- Think of a time when you chose a positive way to handle conflict. Describe some things you did and the outcome of the conflict. How did your choice impact your relationship with the other person?

- Which of the positive responses on the list might be most difficult for you to adopt when you're in the middle of a conflict? Why? What might happen if you were able to respond that way more often?

- Next time you face a conflict, which of the responses on this list will you try? Explain why you think this response (or responses) would be useful.

From *Create a Culture of Kindness in Middle School* by Naomi Drew, M.A., with Christa M. Tinari, M.A., copyright © 2017. This page may be reproduced for individual, classroom, or small group work only. For all other uses, contact Free Spirit Publishing Inc. at www.freespirit.com/permissions.

Dealing with Anger

CHARACTER CONNECTIONS

self-control / personal responsibility / anger management

Lesson 36 helps students gain greater control over anger, especially when conflicts arise.

Note: Be sure students have completed the "Anger Checklist" (page 36) prior to this lesson.

Students will

- review the Stop, Breathe, Chill process from Lesson 8, "Using Stop, Breathe, Chill to Respond, Not React"
- mentally rehearse using Stop, Breathe, Chill as a way to disconnect from anger, especially during conflicts
- role-play combining Stop, Breathe, Chill with the Win/Win Guidelines

Materials

- handouts: "Brain Graphic" (page 30), "Anger Checklist" (page 36), "Using the Win/Win Guidelines for Working Out Conflicts" (page 156), and "Getting a Handle on Anger" (page 177)

Preparation

Have students bring back their completed "Anger Checklist" handouts from Lesson 5, or give them new copies to fill out prior to today's lesson.

Distribute copies of the "Using the Win/Win Guidelines for Working Out Conflicts" handout from Lesson 31. Also write the words *Stop, Breathe,* and *Chill* on the board.

Introduction

Ask: **Have you ever tried to work out a conflict while you were still mad? How did that go?** If desired, briefly share a story of when you had this experience yourself. Ask: **Why is it essential to cool off before trying to resolve any conflict? What part of the brain are we stuck in when we don't cool off?** (Answer: The reptilian brain.) Refer to the "Brain Graphic" poster or handout. Ask why the reptilian brain is a bad place to be stuck. (Possible answers: Because you won't be able to think clearly; because you'll just react.) Entertain one or two responses.

Say: **Today we're going to practice ways to calm down when you're in a conflict and feeling angry. Take a look at your "Anger Checklist" and find one or two areas you'd most like to improve.** Encourage students to discuss their responses. Share something on the checklist that *you'd* like to get better at, too.

Discussion and Activity

Read the following quote from a seventh-grade girl: *"In middle school, people have mood swings and get angry more easily than when we were younger. We're getting more homework and have after-school pressures, plus other stuff, too. It's easier to release stress toward other people than deal with it ourselves."* Ask: **Can you relate to these words?** Invite reflection and responses.

Put kids in pairs. Say: **Think of a conflict that started because you or someone else was in a bad mood and ended up getting mad. Tell each other about it briefly, but don't use any real names.** After about four minutes, ask for a few students to share their stories with the whole group. Then say: **Even though anger is a natural and normal emotion, it can become a destructive force if we don't know how to handle it.**

Say: **Now tell your partner what strategies help you gain greater control over anger.** Give pairs another few minutes to share, then ask for a response or two in the large group.

Point to "Stop, Breathe, Chill" on the board. Say: **Each time we use this strategy we strengthen the neural pathways in the brain that help us manage anger.** On the "Brain Graphic" poster, indicate the neocortex—the part of the brain that Stop, Breathe, Chill helps us access. Say: **Now we're going to do some mental rehearsal to practice handling conflict and anger in the most effective ways possible.** Remind students that mental rehearsal is a powerful tool that many professional athletes and performers use.

Ask students to think of the conflict they told their partner about. Have them close their eyes, cover them, or look down, and briefly picture what happened. Say: **Picture the moment when you felt the angriest. Recall the feelings in your body. Now imagine holding up a big stop sign in your head.** (Pause.) **Take a slow deep breath and let it out. Take another. As you take the next breath, silently say a calming statement to yourself.** (Pause.) **Now picture yourself being composed enough to say to the other person, "I need to take a break. Let's talk in a little while." Imagine yourself walking away, and coming back better able to talk over the problem."**

Have students open their eyes. Ask: **Were you able to see yourself calming down? Was there anything that stood in the way of you becoming calmer? What else could you say besides, "I need to take a break"?**

Entertain responses and ask if anyone has questions. Here are a few that might come up:

- What if the other person still acts mad? (Answer: Suggest taking more time out and talking things out at a later time.)
- What if the other person calls you names? (Answer: Try to be the bigger person. Say something in response, but keep it respectful. For example, "I'm not calling you names, and I'd appreciate the same respect from you.")
- What if the other person starts bullying you with threats, humiliation, or physical attacks? (Answer: Stop trying to work things out and talk to an adult who can help you. No one has the right to attack you. Ever.)

Let students know that no strategy is foolproof, but that all the strategies they're learning will help them handle their anger and resolve conflicts better than before. Next, direct students' attention to the Win/Win Guidelines and Rules for Win/Win. Invite volunteers to come to the front of the room to do the following three role-plays. Guide students loosely through the Win/Win Guidelines as they act out the scenarios. They don't have to do every step as long as they stay in the spirit of the process.

Two students are needed for each of these role-plays.

- *You thought you saw your friend flirting with your girlfriend. You decide to say something to your friend at lunch. Do Stop, Breathe, Chill before you speak.*
- *You heard that a friend was gossiping about you. You stop the friend after class to say something. "Do Stop, Breathe, Chill before you speak.*
- *Your older sibling likes to tease you and thinks it's funny, but you find it hurtful. Today you decide to address the problem honestly. Do Stop, Breathe, Chill before you speak and each time your sibling tries to make light of your feelings.*

After each role-play, discuss it briefly with the group. Ask: **Did the people involved in this situation cool off enough before trying to resolve their conflict? Did they work toward compromising rather than placing blame? Did they take responsibility for any negative things they did, such as speaking sarcastically or rolling their eyes? Were they able to work out the problem in a fair, respectful way? Why or why not? What other things could they have done or said as they tried to resolve their conflict?**

Wrap-Up

Distribute the "Getting a Handle on Anger" handout. Ask a student to read aloud the words at the top. Urge students to always honor the Rule of Three when they get angry: "Never hurt yourself, others, or property." Stress the importance of reaching out to a trusted adult if students find that their anger or someone else's is a major issue.

Follow-Up

Take time to go over responses to the "Getting a Handle on Anger" handout with the group. If any red-flag issues arise, consult with your school counselor or other appropriate personnel.

Enrichment Activities

- Have students create posters for any of the following: Stop, Breathe, Chill; Win/Win Guidelines; Rules for Using Win/Win; or Rule of Three. Have them present the information on the posters to younger grades.
- See the 10-Minute Time Cruncher "Role-Playing Ways of Dealing with Anger" on page 178 for more role-plays relating to this lesson.
- Arrange for students to teach favorite strategies from this lesson to another group. You might want to work with a colleague to do this, partnering students in each of your groups. Pairs can then role-play a chosen strategy. Encourage students to create graphics or handouts that illustrate the strategies.

Getting a Handle on Anger

Anger is a natural emotion. There's nothing wrong with feeling angry, but what we *do* with our anger can turn it into a negative force. When you get angry, always honor the Rule of Three:

Never hurt yourself, others, or property.

Think about the Rule of Three as you read what some middle schoolers said about anger. Then answer the questions that follow.

> *"If you feel you're going to do physical harm to yourself or others, you should have other ways to get the anger out." —7th-grade girl*
>
> *"When my brother gets me mad, the thought that comes to me is, 'I'm gonna beat the crap out of you.' I don't actually do it, but I think it." —6th-grade boy*
>
> *"I get the anger out with physical activity like riding my bike or running." —9th-grade boy*
>
> *"I used to break stuff when I was mad. Now I do push-ups." —8th-grade girl*

- What thoughts pop into your head when you get mad?

- What calming statement can you use to stop angry thoughts from taking over your brain?

- What helps you calm down and cool off when you're angry?

- How can you help yourself live by the Rule of Three?

- If you could "talk to" your anger, what would you say?

- If you could talk to someone else's anger, what would you say?

- Who can you talk to if handling anger—your own or someone else's—is a problem for you?

Note: If someone's anger is out of control and you need a caring person to talk to, this support hotline for kids is available twenty-four hours a day, seven days a week, and you won't be put on hold: 1-800-USA-KIDS (1-800-872-5437).

From *Create a Culture of Kindness in Middle School* by Naomi Drew, M.A., with Christa M. Tinari, M.A., copyright © 2017. This page may be reproduced for individual, classroom, or small group work only. For all other uses, contact Free Spirit Publishing Inc. at www.freespirit.com/permissions.

Role-Playing Ways of Dealing with Anger

CHARACTER CONNECTIONS

self-control / personal responsibility / anger management

This time cruncher coordinates with Lesson 36, "Dealing with Anger" (page 174). It gives students additional practice in applying Stop, Breathe, Chill and the Win/Win Guidelines.

Materials

- handouts: "Using the Win/Win Guidelines for Working Out Conflicts" (page 156) and "Maintaining a Win/Win Mode" (page 159)

Directions

On the board, write these three words, one above the other: *Stop, Breathe, Chill.* Draw a stop sign next to the word *Stop.*

Distribute both handouts and choose several students to come to the front of the room to role-play the following conflict scenarios. Guide them to use Stop, Breathe, Chill to calm themselves, then use the Win/Win Guidelines to resolve the conflict. Have the group carefully observe and prepare to give feedback at the end of the role-play. Encourage observers to refer to the "Maintaining a Win/Win Mode" handout as they observe.

Role-Play Scenario #1

Your friend has been acting cold and unfriendly toward you. Each time you see her, you wonder if something is wrong. You noticed that she posted a picture on Facebook of herself and another friend you both normally hang out with. You feel left out, annoyed, and anxious. You decide to talk to her. Background: *Two weeks ago you went to the movies with another friend and didn't invite her because you thought she had a soccer game that day, but you had your dates mixed up.*

Role-Play Scenario #2

Yesterday at lunch, a guy you hang out with was acting overly friendly with your girlfriend at the lunch table. You decide to confront him. You're angry and want some answers. Background: *The guy lives next door to your girlfriend and they've known each other for many years.*

Remind role-players to do Stop, Breathe, Chill before talking to the person they have the problem with. Then have them go through the Win/Win Guidelines on the "Using the Win/Win Guidelines for Working Out Conflicts" handout to talk out the conflict. Have the group give feedback after each role-play. Pose the following questions for them to consider:

- Did the conflict get resolved effectively? If yes, what did each person do that enabled this to happen? If not, what got in the way?
- If the conflict *wasn't* resolved effectively, what could be done differently next time?
- If the conflict *was* resolved effectively, what specifics did you observe that you could apply in real-life conflicts?

Willingness Blocks

CHARACTER CONNECTIONS

self-control / integrity / conflict resolution

Lesson 37 helps students identify and remove their blocks to working out conflicts and fosters a growth mindset around the issue of resolving conflicts.

Students will

- understand that recognizing their blocks to working out conflicts is the first step in removing them
- determine which willingness blocks they're holding on to
- role-play trying to resolve conflicts with and without willingness blocks

Materials

- two wooden blocks or two shoeboxes
- brown construction paper
- a marker
- student journals
- handouts: "Using the Win/Win Guidelines for Working Out Conflicts" (page 156) and "Willingness Blocks" (page 181)

Preparation

Find two wooden blocks, or cover two shoeboxes with brown construction paper. On the side of each one, write *Willingness Block* in large letters.

Introduction

Ask: **Have you ever noticed that if you think you can't do something, you often can't—but that if you think you *can* do something, it's easier to give it a try?** Invite students to share examples.

Ask students if they have any negative beliefs about their ability—or the ability of others—to work out conflicts. Are they sometimes simply unwilling to try to work out a conflict with someone else? If so, why? (Possible answers: It seems hopeless and won't work anyway; they're too angry; the other person won't listen; or they just don't want to.) In their journals, have students do about two minutes of automatic writing on these questions to see what negative beliefs emerge. Tell them that they can think of these beliefs as "willingness blocks."

Discussion and Activity

Ask students what negative beliefs were revealed through the process of automatic writing. Discuss briefly before distributing the "Willingness Blocks" handout. Say: **Let's see what other negative beliefs might get in the way of resolving conflicts.**

Ask a student to read aloud the words at the top of the handout, beginning with, "When you hold onto willingness blocks." Have students complete the willingness blocks checklist on the handout. Discuss results.

Next, ask for two students to come to the front of the room to role-play the following conflict with willingness blocks in place: *The kid who sits next to you in math is constantly tapping his pencil during quizzes and tests. It drives you crazy. He says tapping helps him think. Try working out this conflict as you hold on to your willingness blocks.*

Have the students imagine that in this conflict they're each intent on proving that they're right and the other person is wrong, and they are each resistant to considering anything but their own point of view. Hand each student a block and have them face each other as they speak.

Afterward, discuss the role-play with the group. Ask: **Did the problem get resolved? What was in the way? How do you think this will affect the relationship between these two people?**

Now take the physical blocks away. Tell role-players to shift their minds out of a place of judgment and into a place of willingness to work out the issue constructively. Direct the role-players' attention to the Win/Win Guidelines and Rules for Using Win/Win. Have them replay the conflict, this time demonstrating a willingness to hear each other out and compromise.

Discuss this second role-play with the group. How did it go this time? Was the outcome different? Why?

Ask: **What are some negative results from holding onto willingness blocks? What other negative things happen when we're unwilling to work out conflicts?** If you like, share a time when *your* resistance to another person or point of view caused you to be unwilling to work out a conflict constructively. What was the negative fallout? Tell your group about this. Have students partner up and discuss a similar situation in their own lives and the ensuing results.

Afterward, in the large group, have students share specific negative results from holding on to the willingness blocks they just discussed. (Possible answers: Escalation of the conflict; loss of a friend; emotional and physical stress; continued hostility or tension; a sense of failure; feeling bad about oneself.) Emphasize that a pattern of unwillingness to work out conflicts constructively can become a way of life and can negatively affect future relationships.

Now ask about the potential benefits of letting go of willingness blocks. List responses on the board. Here are a few to guide students toward:

When we let go of willingness blocks we often . . .

- get along better with people
- have healthier relationships
- feel positive about ourselves and the way we handle conflict
- are considered easy to get along with
- experience less stress
- are able to more skillfully handle difficult people and difficult situations
- gain better control over our reactions to conflict
- set up a lifetime pattern of dealing with conflicts in a positive way
- have a happier life because we know how to handle conflict effectively

Ask: **What can you do to help yourself let go of your willingness blocks?** Stress that being aware of these blocks is an important first step. Taking responsibility for your role in a conflict is the second. Discuss other ways to move beyond willingness blocks. What can we say to ourselves to help shift out of a mindset of resistance and into one of willingness to compromise? What words can we use to show we're willing to hear out the other person? Remind students that each time they take steps to let go of a willingness block, they change their brain in a positive way, strengthening the neural pathway that enables them to handle conflict and get along better with others.

Wrap-Up

Have students look at the "Willingness Blocks" handout and choose at least one they'd like to work on letting go of. As time allows, invite students to share these goals with the group.

Follow-Up

Encourage students to keep the "Willingness Blocks" handout somewhere they can easily revisit it. Each time they let go of another willingness block, have them cross it off the checklist. Encourage them to journal about the progress they make.

Enrichment Activities

- Start a Willingness Blog where students can comment on willingness blocks they're dealing with and what they're doing to let go of them.
- To give students more practice in letting go of willingness blocks, do the 10-Minute Time Cruncher "Willingness Blocks Role-Play" on page 182.

Willingness Blocks

When you hold onto willingness blocks, conflicts are less likely to get worked out. In fact, they may escalate. Take a look at the following list. When you're in a conflict, which willingness blocks most apply to you? Place a check mark next to each block you're holding on to. If you have different willingness blocks than those listed below, write them in the spaces provided. Be honest with yourself even if it's difficult. That's an important first step in changing the way you handle conflict. When you've completed the checklist, answer the questions that follow.

- ☐ I want to show I'm "right" and the other person is "wrong."
- ☐ I really don't believe you can work out conflicts in a positive way. It's not realistic.
- ☐ I don't want to come across as a wimp or a loser.
- ☐ I think people will take advantage of me if I compromise.
- ☐ I want to be in control.
- ☐ If I don't like the other person, I don't want to hear him or her out.
- ☐ I'm afraid I'll sound stupid if I try to talk things out.
- ☐ Sometimes I'm too angry to work things out.
- ☐ It takes too long to talk things out.
- ☐ Sometimes I just want to get even.
- ☐ I'd rather blame the other person than take responsibility.
- ☐ I don't want to change how I've always done things.
- ☐ I'm not good at expressing myself, so I assume the other person will probably win.
- ☐ I think I have the skills to resolve a conflict, but I assume the people I get into conflicts with don't, so there's no point in trying.
- ☐ I don't think I can ever learn how to handle conflicts better.
- ☐ Other:
- ☐ Other:
- ☐ Other:

- Which willingness blocks would you most like to let go of?

- What would be the benefit of letting go of these blocks?

- The next time a conflict arises, what can you do differently to let go of these willingness blocks?

REAL-LIFE CHALLENGE

» Show this checklist to someone you trust. Explain that you're working on releasing your willingness blocks so you can handle conflict better. Ask which willingness blocks he or she sees in you. Thank this person for being honest and see if he or she wants to join you in this effort to let go of willingness blocks.

From *Create a Culture of Kindness in Middle School* by Naomi Drew, M.A., with Christa M. Tinari, M.A., copyright © 2017. This page may be reproduced for individual, classroom, or small group work only. For all other uses, contact Free Spirit Publishing Inc. at www.freespirit.com/permissions.

Willingness Blocks Role-Play

CHARACTER CONNECTIONS

self-control / integrity / conflict resolution

This time cruncher coordinates with Lesson 37, "Willingness Blocks" (page 179). It gives students a chance to reflect on how to release willingness blocks that may prevent them from effectively resolving conflicts.

Materials

- handouts: "Using the Win/Win Guidelines for Working Out Conflicts" (page 156) and "Maintaining a Win/Win Mode" (page 159)

Directions

Have students pair up for three minutes to strategize about specific ways to put aside a willingness block and handle the following situation effectively: *Imagine you're already in a bad mood when a kid you've never liked makes a snide remark about your complexion. You want to say something mean in response, but you know that it will only make things worse. But you really don't like this person. That's your willingness block. Is there a way to handle this situation so your willingness block doesn't control your actions and the conflict doesn't escalate?*

Circulate and give coaching where needed as students brainstorm. Then choose one pair to role-play an idea they came up with, specifying what the willingness block is. Afterward, have the group give feedback on the following three elements:

- Were the role-players able to let go of their willingness blocks?
- Were they able to resolve the conflict effectively?
- If so, how did they make it happen? If not, what went wrong?

Being Assertive

CHARACTER CONNECTIONS
compromise / fairness / personal responsibility

Lesson 38 helps students hone the skill of assertiveness.

Note: Prior to doing this lesson, do Lesson 18: "The Dignity Stance" (page 93).

Students will

- understand what it means to be assertive and distinguish assertiveness from aggressiveness and passivity
- practice using assertive body language, tone of voice, and facial expressions
- role-play working out a conflict in an assertive manner

Materials

- notecards and markers
- handouts: "Dignity Stance" (page 96) and "Be Assertive: Speak Your Voice with Strength and Respect" (pages 186–187)

Preparation

Write each of the following words on a different notecard: *assertive, passive, aggressive.*

On the board, write the following:

Being assertive means speaking what's on your mind clearly, honestly, and respectfully. It requires a strong yet neutral facial expression, voice, and body language.

Being aggressive means trying to gain power over another by attacking, demeaning, threatening, or harming. Like assertiveness, aggressiveness can be shown through words, body language, facial expression, or tone of voice.

Note: Hide these definitions before the start of the lesson.

"Too often we say nothing and wonder why others don't understand how we feel." —Sheila Heen

Introduction

Ask: **What does being assertive mean?** Entertain responses, then show the definition on the board. Ask a student to read it aloud.

Ask: **What does it mean to be aggressive?** Entertain responses and then show the definition. Ask a student to read it aloud. Ask: **What is the difference between being assertive and being aggressive?** Help students understand the contrast between the two.

Ask for examples of assertive statements. Ask: **If the person next to you in class is talking too loudly, for example, what could you say that's clear, direct, and respectful?** Take responses. Help students notice if their tone of voice, body language, or facial expression delivers a message different from their words. Let students know that sarcasm is usually interpreted as aggressive.

Now ask for examples of aggressive responses. Ask: **Other than our words, what else can communicate aggression?** (Answers: Tone of voice, body language, and facial expression.) Reiterate that sarcasm, even when it's intended to be funny, is often seen as aggressive, and often *is* aggressive, if it's meant to embarrass others or put them down.

Discussion and Activity

Ask: **What's the direct opposite of aggressive behavior?** (Answer: Passive behavior.) Ask students for examples. Ask a student to read aloud the Sheila Heen quote from the board as a common example of passivity: *"Too often we say nothing and wonder why others don't understand how we feel."* Ask students if they can relate to this. Briefly discuss.

Ask about other ways people may unintentionally convey passivity. (Answers: Meek tone of voice, avoiding eye contact, submissive body language.) Demonstrate a passive demeanor—slumped shoulders, head lowered, hands gripped low in front of the body. Now have each student face a partner, avoid eye contact, and say something in a passive voice and using passive body language.

Ask: **Which is the most effective mode of communication—assertive, aggressive, or passive? Why?** Take responses.

Refer to the "Dignity Stance" handout. Ask which type of communication this stance represents. (Answer: Assertive.) Have students stand and assume the Dignity Stance. Scan the room to see if students have heads held high, shoulders back, bodies straight and tall but not stiff, with arms at sides or linked in back rather than crossed or linked in front.

Have students sit down. Ask: **What might an assertive voice sound like?** (Possible answers: Confident, strong, neutral, calm.) Ask for one or two volunteers to say the following statement aloud in an assertive voice: "I'd prefer not to do that right now." Have the group let each volunteer know if his or her statement came across as assertive or not. If not, how did it come across, and why?

Tell the group you're going to demonstrate a statement in all three modes. Use your voice as well as your facial expression and body language to convey each mode. Say the following statement in all three ways: "I need to talk to that person in the blue shirt."

After each recitation of this statement, ask students to identify what you conveyed—assertiveness, aggressiveness, or passivity. Ask what cues signaled which mode was which.

Now ask for three volunteers to come to the front of the room. Hand each volunteer a notecard that only he or she can see. Tell students that each person is going to say the same statement in a different way. Say: **Listen to the person's tone of voice and notice his or her body language and facial expression. Use these cues to determine whether the person is showing assertiveness, aggressiveness, or passivity.**

Have each volunteer say the following statement in the mode written on their notecard: "We should really leave for math class now."

Afterward, have the group determine which volunteer represented which type of communication. Again, have students name specific things they saw or heard that conveyed each mode.

Repeat the same process with the following statements, choosing new volunteers for each one:

- "I'd rather not play that game."
- "That thing you texted last night really bothered me."
- "I think you should stop picking on her."

Next, read the following real story from a middle schooler: *"Some kids make fun of kids who eat different foods and are from other countries. Some of us try to say something like, 'Stop being mean,' but the people who are making fun just get mad. If I speak up and say something, they accuse me of overreacting."*

Ask for three volunteers to come to the front of the room. Have each one role-play an assertive response to kids who make fun of students from other countries. An example would be, "Hey, what if we were the ones from another country?" Coach students to deliver their statements in an assertive manner, and help them be aware of body language, facial expression, and tone of voice.

Wrap-Up

Ask the group if the role-players conveyed assertiveness effectively. Have them point out if anything came across as aggressive or passive rather than assertive. Ask: **What are some disadvantages of coming across aggressively? Passively? Why is assertiveness the most effective way to communicate when we're standing up for someone, when we're in a conflict, or when we just need to be heard?** Guide students to understand that aggressive responses typically trigger defensiveness and escalate conflicts. Passive responses don't make an impact and are easy to ignore. Assertive responses effectively convey the message you want to deliver and tend *not* to trigger aggressive responses.

Distribute the "Be Assertive: Speak Your Voice with Strength and Respect" handout. Have students complete it as homework and bring it to the next lesson.

Follow-Up

- Have students bring their completed handouts to the next meeting, and discuss their responses to the scenarios presented.
- Give students this real-life challenge: Next time you feel like you need to speak up about something, think about the best words to use and the best way to deliver them. Then take a breath and say what you have to say. Remember—assertive body language, facial expression, and tone of voice count just as much as your words.

Enrichment Activities

- Periodically check in with students to see how they're applying what they've learned about assertive behavior in real life.
- Have students journal about their experiences. What challenges are they encountering as they try to be assertive during conflicts? Under what circumstances do they notice themselves switching into more aggressive or passive modes, and why?
- Set up a question box where kids can leave you notes with questions, comments, and requests for help as they attempt to communicate in more assertive ways.
- Review assertiveness by using the 10-Minute Time Cruncher "Practicing Assertiveness" on page 188.

Be Assertive: Speak Your Voice with Strength and Respect

Being assertive means speaking what's on your mind clearly, honestly, and respectfully. It requires awareness and practice. Use the following scenarios to hone your assertiveness skills.

- Picture yourself with a group of classmates. You find one kid in the group intimidating. Imagine that he or she just ignored you and made a face when you tried to join in the conversation. Normally you would get quiet and withdraw. This time, you look the person in the eye and speak up. What do you say? Remember to be assertive, not aggressive. Brainstorm a few ideas before you decide on the best one. Try saying it in a mirror first.

  Write down what you would say:

  Now close your eyes and picture yourself actually speaking these words. See yourself standing tall and confident, even if you don't totally feel that way. Picture yourself claiming the strength of your dignity and the power of your own words. Say your statement out loud now.

- Picture yourself with friends at school. One of your friends often makes mean comments about someone you know. These comments really bother you, but you always let them go. This time, you decide to speak up. Remember to be assertive, not aggressive. Brainstorm a few ideas before you decide on the best one. Try saying it in a mirror first.

  Write down what you would say:

  Now close your eyes and picture yourself speaking these words in real life. See yourself standing tall and confident, even if you don't feel that way inside. Picture yourself feeling strength and dignity as you make your statement. Say your statement out loud now.

 From *Create a Culture of Kindness in Middle School* by Naomi Drew, M.A., with Christa M. Tinari, M.A., copyright © 2017. This page may be reproduced for individual, classroom, or small group work only. For all other uses, contact Free Spirit Publishing Inc. at www.freespirit.com/permissions.

- Picture yourself with a friend who always bosses you around. You often go along with what this friend says because you don't want to make waves. Today your friend is pushing you to do something after school that you *really* don't want to do. This time, you speak up. Remember to be assertive, not aggressive. Brainstorm a few ideas before you decide on the best one. Try saying it in a mirror first.

  Write down what you would like to say:

  Now close your eyes and picture yourself speaking these words in a real-life situation. See yourself standing tall and confident, even if you feel otherwise. Picture yourself feeling full of dignity and inner strength as you speak. Say your words out loud now.

- Picture yourself having a conflict with someone who likes to be right all the time. Normally, when you're in a conflict with this person, you back down. Today you realize that what you have to say is important, too. This time you don't back down, but you don't go on the attack, either. Remember to be assertive, not aggressive. Brainstorm a few ideas before you decide on the best one. Try saying it in a mirror first.

  Write down what you would say:

  Now close your eyes and picture yourself speaking these words to someone in real life. See yourself standing tall and strong, even if you feel nervous. Feel the power of your confidence and dignity. Now say your words out loud.

- Picture yourself having an argument with your younger sibling. Normally you get aggressive because you know you can. This time you decide to be a little kinder and a lot more fair. Imagine yourself really listening to what your sibling has to say instead of using your position as older sibling to boss him or her around. Picture yourself feeling proud of the way you're behaving this time. How might doing this change your relationship with your sibling? How might it affect how you feel about yourself?

  Write down what you would do or say:

  Now close your eyes and picture yourself actually doing this if a similar situation arose in your life.

From *Create a Culture of Kindness in Middle School* by Naomi Drew, M.A., with Christa M. Tinari, M.A., copyright © 2017. This page may be reproduced for individual, classroom, or small group work only. For all other uses, contact Free Spirit Publishing Inc. at www.freespirit.com/permissions.

Practicing Assertiveness

CHARACTER CONNECTIONS
compromise / fairness / personal responsibility

This time cruncher coordinates with Lesson 38, "Being Assertive" (page 183). It gives students practice delivering assertive statements in assertive ways.

Directions

Have students pair up and practice saying the following statements first passively, then aggressively, and finally assertively:

- "I don't like being spoken to that way."
- "I find that joke offensive."
- "I'm uncomfortable hearing you put him down that way."

Now have each pair work together to compose an assertive statement as a response to the following scenario: *Your friend just said to you, "What's your problem today? You're acting like a jerk."*

While still in pairs, have students each deliver the statements they've drafted in an assertive way, being mindful of body language, facial expression, and tone of voice. Circulate and offer guidance as needed.

Learning to Detach from Negativity

CHARACTER CONNECTIONS

self-control / self-respect / anger management / courage

Lesson 39 gives students healthy ways to detach from their reactions to other people's mean words and behaviors.

Students will	Materials
• reflect on the impact of mean words and actions • understand that it's both possible and necessary to lessen the impact of mean words and actions • practice specific strategies that can help them detach in a healthy way	• writing paper • handouts: "Quotes from Middle Schoolers" (page 191), "Use the Power of Your Brain to Triumph Over Mean Behaviors" (page 192), and "Advice from Teens on Detaching from Mean Words and Actions" (page 193)

Preparation

Make one copy of "Quotes from Middle Schoolers" and cut it into four strips. On the board, write the following:

> *Detaching is about not letting someone else's meanness take over our brain. It's about claiming our own power instead of giving it away to someone who wants to hurt us.*

Introduction

Say: **We all know that mean words and actions can take a toll on people's emotions and self-esteem. Today we're going to talk about ways we can detach from the impact of meanness. How does it feel to be the target of someone's meanness? What kind of emotional toll can it take?** Allow students to talk in generalities if need be, since speaking personally about this can sometimes be too raw and self-revealing.

Discussion and Activity

Tell the group they're going to hear from some middle schoolers who shared how they felt after hearing mean words. Hand out the four "Quotes from Middle Schoolers" strips to four different students. Have each student come to the front of the room and read aloud his or her quote.

Ask for students' responses to these words. Then ask: **What if the other person says he or she was just joking around, but it still hurts someone's feelings?** Make it clear that the responsibility doesn't rest with the recipient of the teasing or put-downs, but with the person who delivers them. If jokes or teasing hurt another person, they're not okay—period.

Put students in groups of four and have them choose one person to take notes and record ideas. Give each recorder a sheet of writing paper. Now ask groups to think of things they do to help *themselves* feel better when they feel hurt or excluded. Encourage students to come up with additional examples of positive self-talk and strategies they can use. Give them about seven minutes to do this.

Next ask each small group to share their list aloud with the full group. Emphasize that the strategies we use for coping and detaching need to be healthy ones. On the board, list the healthy strategies that students propose. You can also suggest the following:

- Be extra kind to yourself when you've been hurt. Seek out a trusted person who can counteract hurtful words with kindness and affirmation.

- Memorize this quote from Gandhi, and repeat it to yourself whenever needed: *"I will not let anyone walk through my mind with their dirty feet."*
- Tell yourself that you will not allow anyone who speaks mean words to "rent space" in your brain. Then do something to release negative energy, such as writing, drawing, talking to a friend or teacher, exercising, running, dancing, or helping someone else. Helping others almost always makes us feel better.

Note: If any destructive strategies come up (such as bingeing on food, TV, or anything else; other forms of numbing; or self-harming) address these, and be sure to follow up with students or caregivers afterward.

Now distribute the "Use the Power of Your Brain to Triumph Over Mean Behaviors" handout. Take students through both of the handout's envisioning processes, "Protective Shield" and "Protective Being." After that, move on to the self-talk strategy, "Self-Compassion." See if students have other healthy strategies to suggest. Encourage creative activities like painting, singing, playing an instrument, and writing. Also encourage physical activities such as running, walking, yoga, or team sports. Meditation is another helpful practice.

Wrap-Up

Tell students to do the envisioning processes on the "Use the Power of Your Brain to Triumph Over Mean Behaviors" handout tonight before they go to sleep. They can combine both into one if they wish. Let them know that doing this may help them sleep better and that if it's done on a regular basis, this will create new neural pathways in the brain that will protect them against the effects of other people's hurtful behaviors. Pass out "Advice from Teens on Detaching from Mean Words and Actions" and tell them to answer the questions on the handout as homework.

Follow-Up

- In their journals, have students write about their protective shields and protective beings in detail. Have them describe the effect of engaging in these processes at night. Encourage them to continue using this practice.
- Discuss the positive statements students wrote on their "Advice from Teens on Detaching from Mean Words and Actions" handouts.

Enrichment Activities

- Have student create artwork, songs, or poems about the two envisioning processes.
- Have students write letters to themselves from the adults they will be twenty years from now. Tell students that these adults should tell their middle school selves all the wonderful qualities they have and acknowledge even the smallest positive traits with kindness and wisdom. Then students should have the adults give their middle school selves advice on dealing with hurtful comments from others.

Quotes from Middle Schoolers

Cut along the dotted lines and pass out a quote to four different students to read aloud during this lesson.

"My friends would make fun of me. When I was with them, I would laugh it off, but when I was alone, it would really hurt. I felt like they were singling me out just to be funny. I hated being the butt of their jokes."
—8th-grade girl

"I kept it inside, but I'd come home every day and I'd be so bummed out."
—8th-grade boy

"At band practice this girl and her friends kept giving me looks. I don't even remember what they were saying, but their looks really hurt. I started to cry so I went to the girls' room. The girl just stared at me as I walked away. I felt completely intimidated."
—6th-grade girl

"When they called me names, I felt ashamed, like there was something wrong with me that everyone else could see."
—7th-grade boy

From *Create a Culture of Kindness in Middle School* by Naomi Drew, M.A., with Christa M. Tinari, M.A., copyright © 2017. This page may be reproduced for individual, classroom, or small group work only. For all other uses, contact Free Spirit Publishing Inc. at www.freespirit.com/permissions.

Use the Power of Your Brain to Triumph Over Mean Behaviors

The following strategies are powerful antidotes to negative feelings that can be triggered by mean words and actions. Practicing them will help you learn to prevent mean behaviors from getting under your skin.

Protective Shield. Envision a shield that completely surrounds you and that no one else can see. Your shield protects you from mean words and actions. It has the power to dissolve the impact of meanness. Picture yourself bathed in protective light within the safety of your shield. You feel safe, strong, and happy no matter what's going on around you. Feel the protective energy inside you. Every night before you go to bed and every morning when you wake up, picture yourself surrounded by your shield and safe within it. If any meanness comes your way, envision your shield protecting you from its effects. Create a "Protective Shield Statement" that helps you feel safe, strong, and untouched by anyone's mean words. Write it here and say it silently to yourself whenever you need to. Here's an example: "I am safe and protected every second of the day."

The Comfort of a Friend. Think about someone in your life who believes in you and thinks you're the best. If no one comes to mind, use your powers of envisioning to create a person who fills this role. Or, use a character from a book or movie. Have this person tell you wonderful, positive things about yourself. You feel powerful, respected, and admired around him or her. See this person now. Picture him or her as clearly as you can. Now have this person tell you something reassuring. Have his or her words soothe any hurt you feel. Let these words fill your brain, your heart, your entire body. Feel the words giving you a sense of comfort. Below, write down some soothing words this person might say.

Self-Compassion. If you feel hurt or diminished by someone else, tell yourself something kind, supportive, and healing, like, "I know this hurts right now, but these words aren't true, and these feelings are temporary." Be as kind and compassionate to yourself as possible. Do something healthy that helps you feel better, like talking to a trusted person, engaging in creative projects, or doing healthy physical activities. What other healthy healing things could you do? List at least four ideas here:

 From *Create a Culture of Kindness in Middle School* by Naomi Drew, M.A., with Christa M. Tinari, M.A., copyright © 2017. This page may be reproduced for individual, classroom, or small group work only. For all other uses, contact Free Spirit Publishing Inc. at www.freespirit.com/permissions.

Advice from Teens on Detaching from Mean Words and Actions

Consider these wise words from teens. They'll help you feel strong and whole in the face of meanness.

"Here's how I look at it: If they're spending their time trying to get a reaction out of you, it's just not worth giving them the satisfaction. There's no point in talking back. It's better to ignore what they're saying and focus on something else." —8th-grade girl

"It's not worth getting into a fight over some of the stuff kids do. I know I'm a different kind of person than they are, and that's okay. It's good just to be your own self and let their words slide off your back." —9th-grade boy

"Sometimes kids call people names just to be cool. They're trying to make you feel powerless and themselves powerful. Try to ignore it. Normally if I walk away and ignore them, they'll just forget about it. Sometimes I ask myself if I did something wrong. If I did I try to fix it. Other times I just realize that it's their loss. If it keeps on happening, I find an adult to talk about it with." —9th-grade girl

"If someone's name-calling I try to ignore them. If you're with people who are disrespectful, you need to hang around with other people." —8th-grade boy

"Let it go. People can talk all they want, but they can't hurt you if you don't let them. If it really bothers you, talk to the school counselor or someone else who can keep it private." —9th-grade boy

Now think about how *you* can detach from mean words. One important way is through positive self-talk. You have the ability to fill your brain with thoughts that make you feel whole and strong. Here are some statements that will do just that. Say them to yourself for an immediate boost:

- I'm not going to let their mean words take up space in my brain!
- I'm a great person just as I am.
- I refuse to give away my power.
- I'm stronger inside than even I realize.
- I know how to make myself feel better, and I'm going to start right now.

What other statements can you add to this list? Write them here.

From *Create a Culture of Kindness in Middle School* by Naomi Drew, M.A., with Christa M. Tinari, M.A., copyright © 2017. This page may be reproduced for individual, classroom, or small group work only. For all other uses, contact Free Spirit Publishing Inc. at www.freespirit.com/permissions.

SECTION 5

COPING WITH AND COUNTERACTING BULLYING

LESSON 40 Bullying vs. Teasing

CHARACTER CONNECTIONS
empathy / personal responsibility / conscience

Lesson 40 helps students understand the difference between bullying and teasing and that bullying hurts everyone involved, including bystanders.

Students will
- learn the definition of bullying
- reflect on the impact of bullying
- consider what they can do to counteract and decrease bullying

Materials
- handouts: "The Definition of Bullying" (page 198) and "A True Story of Bullying" (page 199)

Preparation

Prior to the lesson, choose a student who will read "A True Story of Bullying" aloud. Give the student a copy of the story to review ahead of time.

On the board, write the following:

Bullying affects everyone:
The person who is bullied
The person who bullies
The bystanders who witness the bullying

Introduction

Say: **We hear a lot about bullying in the news and at school, so it's important to clearly understand exactly what bullying is and what it means.** Pass out "The Definition of Bullying" handout and ask a volunteer to read the full definition aloud. Emphasize that bullying is always meant to do harm. Teasing, on the other hand, can be annoying and may make people mad, but it's generally not intended to do harm. Say: **If someone says or does something to purposely harm you or hurt your feelings, that's bullying.** Entertain responses and questions.

Ask for examples of teasing in contrast to bullying. Make it clear that even when teasing isn't meant maliciously, if it bothers one of the parties involved, it isn't okay to do. Also, there are times when teasing might start off as playful but tips over the edge into being mean. Be clear that if it upsets the other person, it's not acceptable. Emphasize that we all have different thresholds of tolerance for teasing. Ask: **How about if you say you were just kidding? Is it up to the other person to see it as a joke?** (Answer: No. If the other person finds it offensive, it's up to you to stop.)

Ask: **What about kids who others think of as "too sensitive"? Is it their responsibility to toughen up, or is it the responsibility of others to be more understanding?** (Answer: If someone's hurt or offended by something we say or do, we need to back off. It's not our role to judge how sensitive he or she should be.) Remind students that we never know what others might be going through, and when they're dealing with a lot of stress, they'll likely be more affected by things people say. It's important to be aware of this when we interact with others.

Discussion and Activity

Direct students' attention to the words on the board, beginning with "Bullying affects everyone."

Ask: **How does bullying affect kids who are targeted?** (Possible answers: Effects might include sadness, shame, depression, a sense of worthlessness, not wanting to go to school, stomachaches, sleep problems, and in some cases suicidal thoughts.) Be clear that not all kids who are bullied have extreme reactions. A lot depends on other factors. For example, if someone is going through a hard time at home, the effects of bullying are likely to be magnified.

Ask: **How does *witnessing* bullying as a bystander affect people?** (Possible answers: Bystanders often feel fearful, anxious, or self-protective. When kids witness bullying and do nothing to help, they're often left with guilt and shame.) Ask: **What does bullying do to the atmosphere at school?** Discuss.

Ask: **Who else is negatively affected by bullying?** (Answer: The person who bullies.) Share the following information: According to stopbullying.gov, kids who bully often end up abusing alcohol or drugs, getting into fights, getting in trouble with the law, or becoming abusive adults. They are also at greater risk for suicide. Take questions and comments in response to this data.

Say: **The story you're about to hear was written by a middle schooler and is a true example of bullying.** Distribute "A True Story of Bullying" and have the student you chose earlier read the story aloud.

Ask: **How was this student bullied?** (Answer: Kids made fun of his religion, culture, language, and accent. They tried to make him feel like he didn't belong.) Say: **Imagine having to leave your home and friends and move to a new land without knowing the language or customs, only to face an entire year of mistreatment. How would you have felt if this were you?**

Ask: **Think about the bystanders in this story. What might they have been thinking as they witnessed this bullying situation? Why do you think no one helped the boy being bullied? What could people have done to help? How might things have been different if even one person had helped?**

Say: **Bystanders are in a powerful position to become upstanders and help people who are bullied. But bystanders sometimes do things that make bullying situations worse. What are some of these things?** (Possible answers: Join in; ignore what's going on; laugh; point.) **On the other hand, what can bystanders do to *help* someone who's being bullied?** (Possible answers: Get help; stand by the side of the person who's being bullied; tell others to stop.)

Note: We'll discuss bystanders further in Lesson 43: "Be an Upstander in the Face of Bullying."

Ask: **If you saw someone going through something similar to what the boy in this story endured, what could you do?** Stress that you don't have to be an upstander alone. Remind students that partnering up with someone else can make it easier to help. Also emphasize that support can come in many forms. Offering a kind word, standing by the person's side, or checking in with the person later can help a lot.

Wrap-Up

Tell students that in an upcoming lesson they'll be learning more things they can do if they're being bullied or if someone they know is. For now, have them answer the questions at the end of both handouts as homework.

Follow-Up

Discuss in depth your students' responses to the questions on the "A True Story of Bullying" handout. Guide them to put themselves in the place of the boy who was bullied, imagining themselves as him. Ask what their lives might be like if they actually were him.

Note: When your students consider how they could have helped, guide them away from giving pat answers they think you want to hear. Encourage them to look honestly at the reality of helping in the face of their own fears. Ask how we can make it less scary for bystanders to intervene in bullying situations.

Enrichment Activity

Depending on where you live, bullying—or certain aspects of it—may be illegal. Have students research what the laws in your area say about bullying and write reports on what they learn. Also, have students read your school's anti-bullying policy and summarize the key points. Afterward, discuss what students learned. Ask them to think about bullying that goes on under the radar—at places or times adults are less likely to notice. Ask what some of those places and times are. In these situations, what's the most important thing they can do? (Answer: Report it confidentially to an adult.)

The Definition of Bullying

bullying: Deliberate, aggressive behavior intended to harm another person. Bullying is usually characterized by an imbalance of power between the people involved, is often repetitive, and can be done face-to-face or through electronic media.

Bullying may include:

- verbal taunts and put-downs
- humiliation
- threats and intimidation
- stealing someone's property or using threats to take their things
- exclusion
- the hurtful use of texting, tweeting, websites, social media, and other digital or online modes of communication
- physical aggression or violence of any kind

Remember, bullying affects *everyone*:

- The person who is bullied
- The person who bullies
- The bystanders who witness the bullying

REAL-LIFE CHALLENGE

» Bullying is always wrong, and we can all do things to stop it. Do some research into what kids can do to help address and reduce bullying. What ideas seem most realistic and useful? Write them down in your journal and add some of your own. Challenge yourself to put these ideas into action. Make a pact with a friend to do this together.

» Search on YouTube for "Stop Bullying: Speak Up Special Presentation." This is a Cartoon Network video. Start at 15:30 and watch straight through to the end. Afterward, write in your journal about the three most important things you learned from the people in this video. Join with a friend to come up with three great ways to pass on the information you learned. Put together something that can be posted on social media. Spread the word!

 From *Create a Culture of Kindness in Middle School* by Naomi Drew, M.A., with Christa M. Tinari, M.A., copyright © 2017. This page may be reproduced for individual, classroom, or small group work only. For all other uses, contact Free Spirit Publishing Inc. at www.freespirit.com/permissions.

A True Story of Bullying

This story was written by a middle school boy who moved from his country of birth with giant hopes, only to face cruel bullying. Imagine what this was like for him as you read his words. Then answer the questions that follow.

I was bullied in sixth grade by a group of mean boys. I had just moved to this country from Asia (leaving my awesome friends and the relatives I loved). I became a new student in my school and couldn't speak English very well. I was in E.S.L. (special classes for learning English as a second language) for two years. I thought kids would be nice to me, but I was wrong. Every day these boys made fun of my religion, my culture, my language, my accent, and everything else. I felt so bad I wanted to go back to my country. So I decided to tell my mom about it. She also couldn't speak English well. My mom told me to ignore the mean kids. I did what she said, but they kept doing it. I endured this situation for a whole year. After the horrible year passed, I asked my mom to ask the board of education to let me repeat sixth grade, because I didn't want to be with those same people in seventh grade. Things got a lot better when I repeated my grade. But I didn't have any friends. Then in E.S.L. I met three awesome kids. Young was from Korea, Alexandros was from Greece, and Raymond was from China. They were my new best friends. Young went back to her country, but we still text each other, and Alex and Raymond are still here. I am now enjoying my life with great people around me. But I won't ever forget my first awful year in this school.

- What is your gut feeling about the way this boy was treated? Explain.

- Imagine being this boy. Describe what it might be like to come to a new country where everything is unfamiliar and then to have to endure what he went through.

- What would you have done to address this situation if you were this boy?

- If you were a bystander witnessing this boy being bullied, what would you do? Consider what might happen if you were to speak up. Try to be as honest as possible.

- If you were a good friend of the boys who were doing the bullying, what could you do about this situation? Again, consider all the implications, and be as honest as possible.

- Years from now when they look back, how do you think the kids who bullied this boy will feel about what they did? If you were one of these kids, how would you feel later?

From *Create a Culture of Kindness in Middle School* by Naomi Drew, M.A., with Christa M. Tinari, M.A., copyright © 2017. This page may be reproduced for individual, classroom, or small group work only. For all other uses, contact Free Spirit Publishing Inc. at www.freespirit.com/permissions.

If Someone Bullies You

CHARACTER CONNECTIONS

self-compassion / personal responsibility / empathy

Lesson 41 gives students steps to take if they're being bullied.

Students will	Materials
• understand that if they are being bullied, it's not their fault • know that it's essential to tell someone if they're being bullied • role-play asking for help	• handouts: "Real Stories About Bullying" (pages 202-203) and "If You're Being Bullied" (pages 204-205)

Introduction

Say: **Bullying is wrong. Period. There is *never* any justification for it. We all need to work toward eliminating it completely. Today we're going to talk about specific things we need to do if we're being bullied.**

Ask: **Why is it never okay to bully someone?** Entertain responses, reminding students that your school takes bullying very seriously and that in many places it's against the law and has real consequences.

Discussion and Activity

Distribute both handouts. Have students look at "Real Stories About Bullying." Say: **Some of these stories might be difficult to hear. If anyone wants to speak with me privately after this lesson, please let me know and I'll make the time.** Ask a student to read aloud the first story, told by a boy who was bullied. Discuss student responses to this story.

Note: These stories may bring up pain and shame in some students. Be aware, and be available. If you're not comfortable handling the difficult feelings or experiences they share, arrange to have them speak with your school counselor or social worker.

Ask: **How is asking for help different from tattling or snitching?** Confront the taboo on "snitching" and emphasize that asking for help is about preserving your well-being and safety. It's *not* about getting someone else in trouble.

Have students set this handout aside and look at "If You're Being Bullied." Ask for student volunteers to read aloud each bullet point. Discuss each one and answer questions as they arise.

- ***Remember that being bullied doesn't mean there's anything wrong with you!*** Tell students that one of the most devastating parts of being bullied is that it can cause us to doubt ourselves. Self-doubt and shame are two of the most common reactions to bullying, and both are damaging. Ask students what they can do to reclaim their confidence and strength if they're being bullied. Have students list ideas on their handouts. Be sure the ideas include talking to a trusted person and releasing pain through activities that fully absorb students and express their interests, talents, or passions. Briefly discuss specific activities kids might engage in. Sports, exercise, art, music, and volunteering are some great choices.
- ***You NEVER need to suffer through bullying alone. Don't try to. Reach out for help.*** Ask: **Why is talking to someone when you need help a sign of strength, not weakness?** Let students know that reaching out for help is a way of acknowledging that they don't deserve to be bullied. Also

remind students that every kid has the right to go to school in peace. All fifty states in the United States have anti-bullying laws for that reason, as do some provinces in Canada.

- *Remember that everyone experiences challenges in life, and these challenges may include being bullied, teased, put down, or excluded.* Help students come up with coping skills to use in the face of bullying, drawing on strategies discussed throughout this lesson and others. Tell them this, too: **Research shows that helping someone else is one of the top ways to counteract anxiety, sadness, and depression.** On the back of their handout, have students write down two ways they can actively help others.
- *Know that being bullied doesn't mean your life will be awful.* Stress that people are resilient and we have the ability to bounce back from difficult experiences. We can rebuild our confidence and optimism in many ways. Often, people who've been bullied gain extra compassion and inner strength. Some people channel the pain of being bullied into motivation to make their lives better than ever. Many people who've been bullied go on to achieve great things. If you like, guide students to look up famous and successful people who were bullied.
- *Remember that you can reprogram your brain back to strength.* Guide your students through the two envisioning processes on the handout. Discuss questions that come up about how these practices can help them cope with bullying. Write some examples of supportive words for the first envisioning process ("Picture yourself surrounded with loving energy") on the board for kids struggling to come up with something positive to say about themselves. They can then copy these words into their journals as "go-to" statements. For example, "You deserve the best because you *are* the best. I'll be by your side no matter what." Tell students they can also practice saying these statements in the mirror at home.
- *Keep talking to people who can help, and don't stop talking to them until the bullying ends.* Remind students that you are available to talk and that they have many other resources at school, too.

Wrap-Up

Have students read all the stories on the "Real Stories About Bullying" handout and answer the questions as homework.

Follow-Up

- Review the "Real Stories About Bullying" handout and go over answers to questions. How did these stories affect your students? Do any of the experiences they read about sound familiar? Remind students that if they need to talk to you about a bullying situation they're involved in or aware of, you'll make yourself available for a private conversation.
- Assign this real-life challenge: Share this lesson's handouts, and what you've learned, with adults in your family. Emphasize that bullying is *not* a rite of passage, nor is it something any kid should have to handle on their own. Let them know how much their support and understanding mean to you.

Enrichment Activity

Have students visit the anti-bullying websites listed on the "If You're Being Bullied" handout and create posters that include five pieces of information they found on these sites.

Real Stories About Bullying

"There are three words in the English language that take the most courage to say. They are, 'Please help me.' And when you say them, your life changes."
—psychologist Dan Gottlieb

Read each story, then answer the questions on the next page.

From a boy who was bullied and didn't speak up:

"It really would have made life a lot easier had I just spoken up sooner . . . after the first day, or first couple of days. I really wish I would have told someone, but instead, I kept it inside . . . People don't realize there's a huge difference between tattling and telling. If you're tattling on somebody, you're just trying to get someone in trouble, but if you're telling someone about a problem like a bully, you're not tattling, you're actually trying to help somebody."

From a girl who experienced a subtle form of bullying:

"I haven't been outright bullied in the usual ways, but there's this person who excludes me constantly. Whenever I'm around her, I get this feeling of insecurity. Her presence alone makes me feel that way. She's really popular and her body language tells me I don't belong. She looks the other way whenever I speak and completely ignores me. She always makes me feel shoved aside. Sometimes after school she walks right past my house with her friends and even if I'm standing right there, she never invites me to join them. It's like I'm invisible. I tried to tell myself I was being paranoid or it was all in my head. But it's not. This is real. Finally I talked to my parents and they helped me realize there was nothing wrong with me, and that she was purposely leaving me out. After that I started to see that this girl isn't someone I would even want to be around. She's not a nice person."

From a teenage boy looking back on being bullied constantly in middle school:

"I didn't really go to the teachers 'cause . . . I would be called a crybaby, a tattletale, and I didn't really want that to be added to the list of names I was called. I definitely should have . . . told my teachers, even gone to the principal, especially because there were specific people that were continuously doing it. And when I didn't stop it, they felt that that was their freedom to just keep doing it. So while I thought that [not telling anyone] was going to stop the name-calling, it was just helping condone it."

From a bystander who watched bullying take place but didn't help:

"I've stood there and done nothing because I'm worried about them. I don't know why I didn't do anything. I could have done a lot of things . . . I could have told the teacher. I could have said something to make the bully go away. But not in a mean voice. I would just say, 'Please leave my friend alone.'"

From *Create a Culture of Kindness in Middle School* by Naomi Drew, M.A., with Christa M. Tinari, M.A., copyright © 2017. This page may be reproduced for individual, classroom, or small group work only. For all other uses, contact Free Spirit Publishing Inc. at www.freespirit.com/permissions.

- Which of these stories do you relate to the most? Why?

- Why does saying "Please help me" require so much courage? Why is it so important to say these words if you're being bullied?

- Why is keeping your feelings inside a harmful idea?

- What should you do if you realize that the way you're treating someone is actually bullying?

- What can you do if you witness bullying taking place?

REAL-LIFE CHALLENGE

» As you go through your day at school and after school, notice if any forms of bullying are taking place. Journal about what you observe and questions you might have. Then talk about all of it with a trusted adult or close friend. Ask for support if you need it, if you're experiencing bullying, if you're witnessing it, or if you're doing it to someone else.

From *Create a Culture of Kindness in Middle School* by Naomi Drew, M.A., with Christa M. Tinari, M.A., copyright © 2017. This page may be reproduced for individual, classroom, or small group work only. For all other uses, contact Free Spirit Publishing Inc. at www.freespirit.com/permissions.

If You're Being Bullied

- **Remember that being bullied doesn't mean there's anything wrong with you!** Bullying is always the responsibility of the person doing the bullying and never the fault of the one being bullied. A survey of 13,000 students in fifth through twelfth grade revealed that reminding themselves of this fact helped them tremendously as they coped with bullying.

  If you begin to doubt yourself or if you feel a lot of negative feelings as a result of bullying, think about what you can do to rebuild your strength and confidence. List three positive steps or activities here:

  1.

  2.

  3.

- **You NEVER need to suffer through bullying alone. Don't try to. Reach out for help.** Getting help from friends, family, teachers, counselors, or other trusted adults is a sign of strength, not weakness. It shows you are strong enough to take a stand for your own well-being.

- **Remember that everyone experiences challenges in life, and these challenges may include being bullied, teased, put down, or excluded.** These experiences are difficult, but they do not define who you are. If you're being bullied, it's natural to feel hurt and embarrassed. A lot of kids feel this way. You can use coping skills to be resilient, and you may find that you're even stronger after facing these difficulties.

  What are three coping skills you can use to help yourself gain resilience?

  1.

  2.

  3.

- **Know that being bullied doesn't mean your life will be awful.** Kids who are bullied also have friends, hobbies, and fun experiences. And most people who are bullied do *not* hurt themselves or others. They get through it and go on to live good lives. You can, too.

- **Remember that you can reprogram your brain back to strength.** To create new neural pathways that will help you feel stronger and more confident, envision the following scenarios every night:
  - Picture yourself surrounded with loving energy. Picture a loving person, either someone you know in real life or someone you create in your imagination, who accepts you unconditionally. Imagine this person speaking to you and telling you all the things that are wonderful about you.
  - Picture yourself feeling confident and powerful, and triumphing over whoever is trying to bring you down. Picture this in great detail. See yourself in the Dignity Stance, standing tall and strong, and speaking to the person who is targeting you. If negative voices come into your mind, refocus on feeling strong and confident.

 From *Create a Culture of Kindness in Middle School* by Naomi Drew, M.A., with Christa M. Tinari, M.A., copyright © 2017. This page may be reproduced for individual, classroom, or small group work only. For all other uses, contact Free Spirit Publishing Inc. at www.freespirit.com/permissions.

- **Keep talking to people who can help, *and don't stop talking to them until the bullying ends.*** Remember, you have the right to get help if you're being bullied. You deserve a happy life and a happy future. Write down the names of three people who can give you the support you need and who will keep supporting and helping you until the bullying ends:

  1.

  2.

  3.

»»»»»»»»»»»»»»»»»»»»»»»»»

Need to talk to someone confidentially? Go to the following sources to find trained people who care.

Boys Town National Hotline: 1-800-448-3000. This number is for boys and girls even though the message says Boys Town national hotline. It's free, confidential, and available 24-7. Be patient. Sometimes there's a short wait.

Boys Town National Textline: Text "Voice" to 20121. Free and confidential. Available 24-7.

Chat or email here: yourlifeyourvoice.org

Want to know more about what you can do about bullying? Visit the following websites for additional information.

No Bullying
nobullying.com
Look for the "Teens" section of this website to learn about how to identify bullying, what can cause it, what forms it can take, and much more.

No Place 4 Hate
www.noplace4hate.org/real-bullying-stories
This site helps kids deal with bullying, prejudice, and bigotry. You can read stories written by kids who've experienced these issues and also learn what to do if you're in a similar situation.

Teens Against Bullying
www.pacerteensagainstbullying.org
This site can help you take action against bullying. Read about kids who've been bullied, find out how they're helping make bullying a thing of the past, and learn specific things you can do if you witness, experience, or initiate bullying.

From *Create a Culture of Kindness in Middle School* by Naomi Drew, M.A., with Christa M. Tinari, M.A., copyright © 2017. This page may be reproduced for individual, classroom, or small group work only. For all other uses, contact Free Spirit Publishing Inc. at www.freespirit.com/permissions.

If You've Bullied Others

CHARACTER CONNECTIONS

integrity / compassion / personal responsibility

Lesson 42 helps students take responsibility for bullying and teaches them how to make amends.

Students will

- reflect on the effects of bullying on people who have bullied
- understand that people who bully are often left with deep regret
- learn how to make amends if they've hurt another person

Materials

- handouts: "Checklist: Am I Bullying Someone?" (page 208) and "Real Words from People Who Have Bullied Others" (page 209)

Preparation

On the board, write the following pledge. You might also want to write these words on poster paper and display them permanently in your space.

> *The No Bullying Pledge*
> *I will not take part in any actions that purposely hurt another person.*
> *I will join with friends to stand up for kids who are being picked on.*

»»» **Online Resource** »»»»»»»»»»»
If desired, visit cyberbullying.org and search for the post "Parenting Kids Today to Prevent Adult Bullying Tomorrow" by Sameer Hinduja, and share it with parents. Encourage them to read it and consider the recommended steps for raising kids who don't bully.
»»»»»»»»»»»»»»»»»»»»»»»»

Introduction

Say: **Some people are aware that they're bullying, while others may bully someone else without even realizing that what they're doing is bullying.** Ask: **What differentiates bullying from teasing?** (Answer: The intent to do harm. Also, bullying is generally repeated over time.) Say: **The confidential checklist I'm about to give you will help you figure out whether you might be bullying. No one will see your answers but you, unless you want to share them with me. Fill it out as honestly as you can. Bullying can only end when we take responsibility for our actions.**

Distribute the "Checklist: Am I Bullying Someone?" handout and have students fill it out. Say: **When you're finished, fold or cover the checklist so only the bottom part of the handout is showing. Put it in your desk. We'll be addressing the section on making amends later in this lesson.**

Discussion and Activity

Give students about five minutes to complete the checklist. Then distribute the "Real Words from People Who Have Bullied Others" handout. Have a volunteer read aloud the introduction at the top, as well as the first quote. Ask: **What was the main feeling this person had?** (Answer: Overwhelming guilt.)

Now ask four different volunteers to read aloud the other four stories from people who have bullied. Pause between each story to have students briefly identify the feelings each person has been living with.

After all five stories have been read aloud, ask the following questions:

- Why did all of these people feel as bad as they did?
- What do you think would be the greatest wish of each person?
- What can we learn from the experiences you just heard about?

Note: Help students understand that if they've bullied others, what they *did* was bad, but this doesn't mean they're bad people. Some of the people from the stories they just heard felt so guilty that they falsely believed they themselves were bad. This is why making amends is so important. It helps heal the person who did the bullying, as well as the person who was harmed.

Now have students look at the last section of their first handout. Go over the ways to make amends and discuss each one. Tell students that these steps can be used in any situation where they've mistreated someone, including friends, classmates, or family members.

Wrap-Up

Direct students' attention to the No Bullying Pledge on the board and have them read it aloud together. Discuss what the pledge means to them. Ask them how easy or difficult it might be to always honor the words of this pledge. Ask students what might stand in their way and what they can do to remind themselves to live by these words.

Follow-Up

During this lesson, pay close attention to students' facial expressions, body language, and other cues to determine if you need to check in with anyone afterward. If your instincts tell you someone might need to talk further, arrange for a private time to do so. Encourage all students to keep making amends for hurting anyone in their lives, whether through bullying or any other unkind behavior. Offer additional guidance to kids who aren't sure how to make amends or feel hesitant about doing so. See what's standing in the way and help them come up with specific things they might say or do. Offer to help them rehearse the process of making amends.

Enrichment Activity

Put students in pairs and have them role-play taking responsibility for bullying another person. Then have them brainstorm a variety of ways to make amends. If there's time, have them role-play asking for forgiveness and making amends.

Checklist: Am I Bullying Someone?

It's possible to bully someone without even realizing that it's bullying. In order to understand clearly what you're doing and pave the way for making things right, consider the following list carefully and honestly. Put a check mark next to any action you have purposely done to the same person more than once or twice.

- ☐ Put him or her down
- ☐ Try to embarrass or humiliate him or her
- ☐ Exclude the person from activities or from sitting with you or your group
- ☐ Text, email, or post demeaning or hurtful messages to or about the person
- ☐ Participate in ranking him or her on embarrassing or demeaning websites
- ☐ Spread rumors or circulate mean or embarrassing gossip about the person
- ☐ Join in with people who are bullying him or her
- ☐ Threaten him or her
- ☐ Inflict physical harm
- ☐ Try to convince other people not to be his or her friend
- ☐ Get someone else to bully the person
- ☐ Make him or her feel less worthy or valuable than you
- ☐ Force the person to do things against his or her will
- ☐ Do any of the above when angry, and justify it by telling yourself the person did something to you first
- ☐ Do any of the above and act like it was just a joke
- ☐ Do any of the above and rationalize it by saying the person reacted because he or she was too sensitive
- ☐ Do any of the above because you believe that person deserves it

If you've done even one of the things on this checklist, it's important that you make amends. It is likely to help the person you've bullied, and it will also help you. To make amends, here's what you need to do:

- First, promise yourself you will never harass or harm this person again.
- Ask for the support of someone you trust to help you stop bullying.
- Reach out to the person you've hurt and apologize for what you've done. You can do this in person, via email or text, or by sending a handwritten note.
- Come up with some way of making things right. For example, you might offer to help the person you've hurt with something he or she could use support in.
- Find a way to speak out against all forms of bullying and to be an upstander for anyone who's being mistreated.
- Help your school form an anti-bullying committee or club if one doesn't already exist. Get involved, stay involved, and get your friends involved.

 From *Create a Culture of Kindness in Middle School* by Naomi Drew, M.A., with Christa M. Tinari, M.A., copyright © 2017. This page may be reproduced for individual, classroom, or small group work only. For all other uses, contact Free Spirit Publishing Inc. at www.freespirit.com/permissions.

Real Words from People Who Have Bullied Others

Many people who've bullied others feel the need to express remorse. This is the case for the people whose words are below. Consider their stories and then answer the questions that follow.

"Bullying is a learned thing. I learned from those who did it to me that I could show power over someone. I hurt a lot of people along my path, and for that I'm truly sorry."

"I was a bully in school. I'm not going to justify my behavior in any way. There are no words to describe how monstrous I was. There was one particular kid, 'Gina,' whom I bullied mercilessly. I am torn up with guilt and haunted by my past actions. I have nightmares about what I did to her."

"I was a bully. I became a bully after enduring years of physical abuse at the hands of my father, as well as psychological and physical abuse by my classmates. I never seemed to fit in at school, had no social skills. When I finally identified a child whom I was capable of bullying, I jumped at the opportunity to release my frustration, at the same time perhaps redeem myself in the eyes of my peers, both of which were a success for me at the time. I am still regretful, some thirty years later."

"I regret not helping a girl who was being bullied, which I guess makes me a bully myself. Last year during school, I witnessed her get bullied to the point of sobbing, screaming, and throwing things at the tormentors outside. The teachers had to have heard or seen it happening, but they did nothing, and neither did anyone else. They just watched it go down. I had wanted to be her friend for a while, and I knew she had been bullied a lot before. I will always regret not trying to stop them, or for not trying to comfort her. I can't imagine having something like that happening to me with so many people watching, only to have them do nothing. I'm so sorry."

"I bullied my younger brother when we were kids. He grew up hating me. He was right. I did all the terrible things he hated me for. Even though I've asked him for forgiveness, I will never be able to heal the wounds I caused. I wish I could turn back the clock and make things right, but that's not possible. When we cause deep wounds in others, we can never make them go away. They remain always, like a jagged scar—a permanent reminder. To all the kids out there who cause wounds in others, think about what you're doing. You will carry the burden of those wounds for the rest of your life. And when the person you harmed recalls their most devastating memories, yours will be the face they see."

- What were some of the feelings these people expressed?

- How have these people suffered as a result of bullying others?

- If you know someone who is bullying others, what can you encourage him or her to do?

- If you're bullying someone, what can you do?

From *Create a Culture of Kindness in Middle School* by Naomi Drew, M.A., with Christa M. Tinari, M.A., copyright © 2017. This page may be reproduced for individual, classroom, or small group work only. For all other uses, contact Free Spirit Publishing Inc. at www.freespirit.com/permissions.

Be an Upstander in the Face of Bullying

CHARACTER CONNECTIONS

kindness / courage / compassion / personal responsibility

Lesson 43 helps students gain the courage to stand up for people who are bullied.

Students will

- understand that it's every person's responsibility to help people who are bullied
- learn and review five upstander strategies
- practice upstander strategies through role-play

Materials

- handouts: "The Dignity Stance" (page 96), "Who Do You Identify With?" (page 212), "Five Upstander Strategies to Know and Use" (page 213), and "Teen Upstanders" (page 214)

Introduction

Say: **When we see bullying taking place, we can either be bystanders or upstanders. What's the difference between the two? Some of you may have already acted as upstanders. If you have, what did you do?** Ask: **Why is it sometimes hard to be an upstander?** Briefly entertain responses.

Discussion and Activity

Distribute the "Who Do You Identify With?" handout. Say: **Do you ever feel like this middle school boy?** Have a student read the quote beginning with, "I feel disappointed in myself."

Explain that when this student said "fight," he wasn't referring to physical fighting, but to standing up and speaking out. Say: **The more kids who do this, the easier it gets for everyone. In schools where it's common for people to speak up, kids create a culture where it's easier to be kind than to be mean.**

Say: **Now let's hear from a middle school girl who had a different experience.** Have another student read the quote beginning, "I've been bullied."

Ask: **How did this girl's experience differ from the boy's? Who do you identify with more? Why?** Have students briefly describe the experiences and feelings behind their answers. Caution them not to use real names or identifying factors.

Say: **Now I'm going to give you five things you can do to strengthen your upstander capabilities.** Distribute the "Five Upstander Strategies to Know and Use" handout. Discuss each strategy, addressing any questions that arise. For the first three strategies, you'll also conduct role-plays demonstrating their use. Keep each role-play brief, and don't have role-players act out the bullying—just the upstander responses to the situations described. Refer to the "Dignity Stance" handout if needed, reminding students to use this posture as they role-play being upstanders.

Support people who are being bullied.
Role-play #1 (3 students): *Student A is new at school. Students B and C notice other kids calling him names and laughing at him. Instead of ignoring what's going on, they walk over to him, stand by his side, and say, "Come on, let's go." As they walk away they say supportive things that help him feel better.*

Distract those who are bullying.
Role-play #2 (5 students): *Students A, B, C, and D are in the lunchroom. When Student E walks in, they start giving her looks and calling her mean names. Student A decides to distract them. She says, "Is anyone going to Alex's party this weekend? I wasn't sure what time it starts. Does anyone know?" By doing so, she brings everyone's attention to a whole new subject.*

Reason with the people who are bullying.
Role-play #3 (3 students): *Student A is mad at Student B. She has an old text from Student B that contains embarrassing personal information about Student B. She tells Student C she's going to send it out to everyone she knows. Student C decides to reason with her. She reminds her that what she's about to do is against the school rules (and maybe against the law). It's considered cyberbullying and she could get in a lot of trouble for doing it. She says, "I'd hate to see that happen."*

Go for help.

Ask the person if he or she is okay.

Wrap-Up

Tell students that upstanders are changing the world and making history. Talk about teenager Jaylen Arnold, who'd experienced severe bullying because of disabilities. This prompted Jaylen to start working on making the world a kinder place for anyone with disabilities. Distribute the "Teen Upstanders" hand-out. As homework, have students read the handout and answer the questions at the end.

Follow-Up

Discuss students' answers to the questions at the end of "Teen Upstanders." Keep encouraging students to follow the examples they've learned about.

Enrichment Activities

- Have students search online or elsewhere for other stories of inspiring upstanders. Ask them to reflect on ways they can emulate the upstanders' actions. Then have students write short plays illustrating upstander behavior. They can perform dramatic readings of these scenarios for their families, your group, or for another group. Encourage them to strive toward similar behavior in real life.
- In their journals, have students write down the name of one person they've observed being mistreated and one thing they can do to help, even if it's just checking in with that person to see if he or she is okay.
- Do the 10-Minute Time Cruncher "Being an Upstander" on page 215.

Who Do You Identify With?

Consider these quotes and then answer the questions that follow each one.

"I feel disappointed in myself. I feel I can be a better advocate for kids being bullied. Instead of talking to a teacher or to the kids face to face, I always choose to ignore and walk away. It's like fight or flight: I always choose 'flight' but I wish I had the courage to choose 'fight' by helping the other person." —8th-grade boy

- Why do you think this boy tends to ignore the bullying he sees?

- How might he overcome his fears and help kids who are being bullied?

"I've been bullied, so I know how bad it makes you feel about yourself. That's why I stick up for other people, like a girl in my class who has trouble learning. This other kid always makes mean comments about her. I know she feels bad, so the other day I said something. I didn't care if the kid said something bad back to me. After being bullied myself I realized that I really don't care what others say. You shouldn't just watch someone getting hurt. You should stand up for people." —7th-grade girl

- What do you think most motivates this girl to stand up for others?

- Describe a situation where you either stood up for someone or wished that you had.

- Who do you identify with more on this handout, the boy or the girl? Why?

 From *Create a Culture of Kindness in Middle School* by Naomi Drew, M.A., with Christa M. Tinari, M.A., copyright © 2017. This page may be reproduced for individual, classroom, or small group work only. For all other uses, contact Free Spirit Publishing Inc. at www.freespirit.com/permissions.

Five Upstander Strategies to Know and Use

Support people who are being bullied. This includes standing next to them, walking away with them, walking to class with them, reassuring them that the bullying isn't their fault, and calling or texting them later to make sure they're okay.

Distract those who are bullying. This strategy works best if you know the kids who are bullying. Think of ways you can bring their attention to something else. Say something like, "Hey, that was some game last night. Did you see it?"

Reason with people who are bullying. Tell them it bothers you to see someone being made to suffer. Or tell them you don't want to see them get in trouble, and remind them that if an adult sees what they're doing, they will.

Go for help. Tell an adult what's going on right away. Remember, asking for help is *not* tattling. It's not about getting someone in trouble. It's about preventing future harm. This true story from a girl in sixth grade is a perfect example:

> *"I was bullied by a girl who called me dirty and told everyone not to be friends with me. I started to think about suicide and how nobody wanted me. One girl who didn't believe what the kids said saw me in the bathroom crying and asked me what was wrong. I told her everything. She hugged me and told me I was going to be all right. She told me that she was going to go to her class and get something. When she came back she came with my counselor and my principal. They helped me deal with everything and said that those girls would get into lots of trouble. By the next month I was in my new friend's class."*

Ask the person if he or she is okay. This simple step can take some of the pain out of bullying. You might send a supportive text or email, too, saying something like, "I think you're a really nice person. That kid had no right to talk to you that way."

Be brave. Never forget that you can make a big difference in someone else's life!

From *Create a Culture of Kindness in Middle School* by Naomi Drew, M.A., with Christa M. Tinari, M.A., copyright © 2017. This page may be reproduced for individual, classroom, or small group work only. For all other uses, contact Free Spirit Publishing Inc. at www.freespirit.com/permissions.

Teen Upstanders

"Sometimes people say mean things about me,
but my whole lunch table stands up for me."
—7th-grade boy

The more kids stand up for people, the easier it becomes for others to follow their lead. Read on to learn about some teen upstanders whose examples you can follow.

Teen Upstander Sidney Davis. When Sidney Davis saw some boys teasing a disabled classmate in the lunchroom, she decided she had to speak up. She calmly asked the boys why they were teasing. They told her they were only kidding, and the boy they were teasing didn't mind. Here's what Sidney did next: "I explained that, from my experience, even though he acted unaffected, the teasing and taunting hurts. I revealed that when I was in lower school, my friends would occasionally joke around and tell me I was fat. I always laughed it off, but it really got to me, and also made me extremely self-conscious regarding my weight. As I was speaking, the boys seemed to understand where I was coming from. Their eyes became sympathetic as they realized what they had been doing."

Teen Upstander Jaylen Arnold. When Jaylen Arnold was younger, he was bullied because of a disability. He turned that experience into a mission that's been helping kids across the country. Search online for "Jaylen's Challenge" to read about all of the amazing things he's done.

Teen Upstanders Travis Price and David Shepherd. In 2007, Travis Price and David Shepherd noticed a new kid at their high school being bullied for wearing a pink shirt. They wanted to help, and they came up with a creative way to do it. Search online for "Pink Shirt Day" to see how their upstander actions turned into a movement that's touched the lives of many teens.

- The world needs *you* to be an upstander. What do you plan on doing next time you see someone being mistreated?

- It's sometimes easier to be an upstander when you join with others. How can you join with a friend to initiate upstander behaviors at your school?

- Look online to read more about Jaylen's Challenge and Pink Shirt Day. How can you get an upstander project going in your school?

REAL-LIFE CHALLENGE

» Get your friends together to form an upstander group. Support each other in being upstanders every single day. If you ever feel like you need more courage, call or text a friend in the group to get some support. There's power in numbers.

» Get inspired! Read about other upstanders who take a stand against injustices of many kinds. Search online for "Upstanders Starbucks" to see and hear their stories. What new ideas for being an upstander do these stories give you?

 From *Create a Culture of Kindness in Middle School* by Naomi Drew, M.A., with Christa M. Tinari, M.A., copyright © 2017. This page may be reproduced for individual, classroom, or small group work only. For all other uses, contact Free Spirit Publishing Inc. at www.freespirit.com/permissions.

Being an Upstander

CHARACTER CONNECTIONS

kindness / courage / compassion / personal responsibility

This time cruncher coordinates with Lesson 43, "Be an Upstander in the Face of Bullying" (page 210). It helps students review ways they can support people who are bullied and consider some strategies they plan to use in real life.

Materials

- handout: "Five Upstander Strategies to Know and Use" (page 213)

Directions

Distribute the "Five Upstander Strategies to Know and Use" handout, or have students refer to their copies from Lesson 43. Put students in pairs and have each pair choose an upstander behavior they plan to use if they witness bullying. Have partners role-play applying the strategy they chose. ***Note:*** Direct students *not* to act out the bullying behaviors but to focus instead on how they would respond. Circulate and give coaching as needed.

What Is Cyberbullying?

CHARACTER CONNECTIONS

conscience / responsibility / self-respect

Lesson 44 presents information about cyberbullying.

Students will

- understand the definition of cyberbullying and discuss key facts about cyberbullying
- review their school's cyberbullying policy
- identify prevention strategies for cyberbullying

Materials

- a copy of your school's cyberbullying policy
- handouts: "Cyberbullying Mini-Quiz" (page 218) and "Tips for Preventing Cyberbullying" (page 219)

Preparation

Educate yourself about (or refresh your memory of) your school's current rules about cyberbullying. If your school has a policy or statement in a handbook or online, print out a copy to share with the group.

Take time to review the facts about cyberbullying that are on the "Cyberbullying Mini-Quiz" (page 218) and learn about the various kinds of cyberbullying behaviors. (Concise information about cyberbullying is available at cyberbullying.org/facts.)

Introduction

Say: **Raise your hand if you've heard the term *cyberbullying*. Keep your hand up if you can explain what cyberbullying is.** Call on a volunteer or two. If further clarification or explanation is needed, say: **Cyberbullying is bullying through the use of technology. The founders of the Cyberbullying Research Center define cyberbullying as a situation in which someone intentionally and repeatedly harasses, makes fun of, or mistreats another person on social media sites, through text messages, or in other ways online.**

Discussion and Activity

Distribute the "Cyberbullying Mini-Quiz" and have students complete it. Afterward, review each question, and share the correct answers and explanations that follow.

Cyberbullying Quiz Answers and Explanations

Cyberbullying is now more common than "traditional" bullying that happens face to face. *FALSE.* Although cyberbullying is on the rise, students report being bullied in person more frequently than being cyberbullied. As teens increasingly communicate via technology, however, this may change. Ask: **Why do you think cyberbullying can be especially devastating?** Discuss briefly.

Teens usually use phones, rather than computers, to cyberbully. *TRUE.* Today's teens are using phones more frequently than computers. Since many teens use their phones regularly throughout the day to text and access social media, unwanted communication from someone who is cyberbullying can be hard to escape. In addition, messages and pictures can be shared quickly with many people, potentially increasing the embarrassment and pain of bullying. Caution students that circulating someone else's negative text makes you just as responsible as the person who started it.

Only 10 percent of teens say they have visited a website bashing another student. *FALSE.* Sources such as the website NoBullying.com state that the actual percentage may be as high as 75 percent. These sites can do a lot of harm by spreading false rumors or revealing personal information about someone. These websites may include insults, threats, and unflattering or digitally altered photos. Be sure to let students know that they can speak to you or drop you a confidential note if they have been the target of such a site—or if they want to help a friend. It may be possible to delete the site and identify the students who were involved in creating it and posting to it. If students feel threatened, be sure to report the situation to your principal, counselor, or designated bullying prevention coordinator.

Cyberbullying actions are permanent. *TRUE.* Although it's possible to remove damaging words and pictures from sites where they have been posted, it's very difficult or even impossible to erase something completely from the Internet. The content may have been shared with other people on other sites, and there may be no way to track it all down. Here's what one teen said about this: *"These days there are so many ways you can get bullied. A picture or embarrassing comment can go viral within hours and everyone in your school will know about it. By then you're a social outcast and you can't do anything to delete it. Even if you block it, everybody already knows about it."*

About 25 percent of teens report being cyberbullied at some point. *TRUE.* The Cyberbullying Research Center conducted a study of 15,000 students and found that about one in four teens said they had been cyberbullied sometime in their life. That means that, on average, a class with twenty-five students would include six or seven students who have experienced cyberbullying.

Ask students if the answers to the quiz match up with their own expectations and experiences. Students may have diverse personal experiences with technology and cyberbullying.

Ask: **What social networking sites and apps are most commonly used by students your age? Which ones do you use? What kinds of interactions are taking place on those sites? Have you ever witnessed cyberbullying?** Take responses from students. Caution them not to use real names if they're relating personal stories.

Say: **Now let's take a look at our school's policy on cyberbullying.** Ask a student to read aloud your school's policy. Ask: **What does the policy state are the possible disciplinary consequences of cyberbullying?** If your school's policy does not mention cyberbullying, ask whether or not students feel a specific policy is needed. Note that there can sometimes be serious legal consequences for cyberbullying, especially if messages include threats or sexting. If necessary, explain that sexting is sending or receiving sexually explicit pictures or messages. Instances of sexting can involve the police, and charges may be brought against someone who sent or saved a sext.

Say: **Let's consider some ways we can prevent cyberbullying.** Give students the "Tips for Preventing Cyberbullying" handout. Ask for volunteers to read the sections of the handout aloud. Answer questions students may have. Ask: **Which of these tips are you already using? Which are new to you, and which do you want to try?**

Wrap-Up

Place students in pairs and give them the following prompt: "Something new I learned about cyberbullying is __________. Something I would like to learn more about is __________." Invite students to share their responses. If there isn't enough time to share, students can complete this prompt in their journals. In either case, take note of what they'd like to know more about, and make plans to follow up on these questions.

Follow-Up

Pay attention to cyberbullying situations in the news. Bring a news story to the attention of your group and discuss the situation. Questions to consider might include, "What happened in the story?" "What could have prevented this situation from happening?" "What can be done now?" Encourage students to look for more stories in the news and consider these same questions.

Enrichment Activity

Have students research school rules or area laws about cyberbullying and create materials such as public service announcements, posters, pamphlets, or blogs to educate other students about these laws. If students feel that stronger measures are needed, encourage them to write letters to the school board or other elected officials stating their concerns and making a case for their positions.

Cyberbullying Mini-Quiz

1. Cyberbullying is now more common than "traditional" bullying that happens face to face.
   - ☐ True
   - ☐ False
2. Teens usually use phones, rather than computers, to cyberbully.
   - ☐ True
   - ☐ False
3. Only 10 percent of teens say they have visited a website bashing another student.
   - ☐ True
   - ☐ False
4. Cyberbullying actions are permanent.
   - ☐ True
   - ☐ False
5. About 25 percent of teens report being cyberbullied at some point.
   - ☐ True
   - ☐ False

 From *Create a Culture of Kindness in Middle School* by Naomi Drew, M.A., with Christa M. Tinari, M.A., copyright © 2017. This page may be reproduced for individual, classroom, or small group work only. For all other uses, contact Free Spirit Publishing Inc. at www.freespirit.com/permissions.

Tips for Preventing Cyberbullying

Choose your words wisely. Think before you click!

- Don't post mean, disrespectful, or embarrassing words or pictures.
- Remember that sarcasm and some jokes that might not be hurtful in person can seem meaner or more offensive online.
- Don't like, retweet, or give other fuel to mean posts.
- Don't visit websites that are dedicated to bashing other people.
- Use social media to boost people up, not tear them down.
- Think about who might see your message before deciding whether to send it.
- Don't participate in sites that allow you and other posters to participate anonymously.

Stay safe online.

- Never share your password with anyone but your parents.
- Adjust your privacy settings so that your messages are communicated only to your chosen audience.
- Be careful about what you post. Keep your personal details and information private.
- Log out of your accounts whenever you're not using them.
- Only accept invites from, or respond to, people you know personally.
- Only follow links that appear safe or are sent to you by people you know.
- Be picky about who you friend, follow, and favorite online.
- Never pretend to be someone you're not.

Know your rights and responsibilities.

- Know that it is against school policy (and some laws) to cyberbully.
- Never make threats online, even as a joke.
- Know that authorities can access your online history.
- Remember that even deleted communications can be retrieved by authorities.
- If you witness cyberbullying, report it to an adult.

REAL-LIFE CHALLENGE

» Create a personal statement about how you want to interact with others online. For example, one seventh-grade girl created a statement for Facebook that read, "I want to communicate with you here, but please, no hating and no bullying. Also, no gossiping about anyone. Oh, and try to keep your language respectful. If you agree, 'like.' If you don't agree to this, you might be unfriended or blocked."

What is *your* personal statement?

From *Create a Culture of Kindness in Middle School* by Naomi Drew, M.A., with Christa M. Tinari, M.A., copyright © 2017. This page may be reproduced for individual, classroom, or small group work only. For all other uses, contact Free Spirit Publishing Inc. at www.freespirit.com/permissions.

Responding to Cyberbullying

CHARACTER CONNECTIONS
assertiveness / compassion / empathy / responsibility

Lesson 45 helps students identify safe and effective ways to respond to cyberbullying.
Note: Be sure to do Lesson 44: "What Is Cyberbullying?"(page 216) prior to presenting this lesson.

Students will

- learn positive ways to respond to cyberbullying
- discuss upstander strategies they can use in the face of cyberbullying
- identify and choose specific helpful actions to respond to cyberbullying

Materials

- handouts: "Anyone Could Be Daniel Cui" (page 222), "Cyberbullying Dilemmas" (pages 223–224), and "Responding to Cyberbullying" (page 225)

Preparation

Search online for the video "Facebook Stories: We Are All Daniel Cui" and preview the video in preparation for showing it to students. (If the video is not available, read the "Anyone Could Be Daniel Cui" handout.)

Introduction

Say: **Today we're going to talk about ways we can respond to and counteract cyberbullying.** Show the video "We Are All Daniel Cui," or distribute the "Anyone Could Be Daniel Cui" handout (or both, if you like). Afterward ask: **How did students respond to cyberbullying and act as upstanders in this story? Have you ever seen or participated in anything like this online? Why do you think this story is titled, "Anyone Could Be Daniel Cui"?** Invite students to share stories from their lives, cautioning them not to use real names.

Discussion and Activity

Break students into small groups and distribute the "Cyberbullying Dilemmas" handout. Have each group choose one of the cyberbullying dilemmas to discuss. Say: **Brainstorm five ways the target or bystanders in this situation could respond to the dilemma. Designate one member of your group to record your ideas.** Give students five minutes or so to come up with responses. When the time has elapsed, say: **Let's hear your ideas for responding to cyberbullying.** Call on group members to share their ideas, reading aloud the dilemma first if desired. Be sure to have students focus on specific, concrete ways they can support someone who is being cyberbullied by using upstander strategies.

Distribute the "Responding to Cyberbullying" handout and say: **Here are some additional suggestions for responding to cyberbullying.** Ask for a student volunteer or two to read the list aloud. Let students know they will have about five minutes to put check marks by the responses they think would be most effective.

Wrap-Up

After students have completed the "Responding to Cyberbullying" handout, say: **Let's hear which actions you would be most likely to use, either as an upstander or as the target of the bullying.** Entertain student responses and answer any questions. Ask them under what circumstances it would be most important to tell an adult. Say: **If a direct threat is made to you or someone else, contact an adult immediately.** Stress that *all* threats—whether a person threatens to hurt himself or someone else—should be taken seriously. An adult may even contact the police, who will conduct an investigation to determine if there is a safety concern and whether or not the law was broken.

Follow-Up

Check in with students on a regular basis about bullying behaviors they might be seeing or experiencing online. Have students jot down their own cyberbullying dilemmas based on their real-life experiences. Collect and read the dilemmas. Choose a few to use during a follow-up discussion on cyberbullying (omitting any personal details if needed). Be sure to ask students to describe the most effective ways to respond, and reiterate ways they can help others.

Enrichment Activity

Search online for information about different methods of cyberbullying. (For example, at ipredator.co/cyberbullying-examples you can access a PDF listing forty-two different kinds of cyberbullying tactics, including flaming, impersonation, catfishing, and trolling.) Talk with the group about a few of these cyberbullying methods and refer back to the "Responding to Cyberbullying" handout to identify the most effective responses to those specific tactics.

Anyone Could Be Daniel Cui

Read this story and then answer the questions that follow.

Daniel Cui was a freshman goalie on his high school's varsity soccer team. The team was having a bad season, with no wins out of ten matches. Then, during a game they thought they might win, the star player of the other team made a great kick that Daniel was not able to block. After the game, a kid at school said he was going to post some pictures of Daniel making great saves throughout the season. However, when the pictures went up on Facebook, they were all pictures that showed Daniel failing to block shots. After the photos were posted, a lot of people were talking about them, and about the loss of the game. Daniel felt so embarrassed that he didn't want to go to school.

Daniel's teammates decided that they needed to do something. They found a picture of Daniel making a great save and they made that picture their Facebook profile picture. Soon, other people followed suit—including all the players on both the boys' and girls' soccer teams. Over 100 students liked the picture and made positive comments on it. Supported by his classmates, Daniel returned to school with his head held high. The next season, he became more confident in his goalie skills and made many great saves for the team.

- How did students respond to cyberbullying and act as upstanders in this story?

- Have you ever seen or participated in anything like this online? If so, write about it here.

- Why do you think this story is titled, "Anyone Could Be Daniel Cui"?

 From *Create a Culture of Kindness in Middle School* by Naomi Drew, M.A., with Christa M. Tinari, M.A., copyright © 2017. This page may be reproduced for individual, classroom, or small group work only. For all other uses, contact Free Spirit Publishing Inc. at www.freespirit.com/permissions.

Cyberbullying Dilemmas

Consider how you would respond to the following dilemmas.

Dilemma #1

You are being sent text messages every hour from a number you don't recognize. The texts say things like, "Let's get together," and "I think you're hot." You have replied simply with, "Who are you?" and "Go away." You are still getting the texts. It's annoying and embarrassing.

- How would you respond if the situation were happening to you?

- How would you like your friends or adults to respond if they knew this was happening to you?

- What would be the most effective strategies an upstander could use to help you?

- Write down five specific responses that you or an upstander could use in this situation:

  1.
  2.
  3.
  4.
  5.

Dilemma #2

You see that your picture and pictures of two other students have been posted on a popular social media site, with the words "THE ugliest!" underneath. People have started writing comments under the post, such as "So ugly" and "Ewww—disgusting!" You are hurt, humiliated, and angry.

- How would you respond if the situation were happening to you?

- How would you like your friends or adults to respond if they knew this was happening to you?

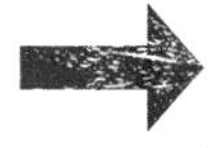

From *Create a Culture of Kindness in Middle School* by Naomi Drew, M.A., with Christa M. Tinari, M.A., copyright © 2017. This page may be reproduced for individual, classroom, or small group work only. For all other uses, contact Free Spirit Publishing Inc. at www.freespirit.com/permissions.

- What would be the most effective strategies an upstander could use to help you?

- Write down five specific responses that you or an upstander could use in this situation:
  1.
  2.
  3.
  4.
  5.

Dilemma #3

You receive several texts and photos from friends who are hanging out together. They are laughing and talking about cool things they're doing and how much fun they're having. You were not aware your friends were getting together. It feels like they are taunting you. You feel rejected and mocked.

- How would you respond if the situation were happening to you?

- How would you like your friends or adults to respond if they knew this was happening to you?

- What would be the most effective strategies an upstander could use to help you?

- Write down five specific responses that you or an upstander could use in this situation:
  1.
  2.
  3.
  4.
  5.

 From *Create a Culture of Kindness in Middle School* by Naomi Drew, M.A., with Christa M. Tinari, M.A., copyright © 2017. This page may be reproduced for individual, classroom, or small group work only. For all other uses, contact Free Spirit Publishing Inc. at www.freespirit.com/permissions.

Responding to Cyberbullying

"There are all kinds of reasons why we might see what's happening to those around us and decide to shrug it off. But remember the stories you've heard and read about people who have been cyberbullied. Some wrestle with serious psychological and emotional problems. . . . Now think about your friends, siblings, or anyone you care about struggling in this terrible way. Wouldn't you want someone to come to their rescue?"
—Justin Patchin and Sameer Hinduja in *Words Wound*

The following are possible responses to being cyberbullied. Put check marks next to the responses that you think would be most effective.

- ☐ Keep a journal to keep track of what is happening.
- ☐ Save the evidence, such as emails, texts, or screenshots.
- ☐ Don't retaliate.
- ☐ Talk about the situation with someone you trust.
- ☐ Ignore it.
- ☐ Laugh it off.
- ☐ Speak up.
- ☐ Block the offender on social media sites, from texting you, and so on.
- ☐ Ask your friends for support.
- ☐ Post positive messages and images online to counteract and drown out the negative.
- ☐ Report harmful and bullying posts to the social media sites where they appear.
- ☐ Talk to an adult such as a parent, teacher, or counselor.
- ☐ Contact the police.

- Which actions would you use if *you* were being cyberbullied?

- Which actions might you use if you wanted to help *someone else* who was being cyberbullied?

- Which actions would you most want other students to use if they knew you were being cyberbullied?

- Under what circumstances would it be most important to tell an adult, or even contact the police?

From *Create a Culture of Kindness in Middle School* by Naomi Drew, M.A., with Christa M. Tinari, M.A., copyright © 2017. This page may be reproduced for individual, classroom, or small group work only. For all other uses, contact Free Spirit Publishing Inc. at www.freespirit.com/permissions.

LESSON

Moral Courage: What's Okay, What's Not?

CHARACTER CONNECTIONS

personal responsibility / kindness / compassion / integrity

Lesson 46 invites students to use the lens of moral courage to consider choices they might make regarding bullying, teasing, and other situations involving moral decision making.

Students will

- understand the meaning of "moral courage"
- gain a greater understanding about what is and is not okay to do
- appreciate that certain behaviors are wrong, even if they find ways of justifying them

Materials

- handouts: "Okay or Not Okay?" (page 228) and "Moral Courage" (page 229)

Preparation

Watch a video in which Irshad Manji, the founder of the Moral Courage Project, describes the incident from ninth grade that inspired her work. To find the video, search online for her name and the term "swastikas in the classroom."

Introduction

Share Irshad Manji's story with students and discuss the need for all of us to have greater moral courage. Say: **Every day we have opportunities to exercise moral courage—the ability to do the right thing in the face of fear—or not to. Very often we make excuses when we don't exercise moral courage. Irshad Manji eventually summoned the ability to act on her moral courage. As a result, she's changing the world.**

Discussion and Activity

Ask: **Under what circumstances might we need greater moral courage?** Distribute the "Okay or Not Okay?" handout. Say: **Today we're going to take another look at some of the concepts we've been talking about relating to teasing and bullying. Consider the question of moral courage as you look at each item on this list. Then answer as honestly as you can.**

Put students in groups of three or four to discuss and fill out the "Okay or Not Okay?" handout. Tell them they don't all need to come to the same conclusions, but they should discuss each item honestly and explain their "it depends" answers. Remind students to listen with an open mind and to refrain from putting down someone else's point of view. Caution students not to pick an answer because they think it's the one you're looking for, but because it's true for them. Give them up to ten minutes to complete this activity. Circulate and make sure groups are staying on topic and listening to each other respectfully.

When students have completed this activity, go over the handout as a big group, one item at a time. For each item, ask students to give a thumbs-up if they chose "okay," or a thumbs-down if they chose "not okay." Ask students to hold up a pen or pencil if they chose "it depends." Choose several students to explain why they chose what they did.

It's important to challenge students' rationalizations of morally questionable choices (without shaming or embarrassing them). Ask one or two students who chose questionable answers to explain their thought process and reasoning. For example, in answering item #8, "Posting something embarrassing online about someone who put you down," a student might suggest that the other person deserves it. Challenge this position by asking why meeting a negative behavior with another negative behavior isn't a positive choice. Ask the group to suggest alternative responses.

As you go through the handout, discuss the concept of moral courage and the importance of doing the right thing simply because we know it's right, even if we feel scared or uncomfortable—and even if we're the only one doing it. Emphasize that having moral courage shouldn't require us to put ourselves at physical risk. However, moral courage might inspire us to take measured and healthy risks when we know it's the right thing to do.

Use item #4 as an example: "Standing by the side of someone who was bullied." Discuss what might be scary about doing this, and acknowledge that it can be difficult to intervene—even silently—in a bullying situation. But emphasize that by summoning our moral courage and acting accordingly, we can make a huge difference in someone else's life—and that we'll probably feel better about ourselves for doing so. (If necessary, reiterate that if students feel a bullying situation puts anyone in danger, they shouldn't intervene on their own, but should seek help from an adult.)

As you go through each item on the list, continue to focus on the concept of moral courage.

Wrap-Up

Have students take out their journals and write down one act of moral courage they will take as a result of this discussion. Tell them that tonight you'd like them to reflect on today's discussion and journal about insights and questions that came up for them. Distribute the handout "Moral Courage" and have them complete it as homework.

Follow-Up

Check in with students about how they're doing on following through with the actions they wrote about in their journals. Go over their responses to the "Moral Courage" handout.

Enrichment Activity

Have students research people who have exhibited moral courage, such as Rosa Parks, Nelson Mandela, Malala Yousafzai, Oskar Schindler, and other historic figures, as well as less famous individuals. Invite students to report on their findings, or to journal about what they learned, along with their insights on moral courage and being an upstander.

Okay or Not Okay?

Read the following statements and decide whether you think each action is okay to do or not, or if it depends on the specific situation. Put a check mark next to your answer, being as honest as you can.

1. Looking the other way when someone's being picked on.
☐ Okay ☐ Not okay ☐ It depends

2. Saying you were kidding when you teased someone and the person didn't like it.
☐ Okay ☐ Not okay ☐ It depends

3. Making a joke at someone else's expense, even if you know it hurts him or her.
☐ Okay ☐ Not okay ☐ It depends

4. Standing by the side of someone who has been bullied.
☐ Okay ☐ Not okay ☐ It depends

5. Laughing when someone's being picked on, as long as you're not picking on them, too.
☐ Okay ☐ Not okay ☐ It depends

6. Deciding someone deserves to be bullied.
☐ Okay ☐ Not okay ☐ It depends

7. Telling your parents that your friends have been texting rumors about someone at school even though your friends told you to keep it secret.
☐ Okay ☐ Not okay ☐ It depends

8. Posting something embarrassing online about someone who put you down.
☐ Okay ☐ Not okay ☐ It depends

9. Ranking people on websites according to attractiveness or other qualities.
☐ Okay ☐ Not okay ☐ It depends

10. Speaking up if your friends exclude someone from the group.
☐ Okay ☐ Not okay ☐ It depends

11. Passing along a text someone sent you in private.
☐ Okay ☐ Not okay ☐ It depends

12. Texting or calling someone your friends have bullied to see if he or she is okay.
☐ Okay ☐ Not okay ☐ It depends

13. Passing on a rumor about someone you don't like.
☐ Okay ☐ Not okay ☐ It depends

14. Telling an adult if you see someone being bullied.
☐ Okay ☐ Not okay ☐ It depends

15. Standing by silently if someone is being gossiped about, made fun of, or bullied.
☐ Okay ☐ Not okay ☐ It depends

16. Bullying someone else because you're being bullied.
☐ Okay ☐ Not okay ☐ It depends

17. Telling someone who is offended by something you said that he or she is too sensitive.
☐ Okay ☐ Not okay ☐ It depends

18. Asking a friend to join you in supporting someone who's being picked on.
☐ Okay ☐ Not okay ☐ It depends

Think About It: What can you do to exercise greater moral courage in any of these situations?

 From *Create a Culture of Kindness in Middle School* by Naomi Drew, M.A., with Christa M. Tinari, M.A., copyright © 2017. This page may be reproduced for individual, classroom, or small group work only. For all other uses, contact Free Spirit Publishing Inc. at www.freespirit.com/permissions.

Moral Courage

Visit the website of the Moral Courage Project at moralcourage.org and click "Get Inspired" to read about the founder, Irshad Manji, and watch a video in which she talks about the moment in ninth grade when she realized what moral courage was all about. Then answer the following questions.

- How do you feel about Irshad's silence at first when she saw what was on the board?
- If you were in Irshad's place, do you think you might have acted similarly? Why or why not? Explain.
- Think about situations in your life where you've remained silent or censored yourself when you should have spoken up. Describe one here.
- How do you feel about the way you reacted in the situation you just described? What might you do differently now?
- What might help you tap into your moral courage in the face of fear so you're better able to speak up in the future?

From *Create a Culture of Kindness in Middle School* by Naomi Drew, M.A., with Christa M. Tinari, M.A., copyright © 2017. This page may be reproduced for individual, classroom, or small group work only. For all other uses, contact Free Spirit Publishing Inc. at www.freespirit.com/permissions.

When Bullying Leads to Self-Harm

CHARACTER CONNECTIONS

compassion / personal responsibility / self-care

Lesson 47 engages students in a discussion about the most devastating reactions to bullying and provides tools for coping with overpowering emotions.

Note: Since this lesson addresses the issues of self-harm and suicide, it may bring out very vulnerable feelings in students. Be aware of this when you conduct this lesson, and be prepared to support students who need it. If you're a classroom teacher, talk to a school counselor to see if he or she would like to co-facilitate with you.

Students will

- talk about the issues of suicide and self-harm
- understand that self-harming behaviors can result from bullying but that this happens rarely
- learn what to do if they self-harm or think about doing so, or if they know someone who does

Materials

- a blank sheet of paper for every student
- a shoebox or other box with a lid
- paper or markers to decorate the box
- one large lump of modeling clay or play dough for each student
- handouts: "Potential Effects of Being Bullied" (page 232), "I'm Truly Sorry: A Letter from a Bully" (page 233), "Tools for Coping with Difficult Feelings" (pages 234–235), and "Tools for Parents: Ways to Address Difficult Feelings and Reduce Self-Harm in Teens" (pages 236–237)

Preparation

Bring in a shoebox or some other box with a lid. Cut a slot in the center large enough to hold a sheet of paper from each student. Have a student volunteer cover or decorate the box and write the word "Personal" on it.

On the board, write the following quote:

> *"Be kind, for everyone you meet is fighting a battle you know nothing about." —Wendy Mass*

Practice reading aloud "I'm Truly Sorry: A Letter from a Bully" or choose a student to do so and give him or her a copy ahead of time to prepare.

If desired, send home the "Tools for Parents" handout before or after doing this lesson.

Introduction

Pass out the "Potential Effects of Being Bullied" handout. Have students look it over and see if they have any questions. Answer their questions as honestly and sensitively as you can.

Say: **Unfortunately, we've probably all heard about situations in which kids have harmed themselves due to bullying. What stories have you heard—in the news or in your life—relating to this?** Encourage honest discussion (but caution students not to use real names or identifying factors if they're discussing situations in their lives). Some of your students might have had suicidal thoughts themselves, or have close friends who have. Others may be engaging in forms of self-harm. Some may have attempted suicide or know someone who has. Be very sensitive to this possibility as you lead this lesson.

Discussion and Activity

Say: **Suicide and self-harm are severe and uncommon reactions to bullying, but news reports can make them seem more common than they actually are, and that can be scary.** Tell students that bullying by itself does not lead to suicide, but that when it's combined with other major stressors, bullying can sometimes be a factor in self-harming or suicidal behavior. (See page 5 for information on common stressors.)

Ask a volunteer to read aloud the Wendy Mass quote on the board. Ask: **What does this mean to you?** Accept a few answers. Say: **Here's what one middle schooler said about this idea: *"You have no idea what's going on in people's heads and their homes. You called this girl fat. Well, guess what? She's anorexic. You made fun of some kid crying. His mom recently got diagnosed with cancer. You should treat people decently, no matter what."*** Ask students to respond to these words.

Read aloud, or have a student read aloud "I'm Truly Sorry: A Letter from a Bully."

Say: **If we ever feel overwhelmed by depression or self-destructive feelings—or if we know someone in this situation—we can respond in healthy ways. Can you name a few?** List student suggestions on the board. Be sure to include talking to a trusted person and not trying to cope alone. Emphasize the importance of support. Kids might bring up hotlines, text lines, and chat lines. Let students know that it's always better to have a live human being by your side, if at all possible, but that hotlines and similar resources are also helpful. Several resources are listed on the handouts they're about to receive. Also suggest healthy outlets like physical and creative activities that can take the edge off overwhelming feelings.

Pass out the "Tools for Coping with Difficult Feelings" handout. Go over each idea and address any questions students might have. Let students know that it's normal for people to feel down at times, but if they're *overwhelmed* by feelings of depression, or feel like they might harm themselves in any way at all, the tools on the handout can help. Additionally, therapy and certain prescription medications may help a lot when difficult emotions are overwhelming. Seeking a trusted adult who can offer guidance and support is the most critical step.

Wrap-Up

Pass out blank sheets of paper and have students write their names at the top. Then ask them to do two to three minutes of automatic writing in response to today's lesson. Assure them that no one but you will see their papers, so they can say anything they like. If they would prefer to draw, that's okay, too. (For some kids, this is the easiest mode of expression.) Have students fold their papers and put them into the box marked "Personal."

When you read through these papers, if any red flags come up, talk to relevant personnel immediately. It's also a good idea to follow up in writing with all your students. This is a serious and difficult topic, and even a brief note of support and acknowledgment can help students feel more comfortable and more willing to open up about what they're dealing with.

Give each student a ball of clay and invite kids to mold the clay into whatever they want. As they do, say: **Our difficult emotions are like this clay. They're changeable. And with the proper tools and support, we can change their shape.**

Follow-Up

Check in with students after this lesson to see if they need to talk. Leave out the box marked "Personal" in case they have additional notes they want to leave for you throughout the coming weeks. Some kids might not be ready to talk right away, so be aware of this.

Potential Effects of Being Bullied

"I was bullied a LOT. I was kicked, humiliated, and made fun of. All the time."
—8th-grade girl

Sometimes bullying can lead to overwhelming feelings. If you're experiencing any of the things listed below, and they continue for more than a few days, talk to someone you trust. *Don't try to go through it alone.* You deserve support, and you have the right to feel better.

Consider this list and make a check mark next to anything that applies to you. Then answer the questions that follow.

- ☐ Feeling afraid to come to school
- ☐ Changes in sleep and eating patterns
- ☐ Stomachaches
- ☐ Headaches
- ☐ Feelings of sadness, loneliness, anxiety, or depression
- ☐ Loss of interest in things you once enjoyed
- ☐ Fearfulness
- ☐ Problems concentrating
- ☐ Lower grades
- ☐ Self-harming behaviors
- ☐ Suicidal thoughts
- ☐ Suicide attempts

- What other negative effects can arise from being bullied?

- What can you do if you know someone who's dealing with anything on the list above?

- What can you do if you are experiencing any of these?

- Why is it important *not* to try handling these feelings all by yourself?

- Who can you talk to at school? At home?

Make this promise to yourself: I will not try to go it alone if I feel overwhelmed by difficult feelings. I will talk to someone I trust.

 From *Create a Culture of Kindness in Middle School* by Naomi Drew, M.A., with Christa M. Tinari, M.A., copyright © 2017. This page may be reproduced for individual, classroom, or small group work only. For all other uses, contact Free Spirit Publishing Inc. at www.freespirit.com/permissions.

I'm Truly Sorry: A Letter from a Bully

I have wronged a lot of people in my life. Many of those I wronged were young, vulnerable, different, and kindhearted. If you are one of the people I was cruel toward, I am truly sorry. I am "think about you and feel ashamed" sorry. Please know that if I knew you now I'd want to befriend you. But it's too late for that. I want you to know that I grew up and made friends with people who were bullied, and they are my favorite people—interesting, kind, unique, bold, and talented.

When I look back, I cringe, but also hope.

I hope that you were not forever scarred or injured by something I said. I hope you were able to turn your rotten interaction with me into something worthwhile. I hope you never think I was right in whatever I said or implied.

If you thought of killing yourself because of me, didn't want to come to school because of me, or cried yourself to sleep because of me, I am sorry. SO, SO sorry. I realize that's not enough. Know that I'm trying to be a better person now.

Sincerely,

Rocky Lewis

From *Create a Culture of Kindness in Middle School* by Naomi Drew, M.A., with Christa M. Tinari, M.A., copyright © 2017. This page may be reproduced for individual, classroom, or small group work only. For all other uses, contact Free Spirit Publishing Inc. at www.freespirit.com/permissions.

Tools for Coping with Difficult Feelings

We all have difficult feelings at one time or another. When we do, it's important to talk to a trusted person who can help. Don't try to go it alone. Along with talking to someone, here are additional ways you can help yourself handle challenging emotions.

1. **Create a coping kit.**
   Put positive and uplifting items in a box or other container to use when you're sad, upset, or fearful, or if you feel the urge to self-harm. You can include anything in your kit—a journal, art supplies, letters from loved ones, or photos of friends, family, pets, or personal heroes. Include anything you find calming, comforting, or inspiring. Keep your kit in a special place at home, but choose one thing to bring with you each day—something small enough to fit in your pocket and hold in your hand when needed.

2. **Use positive imagery.**
   Visualizing a beautiful, serene place is a powerful way to reduce anxiety and painful emotions. Picture a soothing landscape like a beach, or recall positive memories of a place you've been. Use vivid details. Do this whenever you feel stressed or upset. It's your go-to place for soothing stress and anxiety.

3. **Know your triggers.**
   Triggers can be conflicts, stress, or upcoming tests, social events, or dentist appointments. Whatever your triggers may be, do your best to identify and anticipate them. Use the strategies on this list ahead of time to prepare yourself and help yourself cope. Talking to someone can be the best help of all.

4. **Substitute other actions in place of self-harming ones.**
   If you feel the temptation to self-harm, hold an ice cube, tear up paper, snap a rubber band, suck a lemon peel, or pound a pillow instead. These are healthy substitutes that can quickly take the edge off stress or anxiety.

5. **Engage in physical activities.**
   Run, dance, take a walk, ride your bike, play with a pet, exercise vigorously, or do something else that gets your body moving. These activities will give you a boost in a healthy way.

6. **Be compassionate with yourself.**
   Stopping self-harming behavior isn't easy, and it'll take time. Be kind to yourself if you have a setback, and acknowledge yourself for every positive step you take.

7. **Continue talking to a trusted person.**
   If you have difficult feelings that still feel overwhelming, talking to a therapist or counselor can be the best coping mechanism of all. Have your trusted person help set this up for you. You'll be empowered by taking this step.

8. **If you are thinking about suicide, talk to an adult right away.**
   Suicide is a permanent response to a temporary situation. Your life is worth way too much to go that route. Lots of people in our school are here to help. Your teacher is one of them.

Steps 1–7 reprinted and adapted with permission from Deborah Serani, Psy.D., from *Depression and Your Child: A Guide for Parents and Caregivers* (Lanham, MD: Rowman & Littlefield, 2013).

 From *Create a Culture of Kindness in Middle School* by Naomi Drew, M.A., with Christa M. Tinari, M.A., copyright © 2017. This page may be reproduced for individual, classroom, or small group work only. For all other uses, contact Free Spirit Publishing Inc. at www.freespirit.com/permissions.

Where to Go for Help

National Suicide Prevention Lifeline: Call 1-800-273-TALK (8255) anytime, 24-7, to talk to someone who can help.

Boys Town National Hotline: 1-800-448-3000. This number is for boys and girls even though the message says Boys Town national hotline. It's free, confidential, and available 24-7. Be patient. Sometimes there's a short wait.

Boys Town National Textline: Text "Voice" to 20121. Free and confidential. Available 24-7.

Chat online or email here: yourlifeyourvoice.org

The Trevor Project Lifeline: 1-866-488-7386. This organization for lesbian, gay, bisexual, transgender, and questioning young people offers a free and confidential helpline 24 hours a day. For more information, visit thetrevorproject.org.

National Association of School Psychologists: If you know someone who you think might be considering suicide, talk to an adult right away. You can also read "Save a Friend: Tips for Teens to Prevent Suicide." Go to nasponline.org and search for "Save a Friend: Tips for Teens to Prevent Suicide." You will learn about signs to watch for and what you can do.

From *Create a Culture of Kindness in Middle School* by Naomi Drew, M.A., with Christa M. Tinari, M.A., copyright © 2017. This page may be reproduced for individual, classroom, or small group work only. For all other uses, contact Free Spirit Publishing Inc. at www.freespirit.com/permissions.

Tools for Parents: Ways to Address Difficult Feelings and Reduce Self-Harm in Teens

1. Create a coping kit together.
   With your child, put together positive and uplifting items in a box or other container. The things in the kit can be anything—a journal, art supplies, letters from loved ones, or photos of friends, family, pets, or personal heroes. Include anything your child finds calming, comforting, or inspiring.

2. Model positive imagery.
   Help your child visualize a beautiful, serene place. It's a great way to reduce anxiety or painful emotions. Have him or her describe a soothing landscape like a beach, or recall positive memories of a place your child has been. Encourage the use of vivid details. Do the same yourself and share the images and details that work for you.

3. Talk about triggers.
   Help your child better understand the types of situations and stressors that can trigger negative feelings and self-harming actions for him or her. Talk about your personal triggers and healthy ways you cope. Help your child come up with several healthy things that will comfort or calm him or her when negative feelings are likely to be triggered—things he or she can do *before* going into triggering situations.

4. Suggest neutral substitutes for severe behaviors.
   If your teen feels the urge to self-harm, encourage him or her to substitute the behavior with less severe activities, such as holding an ice cube, tearing up paper, snapping a rubber band, sucking a lemon peel, or pounding a pillow.

5. Suggest engaging in physical activities.
   Running, dancing, sports, and other forms of exercise are healthy channels that can reduce the urge toward self-harm. Go for a walk or run together, or choose something physical you both enjoy.

6. Be compassionate about setbacks.
   Stopping self-harming behavior isn't easy, and it'll take time. Your child may have setbacks. The best approach if a setback occurs is to offer nonjudgmental support.

7. Seek professional help if your child's symptoms or distress continue.
   If you're not sure who to reach out to, speak to your school counselor. He or she will be able to help you find the resources and help you and your child need.

Reprinted and adapted with permission from Deborah Serani, Psy.D., from *Depression and Your Child: A Guide for Parents and Caregivers* (Lanham, MD: Rowman & Littlefield, 2013).

 From *Create a Culture of Kindness in Middle School* by Naomi Drew, M.A., with Christa M. Tinari, M.A., copyright © 2017. This page may be reproduced for individual, classroom, or small group work only. For all other uses, contact Free Spirit Publishing Inc. at www.freespirit.com/permissions.

Helpful Hotlines and Links

National Suicide Prevention Lifeline: Call 1-800-273-TALK (8255) anytime, 24-7, to talk to someone who can help.

Boys Town National Hotline: 1-800-448-3000. This number is for boys and girls even though the message says Boys Town national hotline. It's free, confidential, and available 24-7. Be patient. Sometimes there's a short wait.

Boys Town National Textline: Text "Voice" to 20121. Free and confidential. Available 24-7.

Chat online or email here: yourlifeyourvoice.org

The Trevor Project Lifeline: 1-866-488-7386. This organization for lesbian, gay, bisexual, transgender, and questioning young people offers a free and confidential helpline 24 hours a day. For more information visit thetrevorproject.org.

Christy Esposito-Smythers, "What Do I Do If My Teen Is Thinking About Suicide?" *The Huffington Post,* May 26, 2013, huffingtonpost.com/christy-espositosmythers/teen-suicide-prevention_b_3333486.html.

American Academy of Child and Adolescent Psychology, "Facts for Families: Teen Suicide," www.aacap.org/AACAP/Families_and_Youth/Facts_for_Families/FFF-Guide/Teen-Suicide-010.aspx.

From *Create a Culture of Kindness in Middle School* by Naomi Drew, M.A., with Christa M. Tinari, M.A., copyright © 2017. This page may be reproduced for individual, classroom, or small group work only. For all other uses, contact Free Spirit Publishing Inc. at www.freespirit.com/permissions.

Ending Bullying in Your School Starts with You!

CHARACTER CONNECTIONS

personal responsibility / kindness

Lesson 48 invites students to plan specific projects and ideas for sparking kindness and ending bullying.

Note: At least two days prior to this lesson, pass out the handout and have students view the videos and read the articles it lists. Have them bring back the handout to complete during this lesson.

Students will

- work in groups to come up with practical ideas for increasing kindness and ending bullying in their school
- create the seeds of ongoing projects and ideas for building a kinder school culture
- lay out specific steps for moving forward with a schoolwide anti-bullying plan

Materials

- handout: "Sparking Kindness and Ending Bullying in Our School" (page 240)

Preparation

Ask a student to write the following quotes on the board:

> *"You cannot get through a single day without having an impact on the world around you. What you do makes a difference, and you have to decide what kind of difference you want to make." —Jane Goodall*

> *"You are an amazing generation of young people. We can learn a lot from you, so don't be afraid to teach us." —Martie Gillin, founder of SpeakUp!*

»»» Online Resource »»»»»»»»»»»»
To get an idea of what can happen when kids have the opportunity to come up with ideas for positive change and adults support them in following through, search YouTube for "Pitt River Middle School, Random Acts of Kindness."
»»»»»»»»»»»»»»»»»»»»»»»»»

Introduction

Say: **We all have the ability to create a tipping point in our school, one that can be the beginning of the end of bullying. You are each the key to that change.**

Have a student read aloud the Jane Goodall quote from the board. Ask: **What do these words mean to you? What kind of difference do *you* want to make, and how?** Remind students that we can each make a difference individually and that collectively we can make an even greater difference.

Have another student read the Martie Gillin quote from the board. Ask students how they feel about these words. Stress that what they think and feel is important, and that they have the power to shape the future.

Discussion and Activity

Put kids in groups of four or five. Remind them of the guidelines for respectful listening, and say: **Today I have a special challenge for you: I want you to put your heads together to come up with specific ways our entire school can spark kindness and end bullying.**

Have students take out their "Sparking Kindness and Ending Bullying in Our School" handouts. Go over the handout together and let students know that each group will have about fifteen to twenty minutes to come up with ideas. Tell them that at the end of that time, small groups will present their ideas and the large group will vote on the ideas they'd most like to follow through on. As students work, circulate and help them streamline their thoughts and consider concrete ways to follow through with their ideas.

At the end of the designated time, have each group share ideas. List them on the board. Have students vote on the top five ideas they want to follow through on, and the next five they'd like to see happen after that.

Wrap-Up

Ask students to voice their visions for sparking kindness and ending bullying. What might your school be like once more people are onboard with the goals that have been set today? What might it be like for kids to come to school—especially those who've been bullied in the past? How might your school become a model for other schools? Affirm students' visions and remind them that they have the power to create positive change.

Follow-Up

If other teachers or counselors in your school are using this book, meet with them to discuss ideas your groups came up with and decide on a mode of follow-through. Choose a delegation of students (drawing from all groups if applicable, or from your group alone) to meet with the principal and other decision-makers in your school. When you hold this meeting, allow the student delegation to present their ideas and explain the thinking behind them. Work with students and administrators to create a timeline and plan for implementing student ideas.

If you encounter resistance from administrators or others at your school, keep trying. Know that this is a big deal for kids. If their proposals are implemented schoolwide and make a difference in the way students treat each other, it can be life-changing—not just for your group, but for everyone in your school.

Enrichment Activities

- Have kids come up with a campaign to make their message and movement of kindness go viral. Videos, online messages, a texting campaign, and more could be a part of this. Invite your students' most expansive creativity.
- Engage students in getting the whole community and local media involved. Have students reach out to the mayor, chief of police, local business owners, head of the board of education, town council, and more. Have them contact local radio and TV stations plus online news platforms that serve the community. Creating kindness in schools is a big deal. Make everyone a part of it!

Sparking Kindness and Ending Bullying in Our School

There are many examples of real-life projects to promote kindness and counteract bullying. You can look for videos, articles, and blogs to get inspired and start thinking about ideas that could work at your school and in your community. If you need a starting point, try searching online for the following names and phrases:

- Pitt River Middle School Random Acts of Kindness
- The Be ONE Project and "How Positive Peer Pressure Could End Bullying in Your School"
- "Nice It Forward"
- "Pink Shirt Day" and "Bullied Student Tickled Pink by Schoolmates' T-shirt Campaign"

Next, think about your own ideas for projects and actions. What can you do to promote kindness and end bullying at our school—and beyond? Write at least three ideas here:

As you think about how to put your plans into action, consider these questions:

- What messages of kindness do you want to share with others? How can you spread these messages at school?
- How can you use the power of social media and the Internet to spread your message even further?
- Do you want to take your campaign into the community? If so, how do you want to get people outside the school involved?
- What kind of ongoing committee do you need to carry out these ideas? Who should be part of this committee, and how often should the committee meet?
- What questions do you have about how to carry out your plans and ideas? Who can you talk to about these questions?

 From *Create a Culture of Kindness in Middle School* by Naomi Drew, M.A., with Christa M. Tinari, M.A., copyright © 2017. This page may be reproduced for individual, classroom, or small group work only. For all other uses, contact Free Spirit Publishing Inc. at www.freespirit.com/permissions.

Writing Prompts

These prompts correlate with the subject matter in each section of the book. Use them to spark further reflection on the topics explored in the lessons. Students can respond informally to the prompts in their journals, or use them as starting points for automatic writing, essays, or even short stories. Do what works for you and your group.

Section 1
The Core Lessons

- Do you think it's possible to create a more peaceful school? If so, how? If not, why not? What do you see as some of the challenges of doing this?
- Imagine you're about to have a discussion with teachers and parents about creating a "peaceful school." How might their ideas be different from or the same as yours? What if you had this discussion with other students?
- Describe the impact one person can make in a classroom, a school, or the world. What kind of difference would *you* like to make?
- Describe a time when someone really listened to what you had to say. What did that person do that showed he or she really heard you and understood what you were saying? How did being listened to affect you?
- Explain in your own words what you have learned about the brain's ability to change. How do your own thoughts and actions impact your brain? How does your brain impact your feelings and actions?
- Describe something you like about yourself. Why is this quality important to you? Describe something you'd like to improve about yourself. What could you do to make this change?
- What is the cool-down strategy that works the best for you when you're angry or upset? Describe it in detail and explain how you use it.
- What are some of the challenges of using Stop, Breathe, Chill when you're in a tough situation? What might make it easier for you to use Stop, Breathe, Chill in difficult moments? Explain your ideas in detail.
- Describe a time you wish you had used Stop, Breathe, Chill. How might things have turned out differently if you had?

Section 2
Fostering Courage, Kindness, and Empathy

- What are some of the hurtful and mean names you hear classmates saying at school? What impact do you think these words have on the kids who are on the receiving end of them? What can you do to stop the cycle of mean name-calling?
- You might have heard this saying: "Sticks and stones may break my bones but words can never hurt me." Describe what this expression means to you. Do you agree with what it says? Why or why not? When could words possibly hurt more than sticks and stones?
- Why do you think some people seem to feel more empathy than others? What do you think blocks some people from feeling more empathy? How can a lack of empathy create problems?
- Sometimes people change their beliefs or attitudes about other people. What do you think could cause someone to change a belief or an attitude? Describe a time when you changed a belief or an attitude about a person, an idea, or a thing.

- Describe a time when you stood up for someone who was being picked on. What did you do? What happened?
- Do you think most of your classmates and friends believe it's cool to be kind? Share an example that illustrates your response.
- Discuss your ideas for a schoolwide kindness campaign. What kinds of activities would you be interested in doing?

Section 3
Celebrating Uniqueness and Accepting Differences

- In what ways are your friends the same as or different from you? Describe some of your major similarities and differences in detail. Describe how these qualities affect your friendships.
- Describe what you know about your family's cultural heritage. If you don't have very much information about it, how can you learn more?
- What would you do if someone made an incorrect assumption about you, based on your gender, race, or something else? Describe a time when this happened to you or someone you know. How did you feel? What did you (or the person you know) do or say?
- Have you, or has anyone close to you, been personally affected by stereotyping? Share your story. What can be done to end stereotyping?
- Why do you think some people engage in gossip and spreading rumors? If your friends were talking about someone else behind his or her back, how would you feel and what would you do?
- What are some advantages and disadvantages of socially including people whose perspectives or experiences are different from your own? What could you do to get to know students who aren't in your current circle of friends?
- What can you do to make new students feel welcome? Imagine someone new has transferred to your school. Write about how you might help that person feel comfortable and included.
- What do you wish people knew or understood about you? Describe some of your unique or special qualities.
- Do you think prejudice is becoming more or less common in our school? Our society? What makes you think that? Do you think people from a different culture than your own would agree or disagree with you, and why?
- If there were no bias, stereotyping, or prejudice, how would the world be different than it is today? In what way would your daily life be different than it is today?

Section 4
Dealing with Conflict

- What kinds of things typically cause you to feel angry? What signs does your body give you when you are experiencing anger? How do you handle it?
- What would you do if you got into a conflict with a friend? What if you got into a conflict with someone you don't know well? How might your reaction or approach be different?
- Explain the differences between being passive, assertive, and aggressive. Share examples from your life when you or someone else has acted in each way. What effect can each type of reaction have in a conflict situation?
- What would you like to change about the way you handle conflict? What are your greatest challenges when it comes to dealing with conflict? What are your strengths?
- Pretend you will be teaching a group of younger children how to resolve conflicts without fighting. Describe what you would tell them.
- Describe a conflict you experienced and explain how it was resolved. If you or the other person used respectful listening, how did that help you resolve the conflict? If respectful listening wasn't used, how could you or the person have used it? What effect might that have had on how the situation turned out?
- Describe a time when you responded to conflict in a negative way. What happened and what did

you do? What have you felt and thought since that situation occurred? If you could do a "replay" of the conflict, discuss three positive responses you would try instead.

Section 5
Coping with and Counteracting Bullying

- Why do you think bullying happens? What are some reasons people might engage in bullying behaviors?
- What would you do if you felt someone was bullying you? What would you do if the first thing you tried didn't work?
- How big of a problem is bullying at your school, in your view? Do you think other students would agree with your opinion? Why or why not?
- What kinds of bullying behaviors do you think happen most at your school? What can be done to stop or counteract these behaviors?
- What do you think can be done to prevent bullying from happening in the first place? What do teachers need to know in order to prevent and stop bullying? What could they teach students to help stop bullying from taking place?
- How is bullying different from teasing or joking between friends? How can you tell which is happening? Give an example of teasing that doesn't hurt and an example of teasing that *does* hurt.
- What would you do if you found out that a friend of yours was cyberbullying someone? What would you do if someone accused *you* of cyberbullying?
- Imagine that you became aware that someone was being bullied, and you wanted to do something to help. Also imagine that you were feeling nervous or unsure about taking action. What could you do to gain the moral courage you need to do the right thing?
- Discuss your ideas for making kindness fun and "cool" among your peers. What kind of actions would you take to encourage your classmates to be kind? Describe the acts of kindness that you think would make the biggest impact on your classroom and school.
- What are some ways you can be an upstander and encourage others to do the same?
- What recommendations would you make to your school principal about your school's policies on bullying?
- Discuss your ideas for organizing a schoolwide upstander campaign.

Conflict, Bullying, Kindness, and Safety at School: What Do You Think?

We want to hear your thoughts about conflict, bullying, and kindness. Your experiences, feelings, and thoughts are very important to us. Please do your best to fill in every box and answer every question. Don't worry about spelling. And remember, your answers to this survey are anonymous. Just give your true and honest responses. Thank you for helping make our school the best it can be!

About You

I identify as: ☐ Boy ☐ Girl

I'm in grade: ☐ 6 ☐ 7 ☐ 8 ☐ 9

Thinking About Conflict

Conflict is a serious disagreement between two or more people that could lead to a fight.

1. **How often do you see conflict happen at school?**

   ☐ Never ☐ Sometimes ☐ Often ☐ Every day

2. **How often do *you* get into conflicts at school?**

   ☐ Never ☐ Sometimes ☐ Often ☐ Every day

3. **What are the main "conflict starters" for you at school? Read the choices and pick your top three conflict starters. If any conflict starters that apply to you are not listed here, add them in the "other" section.**

   ☐ Name-calling
   ☐ Being teased or made fun of
   ☐ Being left out
   ☐ Boyfriend or girlfriend issues
   ☐ Rumors or gossip
   ☐ Friendship issues
   ☐ Someone being unfair
   ☐ Threats
   ☐ Other:
   ☐ Other:
   ☐ Other:

4. **What do you usually do when you have a conflict? Please explain.**

5. **Are you satisfied with your ability to handle conflict?**

   ☐ No ☐ Sometimes ☐ Yes

   Explain:

Thinking About Kindness

Kindness is treating others with care and respect.

6. **How often do kids at your school treat each other with kindness and respect?**

   ☐ Never ☐ Sometimes ☐ Often ☐ Every day

 From *Create a Culture of Kindness in Middle School* by Naomi Drew, M.A., with Christa M. Tinari, M.A., copyright © 2017. This page may be reproduced for individual, classroom, or small group work only. For all other uses, contact Free Spirit Publishing Inc. at www.freespirit.com/permissions.

7. **Do you think kindness is seen as "cool" at your school?**
   ☐ No ☐ Sometimes ☐ Yes
   Explain:

8. **Do you think it's important for kids to be kind and respectful to one another?**
   ☐ No ☐ Sometimes ☐ Yes
   Explain:

Thinking About Teasing and Meanness

Meanness is unkind behavior that hurts someone's feelings. Teasing is making fun of someone.

9. **What are the main reasons kids are teased by other kids at school? Read the following choices and pick the top three reasons. If one of your reasons is not listed here, add it in the "other" section.**
   - ☐ Looks or physical appearance (including weight or height)
   - ☐ How a person dresses
   - ☐ Race
   - ☐ Religion
   - ☐ Amount of money the person's family has
   - ☐ Popularity
   - ☐ Physical abilities or disabilities
   - ☐ How smart someone is, or is not, perceived to be
   - ☐ Gender
   - ☐ Sexual orientation
   - ☐ Language ability or accent
   - ☐ Other:
   - ☐ Other:
   - ☐ Other:

10. **Do you think it's possible for kids who act mean to change?**
    ☐ No ☐ Sometimes ☐ Yes
    Explain:

11. **Are you satisfied with the way you respond when kids act mean to you or other people?**
    ☐ No ☐ Sometimes ☐ Yes
    Explain:

12. **Do you think some people deserve to be picked on?**
    ☐ No ☐ Sometimes ☐ Yes
    Explain:

From *Create a Culture of Kindness in Middle School* by Naomi Drew, M.A., with Christa M. Tinari, M.A., copyright © 2017. This page may be reproduced for individual, classroom, or small group work only. For all other uses, contact Free Spirit Publishing Inc. at www.freespirit.com/permissions.

13. How often do you help someone out when they are being picked on or bullied (whether in person or online)?

☐ Never ☐ Sometimes ☐ Often ☐ Always

What do you do to help?

Thinking About Bullying

Bullying is deliberate and repeated behavior intended to harm, embarrass, exclude, or frighten another person. Cyberbullying is bullying through technology, such as social media sites, texts, and other digital methods.

14. How often does bullying happen among your friends, classmates, and other people your age?

☐ Never ☐ Sometimes ☐ Often ☐ Every day

15. Do you think cyberbullying among kids is a problem at our school?

☐ No ☐ Sometimes ☐ Yes

Explain:

16. What are the top places where bullying takes place at school? Read all the choices and choose the top three places. If a place is not listed here, add it in the "other" section.

☐ Classrooms
☐ Hallways
☐ Lunch
☐ Bathrooms
☐ Gym class or locker room
☐ Bus (or walking to school)
☐ Sports practice
☐ Online
☐ Other:
☐ Other:
☐ Other:

17. What do you usually do when you see someone being bullied? Place check marks next to all the items that apply to you. If something you do is not listed here, add it in the "other" section.

☐ Report the situation to an adult
☐ Distract the students away from the situation
☐ Confront the person who is bullying
☐ Laugh
☐ Spend time with the person who is being bullied
☐ Say something nice to the person who is being bullied
☐ Ignore it
☐ Join in the bullying
☐ Other:
☐ Other:
☐ Other:

18. If you had a problem with conflict or bullying, who would you most likely go to for help? Choose all that apply. If a person is not listed here, add him or her in the "other" section.

☐ No one
☐ Parent
☐ Friend
☐ Teacher
☐ Sibling
☐ Other:
☐ Other:
☐ Other:

 From *Create a Culture of Kindness in Middle School* by Naomi Drew, M.A., with Christa M. Tinari, M.A., copyright © 2017. This page may be reproduced for individual, classroom, or small group work only. For all other uses, contact Free Spirit Publishing Inc. at www.freespirit.com/permissions.

19. If you were being bullied or picked on, what would you most want other kids to do for you? Choose all that apply. If what you would want is not listed here, add it in the "other" section.

- ☐ Spend time with you
- ☐ Assure you that you don't deserve to be picked on
- ☐ Report the situation to an adult
- ☐ Confront the kids who are bullying
- ☐ Give you advice about what to do
- ☐ Help you get away from the situation
- ☐ Other:
- ☐ Other:
- ☐ Other:

20. If you were being bullied or picked on, what would you most want adults at school to do?

21. Do you feel safe at school?

☐ No ☐ Sometimes ☐ Yes

Explain:

22. Have you ever bullied someone? If so, please describe the situation.

23. What do you think would help decrease or end bullying at school?

24. If you could make one change at school regarding how kids treat one another, what would it be?

25. Is there anything else you'd like to say or ask?

Thank you for completing this survey!

From *Create a Culture of Kindness in Middle School* by Naomi Drew, M.A., with Christa M. Tinari, M.A., copyright © 2017. This page may be reproduced for individual, classroom, or small group work only. For all other uses, contact Free Spirit Publishing Inc. at www.freespirit.com/permissions.

Recommended Resources

Books for Students

We love the "Empathy Reading List" carefully compiled and annotated by the Allen-Stevenson School in New York, so we asked if we could share it with you. Happily, they said yes. Enjoy this great collection of resources.

Note: *To accommodate the needs of students with a wide range of reading abilities, we've included books with reading levels between third and sixth grade, as well as books intended for older or more proficient readers.*

Empathy Reading List from Allen-Stevenson School

One way to develop empathy is to read books in which characters deal with circumstances very different from our own. The characters in these books lead unusual and often challenging lives. These books are all wonderful stories and are particularly suitable books for discussion.

Grades 3–6

Brendan Buckley's Universe and Everything in It by Sundee T. Frazier. Yearling, 2007. Brendan Buckley is a biracial ten-year-old who has never met his white grandfather. Finally, Brendan meets him at a rock-collecting club meeting and finds out that his grandfather is a scientist, just like him. What Brendan does not know is why his mother does not want the two of them to meet.

Bud, Not Buddy by Christopher Paul Curtis. Yearling, 1999. Guided only by an old advertisement for a Cab Calloway jazz concert, Bud—a runaway orphan—sets out to find the leader of the band, who he believes is the father he has never met.

Donuthead by Sue Stauffacher. Alfred A. Knopf, 2003. Pathologically afraid of germs and potential dangers, Franklin Delano Donuthead is frequently alone, until his mother befriends the new girl at school, and Franklin is forced to spend time with a bedraggled girl—his worst nightmare!

Extra Credit by Andrew Clements. Atheneum Books for Young Readers, 2009. Smart but bored, eleven-year-old Abby finds she must earn extra credit if she does not want to repeat sixth grade. She becomes pen pals with Sadeed, a boy at a small school in Afghanistan. Before they know it, their letters are crossing much more than an ocean; they are crossing a huge cultural divide.

How to Steal a Dog by Barbara O'Connor. Square Fish, 2007. One day Georgina has a home, a best friend, and plenty to eat. The next, she's living in a car with her mother and brother. Desperate to improve their situation, Georgina persuades her younger brother to go along with an elaborate scheme to kidnap a dog and collect the reward the dog's owners are bound to offer.

The Hundred Dresses by Eleanor Estes. Harcourt, 1972. Wanda faces mockery at school, both because of her unusual last name and because she claims that she has one hundred dresses at home—even though she wears the same dress to school each day.

Joey Pigza Swallowed the Key by Jack Gantos. Farrar, Straus and Giroux, 1998. Joey just can't sit still at school or focus on what the teacher is saying. He can't help himself. He knows he's a good kid but he wonders if his teachers will ever figure out how to help him put a stop to his wild antics.

The Year of Miss Agnes by Kirkpatrick Hill. Aladdin Paperbacks, 2000. A new teacher has arrived among the Athabascans in Alaska in 1948. Ten-year-old Frederika knows that this teacher is different from all the teachers who have come before her. No other teacher plays opera recordings and talks about Athabascan kids becoming doctors or scientists. And no other teacher has ever said that Frederika's deaf older sister should come to school, too.

Grades 7 and Up

The Astonishing Life of Octavian Nothing, Traitor to the Nation by M. T. Anderson. Candlewick Press, 2006. Raised by a mysterious group of rational philosophers known only by numbers, an African-American boy and his mother—a princess in exile from a faraway land—are the only people in their household assigned names. Octavian begins to question the purpose behind his guardians' studies but it is only when he dares to open a forbidden door that he learns the truth about their experiments—and his own chilling role in them.

Athletic Shorts: Six Short Stories by Chris Crutcher. Greenwillow Books, 1991. A collection of short stories featuring characters from earlier books by Chris Crutcher. These are stories of love, death, bigotry, heroism, and coming of age.

Black and White by Paul Volponi. Viking, 2005. Marcus is black and Eddie is white. They have been best friends for years and are the stars of Long Island City High School's basketball team. Both have realistic chances for college scholarships and pro basketball careers. Then one night they make a bad mistake and are arrested. Now they cannot turn back and one of them will have to pay. Told in their two voices, this is a fascinating look at how each boy experiences the justice system.

The Curious Incident of the Dog in the Night-Time by Mark Haddon. Vintage Books, 2003. Christopher is a mathematically gifted fifteen-year-old boy with autism. Despite his fear of interacting with people, he decides to investigate the murder of his neighbor's dog and discovers secret information about his mother.

Daniel Half Human by David Chotjewitz. Atheneum Books for Young Readers, 2004. In 1933, best friends Daniel and Armin admire Hitler and also swear eternal brotherhood to each other. As anti-Semitism rises and Hitler comes to power, Daniel learns he is half Jewish, threatening Daniel and Armin's friendship.

Food, Girls, and Other Things I Can't Have by Allen Zadoff. Carolrhoda Lab, 2011. Fifteen-year-old Andrew Zansky, who has always been an outcast, is recruited to join his high school's varsity football team. He joins to get the attention of a new girl at school but gradually realizes that his teammates had ulterior motives when they recruited him. He must find a way to respond to the situation and remain true to himself.

I Am the Messenger by Markus Zusak. Alfred A. Knopf, 2002. After capturing a bank robber, nineteen-year-old cab driver Ed Kennedy begins receiving mysterious messages that direct him to addresses where people need help. Along the way, he begins to learn some interesting things about himself.

Inexcusable by Chris Lynch. Atheneum Books for Young Readers, 2005. High school senior and football player Keir sets out to enjoy himself on graduation night, but when he attempts to comfort a friend whose date has left her stranded, things go terribly wrong. As Keir recalls the events leading up to that fateful night, he realizes that the way things look are definitely not the way they really are—and that it may be all too easy to do something terribly wrong.

Inventing Elliot by Graham Gardner. Dial Books, 2004. Fourteen-year-old Elliot Sutton arrives at Holminster High determined not to stand out and be a target as he was at his old school. He invents a whole new Elliot, one who is tough and impenetrable. When a group of upperclassmen called the Guardians, who are obsessed with power, try to recruit him, Elliot must make a difficult decision.

The Perks of Being a Wallflower by Stephen Chbosky. Pocket Books, 1999. Charlie, a freshman in high school, explores the dilemmas of growing up through a collection of letters he sends to an unknown receiver.

Silent to the Bone by E. L. Konigsburg. Aladdin Paperbacks, 2000. When he is wrongly accused of gravely injuring his baby half-sister, thirteen-year-old Branwell loses his power of speech. Branwell's best friend Connor is convinced that Branwell could not have hurt his baby half-sister. But how can he prove Branwell is innocent when Branwell cannot speak for himself?

Speak by Laurie Halse Anderson. Farrar, Straus and Giroux, 1999. Melinda Sordino is a high school outcast. She ruined an end-of-summer party by calling the police, so her old friends will not talk to her, while people she doesn't know hate her from a distance. Even being alone is difficult for Melinda because there's something she's trying not to think about, something about the night of the party that if she admitted it and let it in, would blow her carefully constructed disguise to smithereens. Then she would have no choice—she would *have* to speak the truth.

Will Grayson, Will Grayson by John Green and David Levithan. Dutton, 2010. When two teens, one gay and one straight, meet accidentally and discover that they share the same name, their lives become intertwined as one begins dating the other's best friend, who produces a play revealing his relationship with them both.

Other Recommended Books Relating to Bullying, Empathy, and Moral Dilemmas

Bluish by Virginia Hamilton. Scholastic, 1999. Friendship isn't always easy. Natalie is different from the other girls in Dreenie's fifth-grade class. She comes to school in a wheelchair, always wearing a knitted hat. The kids call her "Bluish" because her skin is tinted blue from chemotherapy.

Dear Bully: 70 Authors Tell Their Stories, edited by Megan Kelley Hall and Carrie Jones. HarperCollins, 2011. Some of today's top authors for teens come together to share their stories about bullying, whether they were silent observers on the sidelines of high school, targets, or perpetrators of bullying.

Doing Time Online by Jan Siebold. Albert Whitman & Company, 2002. Twelve-year-old Mitchell played a prank that led to an elderly woman's injury. Now he finds himself at the police station and given a "sentence" requiring him to chat online with a nursing home resident twice a week for the next month. Although Mitchell is resentful at first, he finds that his new friend gives him courage to finally admit that he is partially responsible for his neighbor's accident.

Freak the Mighty by Rodman Philbrick. Blue Sky Press, 1993. Two boys—a slow learner stuck in the body of a teenage giant and a tiny Einstein in leg braces—forge a unique friendship when they pair up to create one formidable force.

Gifts from the Enemy by Trudy Ludwig. White Cloud Press, 2014. This moving story is based on a Holocaust survivor's true experience. As a prisoner during World War II, Alter Wiener was the recipient of a repeated act of kindness, from an unexpected upstander. *Note*: This is not a chapter book, but an illustrated picture book that shares a simple but powerful message with children and adults.

LGBTQ: The Survival Guide for Lesbian, Gay, Bisexual, Transgender, and Questioning Teens (Revised & Updated Edition) by Kelly Huegel. Free Spirit Publishing, 2018. Created with feedback and suggestions from PFLAG, GLSEN, GLAAD, and others, this frank, sensitive book is written for young people who are beginning to question their sexual orientation or gender identity, those who are ready to work for LGBTQ rights, and those who may need advice, guidance, or reassurance that they are not alone.

Hana's Suitcase: The Quest to Solve a Holocaust Mystery by Karen Levine. Penguin Random House, 2012. This award-winning book is the true story of Hana, a young girl who died in Nazi Germany during the Holocaust, and of Fumiko Ishioka, the director of the Tokyo Holocaust Center.

Mockingbird by Kathryn Erskine. Philomel Books, 2010. Caitlin has Asperger's syndrome. Before, when things got confusing, Caitlin went to her older brother, Devon, for help. But Devon has died, and Caitlin's dad is so distraught that he can't be helpful. Caitlin wants everything to go back to the way things were, but she doesn't know how to make that happen.

Number the Stars by Lois Lowry. Houghton Mifflin Harcourt, 1989. As the German troops begin their campaign to "relocate" all the Jews living in Denmark, Annemarie Johansen's family takes in Annemarie's best friend, Ellen Rosen, and conceals her as part of the family.

Rules by Cynthia Lord. Scholastic, 2006. This 2007 Newbery Honor Book is a humorous and heartwarming story about feeling different and finding acceptance. Twelve-year-old Catherine just wants a normal life—which is near impossible when you have a brother with autism and a family that revolves around his differences. She has spent years trying to teach David the rules—from "a peach is not a funny-looking apple" to "keep your pants on in public"—in order to head off David's embarrassing behaviors.

Saving Jasey by Diane Tullson. Orca Book Publishers, 2001. Thirteen-year-old Gavin's home life is far from perfect. His older brother bullies him, his father has no time for him, and his mother hasn't been the same since she hit a pig on the highway. Gavin finds sanctuary in his friend Trist McVeigh's seemingly perfect home. But all is not as it seems in the McVeigh home.

Share This Journal: A Public Journal Documenting Random Acts of Kindness by Amy Gopel and Keryl Pesce. Vega Publishing, 2014. This journal encourages and documents random acts of kindness, and is intended to be returned to the original owner when all acts of kindness in the book are complete. When returned, the original journal owner is able to see the chain reaction that began with his or her original kind act.

To Kill a Mockingbird by Harper Lee. Lippincott, 1960. Viewed through the eyes of a young girl, this classic novel tells the story of one man's heroic struggle for justice in a town steeped in racial prejudice and hypocrisy.

Words Wound: Delete Cyberbullying and Make Kindness Go Viral by Justin W. Patchin and Sameer Hinduja. Free Spirit Publishing, 2014. This nonfiction book presents many true stories shared by teens about cyberbullying and related topics. The authors give succinct and actionable advice about how to stop and prevent cyberbullying, and how to instead use digital communications to create a kinder world.

Wringer by Jerry Spinelli. HarperCollins, 1997. This novel shows an excellent example of a young man standing up to others for a cause he believes to be important.

Books for Middle School Educators

Empathy: Why It Matters, and How to Get It by Roman Krznaric. Perigee, 2014. In this lively and engaging book, Krznaric argues that our brains are wired for social connection and that empathy—not apathy or self-centeredness—is at the heart of who we are. He presents six life-enhancing habits of highly empathetic people whose skills enable them to connect with others in extraordinary ways.

The Educator's Guide to Emotional Intelligence and Academic Achievement: Social-Emotional Learning in the Classroom, edited by Maurice J. Elias and Harriett Arnold. Corwin Press, 2006. This book reviews the scientific findings that connect social-emotional learning (SEL) and academic achievement and includes chapters on SEL programs and approaches.

Empowering Bystanders in Bullying Prevention by Stan Davis with Julia Davis. Research Press, 2007. This book clearly explains and illustrates the foundational practices that prevent bullying behaviors and promote empathy and respect at school.

Kids Working It Out: Stories and Strategies for Making Peace in Our Schools, edited by Tricia S. Jones and Randy Compton. Jossey-Bass, 2003. This book contains a compilation of informative stories and examples of school-based practices in conflict resolution, social-emotional learning, restorative practices, bullying prevention, peer mediation, and more.

Mindfulness for Teachers: Simple Skills for Peace and Productivity in the Classroom by Patricia A. Jennings. W.W. Norton & Company, 2015. Drawing upon basic and applied research in the fields of neuroscience, psychology, and education, this book offers valuable information about how mindfulness can help teachers manage the stressful demands of the classroom, cultivate an exceptional learning environment, and revitalize teaching and learning

The Teenage Brain: A Neuroscientist's Survival Guide to Raising Adolescents and Young Adults by Frances E. Jensen with Amy Ellis Nutt. HarperCollins, 2015. Drawing on her research knowledge and clinical experience, internationally respected neurologist—and mother of two boys—Frances E. Jensen offers a revolutionary look at the science of the adolescent brain, providing remarkable insights that translate into practical advice for both parents and teenagers.

Think, Care, Act: Teaching for a Peaceful Future by Susan Gelber Cannon. Information Age Publishing, 2011. This book chronicles a teacher's journey with her middle school students as they think about, care about, and then act on social justice issues of importance to them. The book contains many examples of how to integrate social-emotional learning and critical thinking into social studies and language arts content, deepen students' engagement in the subject matter, and facilitate their moral development.

Youth Voice Project: Student Insights into Bullying and Peer Mistreatment by Stan Davis and Charisse L. Nixon. Research Press, 2013. This book provides clear summaries of the findings from the Youth Voice Project, which surveyed more than 13,000 students in fifth through twelfth grade from thirty-one schools in twelve different U.S. states. The authors identify the peer and adult actions that are most helpful to targets of bullying. This is an excellent resource that presents research-based information on the best skills and strategies for preventing bullying and reducing the harm that bullying can inflict on students.

Videos and Other Resources

Let's Get Real by Groundspark (groundspark.org/our-films-and-campaigns/lets-get-real). This thirty-five-minute film features adolescents and their true stories about bullying and harassment. From the kids who are targeted, to the students who pick on them, to those who find the courage to intervene, *Let's Get Real* examines bullying from a full range of perspectives. The accompanying curriculum guide provides excellent, age-appropriate lessons to further student learning on issues such as diversity and bullying. *Note*: This video shows students sharing names and slurs they've been called.

The Feel & Deal Activity Deck by Christa M. Tinari (peacepraxis.com). This unique activity deck for first through eighth grade includes cards with boy and girl illustrations that realistically depict facial expressions corresponding with sixteen different emotions. The deck also contains sixteen teacher cards that present thirty-five engaging activities (some with Language Arts Common Core Standards connections) to help students build emotional intelligence skills and positive relationships with one another.

Organizations and Websites

Association for Mindfulness in Education (AME)
mindfuleducation.org
AME is a collaborative association of organizations and individuals working together to provide support for mindfulness training as a component of K–12 education.

Bully Police USA
bullypolice.org
This site lists and evaluates U.S. bullying legislation state by state. Learn how each state's bullying laws are graded and pick up best practices from states and schools that are highly ranked.

Center for Building a Culture of Empathy
cultureofempathy.com
The Center's mission is to build a movement for creating a global culture of empathy and compassion. The Center collects, curates, and organizes materials and information on empathy. This site contains the largest online collection of articles, expert interviews, history, videos, and research on empathy and compassion.

Centers for Disease Control and Prevention (CDC)
cdc.gov
The CDC has produced several research-based fact sheets on bullying that present complex information in clear, straightforward language. Search "bullying" on the homepage to find a list of clickable links and documents, including factsheets on electronic aggression, youth violence, and the relationship between bullying and suicide.

Character.org
character.org
This nonprofit organization (formerly known as Character Education Partnership) strives to ensure through character education that young people everywhere are educated, inspired, and empowered to be ethical and engaged citizens. Schools can apply to be recognized as National Schools of Character.

Collaborative for Academic, Social, and Emotional Learning (CASEL)
casel.org
CASEL advances the research, policy, and practice of social-emotional learning. This site maintains an annotated guide to evidence-based, effective social-emotional learning programs for kids in preK through high school.

The Cyberbullying Research Center
cyberbullying.org
This site includes research, stories, cases, factsheets, strategies, and current news on cyberbullying, plus downloadable materials for educators and parents to use and distribute.

Edutopia
edutopia.org
Edutopia, the George Lucas Educational Foundation's website and online community, is dedicated to transforming K–12 education so all students can thrive in their studies, careers, and adult lives. The Foundation focuses on practices and programs that help students grow personally and academically. The website contains free, easily accessible videos that highlight educational innovations. Particularly recommended are their videos on social-emotional learning.

Greater Good Science Center
greatergood.berkeley.edu
Located at the University of California, Berkeley, the Greater Good Science Center sponsors groundbreaking scientific research on empathy, gratitude, altruism, and happiness. Their website and free e-newsletter report findings from psychology, sociology, and neuroscience and share best practices for living a meaningful life.

Learning for Justice
learningforjustice.org
Formerly known as Teaching Tolerance, this website includes teaching materials for every grade level on a large variety of issues related to promoting justice and equality. Their magazine contains excellent articles about diversity issues in education. You can also access their lesson bank and free educator resources.

Morningside Center for Teaching Social Responsibility
morningsidecenter.org
The Morningside Center works closely with schools to help young people develop the values, personal qualities, and skills they need to thrive in the classroom and in their communities. With a strong focus on social justice, the Center provides teacher training and posts free lessons on their website.

Operation Respect
operationrespect.org
This nonprofit organization works to ensure a respectful and compassionate climate of learning, free of bullying, ridicule, and violence, for all students. They offer a free middle school curriculum called "Don't Laugh at Me." The "Don't Laugh at Me" song has been covered by many different artists and communicates a powerful message of empathy and respect.

PREVNet
prevnet.ca
This comprehensive site outlines Canadian laws on bullying by province and territory, along with resources and factsheets for teens, parents, and educators, plus up-to-date news on bullying in Canada.

Random Acts of Kindness Foundation
randomactsofkindness.org
This internationally recognized nonprofit organization is founded upon the powerful belief in kindness and is dedicated to providing resources and tools that encourage acts of kindness.

StopBullying.gov
stopbullying.gov
This site provides information from various U.S. government agencies on what bullying is, what cyberbullying is, who is at risk, and how you can prevent and respond to bullying.

Crisis Hotlines

Boys Town National Hotline: 1-800-448-3000. This number is for boys and girls even though the message says Boys Town national hotline. It's free, confidential, and available 24-7. Be patient. Sometimes there's a short wait.

Boys Town National Textline: Text "Voice" to 20121. Free and confidential. Available 24-7.

National Suicide Prevention Lifeline: Call 1-800-273-TALK (8255) anytime, 24-7, to talk to someone who can help.

The Trevor Project Lifeline: 1-866-488-7386. This organization for lesbian, gay, bisexual, transgender, and questioning young people offers a free and confidential helpline 24 hours a day. For more information visit thetrevorproject.org.

Your Life Your Voice: Visit yourlifeyourvoice.org to chat online or email someone for support.

References

Introduction

1. James H. Fowler and Nicholas A. Christakis, "Cooperative Behavior Cascades in Human Social Networks," *Proceedings of the National Academy of Sciences* 107, no. 12 (2010): 5334–5338, doi: 10.1073/pnas.0913149107.

2. Rick Weissbourd and Stephanie Jones, with Trisha Ross Anderson, Jennifer Kahn, and Mark Russell, "The Children We Mean to Raise: The Real Messages Adults Are Sending About Values" (Cambridge, MA: Harvard Graduate School of Education, 2014), sites.gse.harvard.edu/sites/default/files/making-caring-common/files/mcc_report_the_children_we_mean_to_raise_0.pdf.

3. Sourya Acharya and Samarth Shukla, "Mirror Neurons: Enigma of the Metaphysical Modular Brain," *Journal of Natural Science, Biology and Medicine* 3, no. 2 (2012): 118–124, doi: 10.4103/0976-9668.101878.

4. Stephen T. Russell et al., "Adolescent Health and Harassment Based on Discriminatory Bias," *American Journal of Public Health* 102, no. 3 (2012): 493–495.

5. Jeroen Pronk, Tjeert Olthof, and Frits A. Goossens, "Factors Influencing Interventions on Behalf of Victims of Bullying: A Counterfactual Approach to the Social Cognitions of Outsiders and Defenders," *Journal of Early Adolescence* 36, no. 2 (2016): 267–291, doi: 10.1177/0272431614562836.

6. Robert Thornberg et al., "Bystander Motivation in Bullying Incidents: To Intervene or Not to Intervene?" *West Journal of Emergency Medicine* 13, no. 3 (2012): 247–252, doi: 10.5811/westjem.2012.3.11792.

7. Ibid.

8. Stan Davis and Charisse L. Nixon, *Youth Voice Project: Student Insights into Bullying and Peer Mistreatment.* (Champaign, IL: Research Press, 2013). Reprinted with permission.

9. Susan P. Limber, Dan Olweus, and Harlan Luxenberg, "Bullying in U.S. Schools: 2012 Status Report" (Hazelden Foundation, 2013); and Catherine P. Bradshaw et. al., *Findings from the National Education Association's Nationwide Study of Bullying: Teachers' and Education Support Professionals' Perspectives* (Washington, DC: National Education Association, 2011).

10. Frances E. Jensen, "Why Teens Are Impulsive, Addiction-Prone and Should Protect Their Brains," interview by Terry Gross, *Fresh Air*, podcast audio (January 28, 2015), www.npr.org/sections/health-shots/2015/01/28/381622350/why-teens-are-impulsive-addiction-prone-and-should-protect-their-brains.

11. Jay Giedd, "Inside the Teenage Brain," interview by *Frontline*, PBS (January 31, 2002), www.pbs.org/wgbh/pages/frontline/shows/teenbrain/interviews/giedd.html.

12. David Scott Yeager, Kali H. Trzesniewski, and Carol S. Dweck, "An Implicit Theories of Personality Intervention Reduces Adolescent Aggression in Response to Victimization and Exclusion," *Child Development* 84, no. 3 (2013): 970–988, doi: 10.1111/cdev.12003.

13. Maryam Kouchaki and Francesca Gino, "Memories of Unethical Actions Become Obfuscated Over Time," *Proceedings for the National Academy of Sciences* 113, no. 22 (2016): 6166–6171, doi: 10.1073/pnas.1523586113.

14. Gianluca Gini, Tiziana Pozzoli, and Marc D. Hauser, "Bullies Have Enhanced Moral Competence to Judge Relative to Victims, But Lack Moral Compassion," *Personality and Individual Differences* 50, no. 5 (2011): 603–608, doi: 10.1016/j.paid.2010.12.002.

15. Danice K. Eaton et al., "Youth Risk Behavior Surveillance—United States 2007," Centers for Disease Control and Prevention (CDC) *MMWR Surveillance Summary* 57, no. 4 (2008): 1–131.

16. Lauren Musu-Gillette et al., "Measuring Student Safety: Bullying Rates at School," *NCES Blog*, National Center for Education Statistics, May 1, 2015, nces.ed.gov/blogs/nces/post/measuring-student-safety-bullying-rates-at-school.

17. Nirvi Shah, "Students Experience Less Bullying, Fear at School, New Data Show," *Rules for Engagement* (blog), *Education Week*, June 3, 2013, blogs.edweek.org/edweek/rulesforengagement/2013/06/students_experience_less_bullying_fear_at_school_new_data_show.html.

18. Joseph G. Kosciw et al., *The 2013 National School Climate Survey: The Experiences of Lesbian, Gay, Bisexual and Transgender Youth in Our Nation's Schools* (New York: GLSEN, 2014), www.glsen.org/article/2013-national-school-climate-survey.

19. National Center for Injury Prevention and Control, Division of Violence Prevention, *The Relationship Between Bullying and Suicide: What We Know and What It Means for Schools* (Chamblee, GA: Centers for Disease Control and Prevention, 2014), www.cdc.gov/violenceprevention/pdf/bullying-suicide-translation-final-a.pdf.

20. Ann P. Haas et al., "Suicide and Suicide Risk in Lesbian, Gay, Bisexual, and Transgender Populations: Review and Recommendations," *Journal of Homosexuality* 58, no. 1 (2011): 10–51, doi: 10.1080/00918369.2011.534038.

21. Stephen T. Russell and Kara Joyner, "Adolescent Sexual Orientation and Suicide Risk: Evidence from a National Study," *American Journal of Public Health* 91, no. 8 (2001): 1276–1281, ajph.aphapublications.org/doi/pdf/10.2105/AJPH.91.8.1276; and American Association of Suicidology, "Suicidal Behavior Among LGBT Youth" (2014), suicidology.org/Portals/14/docs/Resources/FactSheets/2011/LGBT2014.pdf.

22. Todd I. Herrenkohl et al., "Longitudinal Examination of Physical and Relational Aggression as Precursors to Later Problem Behaviors in Adolescents," *Violence Victimization* 24, no. 1 (2009): 3–19, www.ncbi.nlm.nih.gov/pmc/articles/PMC2659462.

23. National Center for Injury Prevention and Control, Division of Violence Prevention, *The Relationship Between Bullying and Suicide: What We Know and What It Means for Schools* (Chamblee, GA: Centers for Disease Control and Prevention, 2014), www.cdc.gov/violenceprevention/pdf/bullying-suicide-translation-final-a.pdf.

24. "Fidgeting in ADHD May Help Children Think, Perform in School," UC Davis Health System, June 10, 2015, ucdmc.ucdavis.edu/publish/news/newsroom/10069.

Lesson 1: Creating a Vision of a Peaceful School

25. Inga Kiderra, "'Pay It Forward' Pays Off," UC San Diego News Center, March 5, 2010, ucsdnews.ucsd.edu/archive/newsrel/soc/03-08ExperimentalFindings.asp.

26. Frank Niles, "How to Use Visualization to Achieve Your Goals," *Huffington Post*, June 17, 2011, www.huffingtonpost.com/frank-niles-phd/visualization-goals_b_878424.html.

Lesson 6: Words Can Change Your Brain

27. Andrew Newberg and Mark Robert Waldman, *Words Can Change Your Brain* (New York: Penguin, 2012).

28. Maia Szalavitz, "The Biology of Kindness: How It Makes Us Happier and Healthier," *Time*, May 9, 2013, healthland.time.com/2013/05/09/why-kindness-can-make-us-happier-healthier.

Lesson 13: Choosing Your Words

29. "Hate Map," Southern Poverty Law Center, www.splcenter.org/hate-map.

30. Norma J. Bailey, "Break the Silence and Make School Safe for All Kids! Awareness and Strategies for Teachers," *Middle Ground*, October 2011, amle.org/BrowsebyTopic/WhatsNew/WNDet/TabId/270/ArtMID/888/ArticleID/178/Break-the-Silence-and-Make-School-Safe-for-All-Kids.aspx.

Lesson 14: Strengthening Your Empathy Muscle

31. Jane E. Brody, "Empathy's Natural, but Nurturing It Helps," *New York Times*, February 15, 2010, www.nytimes.com/2010/02/16/health/16brod.html.

Index

Page numbers in **bold** indicate reproducible forms and handouts.

About the Authors

Naomi Drew, M.A., is the award-winning author of eight books. She is recognized around the world for her work in conflict resolution, peacemaking, and anti-bullying. Her work has been instrumental in introducing the skills of peacemaking to public education and has been recognized by educational leaders throughout the world. United Nations staffer Michiko Kuroda praised her work saying, "Naomi Drew has adapted the techniques of negotiation to the needs of children." She has been called "A master teacher and pathfinder in our culture." Her work has been featured in magazines and newspapers, and on radio and national TV, including NBC, *The New York Times*, *Time* Magazine, and *Parents* Magazine. She has also served as a peaceful parenting expert for *Classroom Close-ups,* an Emmy-winning public television show.

Naomi is a dynamic speaker who has inspired audiences far and wide. She has served as a consultant to school districts, parent groups, and civic organizations and has headed up the New Jersey State Bar Foundation's Conflict Resolution Advisory Panel for nine years, training trainers to create more harmonious schools. Her work is rooted in a deep desire to create a more peaceful future for all young people, her own two sons being the genesis of this. Imprinted in her brain are Gandhi's words: "If we are to reach lasting peace in the world, we shall have to begin with children." She follows in the footsteps of her mother, whose only birthday wish each year was for a peaceful world.

Christa M. Tinari, M.A., is a nationally recognized speaker, author, trainer, educational consultant, and peacebuilder. She offers expert advice on bullying prevention, social-emotional learning, and school climate improvement to schools and youth-serving organizations across the country. Christa is creator of the Peaceful School Institute teacher training program, and the Feel & Deal Activity Deck, an empathy-building tool for children used on six continents. She is adjunct instructor in the College of Education at Temple University, and she frequently presents at international and national conferences such as the Association for Middle Level Education, ASCD, the Character Education Partnership, and the International Bullying Prevention Association. Christa has helped thousands of educators transform their teaching practices and improve school climate—creating more caring and safe environments for students of all ages.

Raised in a family of educators and passionate about the power of education to bring justice and peace to our classrooms, neighborhoods, and beyond, Christa believes that in order to shape and nurture "the whole child," education must inspire hearts as much as expand minds. "Inspired" is her favorite state of being; working with educators and students, she gets to experience it every day!

Other Great Resources from Free Spirit

Create a Culture of Kindness in Elementary School
126 Lessons to Help Kids Manage Anger, End Bullying, and Build Empathy
by Naomi Drew, M.A.

Grades 3–6.
304 pp.; PB; 8½" x 11"; 1-color; includes digital content

The SEL Solution
Integrate Social and Emotional Learning into Your Curriculum and Build a Caring Climate for All
by Jonathan C. Erwin, M.A.

Grades K–12. 60 lessons and activities.
200 pp.; PB; 8½" x 11"; includes digital content

Building Everyday Leadership in All Teens
Promoting Attitudes and Actions for Respect and Success
(Revised & Updated Edition)
by Mariam G. MacGregor, M.S.

Teachers and youth workers, grades 6–12.
240 pp.; PB; 8½" x 11"; includes digital content

The PBIS Team Handbook
Setting Expectations and Building Positive Behavior
(Revised & Updated Edition)
by Char Ryan, Ph.D., and Beth Baker, M.S.Ed.

PBIS coaches and team members, and other school staff members, grades K–12.
224 pp.; PB; 8½" x 11"; includes digital content

Free PLC/Book Study Guide
freespirit.com/PLC

What Do You Stand For? For Teens
A Guide to Building Character
by Barbara A. Lewis

Ages 11 & up.
288 pp.; PB; 8½" x 11"; B&W photos; illust.

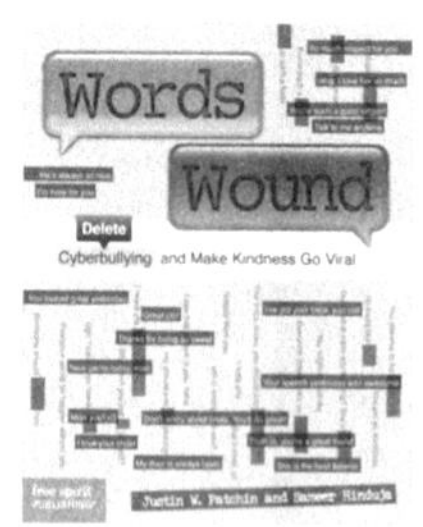

Words Wound (eBook)
Delete Cyberbullying and Make Kindness Go Viral
by Justin W. Patchin, Ph.D., and Sameer Hinduja, Ph.D.

Ages 13 & up.
200 pp.; PB; 6" x 7½"; 2-color

Free Leader's Guide
freespirit.com/leader

End Peer Cruelty, Build Empathy
The Proven 6Rs of Bullying Prevention That Create Inclusive, Safe, and Caring Schools
by Michele Borba, Ed.D.

Administrators, teachers, counselors, youth leaders, bullying prevention teams, and parents, grades K–8.
288 pp.; PB; 7¼" x 9¼"; includes digital content

Interested in purchasing multiple quantities and receiving volume discounts?
Contact edsales@freespirit.com or call 1.800.735.7323 and ask for Education Sales.

Many Free Spirit authors are available for speaking engagements, workshops, and keynotes.
Contact speakers@freespirit.com or call 1.800.735.7323.

For pricing information, to place an order, or to request a free catalog, contact:

Free Spirit Publishing Inc. • 6325 Sandburg Road, Suite 100 • Minneapolis, MN 55427-3674
toll-free 800.735.7323 • local 612.338.2068 • fax 612.337.5050
help4kids@freespirit.com • freespirit.com